THE

EVERYTHING®

EASY LARGE-PRINT CROSSWORDS BOOK, VOLUME V

Dear Reader,

Crossword puzzles are great, but many of them can be really difficult to solve. These puzzles are different. They're not for experts. I designed them to be frustration-free, even for beginners. And the nice thing about crossword puzzles is that you always get a second chance. If you can't solve the clues going across, then try the ones going down. These puzzles are also easy on your eyes. The large-print format makes them less tedious.

According to research, solving crossword puzzles can boost our brainpower, especially as we grow older. It makes sense to me: we need to keep our minds active to keep them in shape. These light-and-easy crossword puzzles can be part of a healthy lifestyle.

All lofty goals aside, the main emphasis here is fun. I think you're going to enjoy solving your way through these pages. But beware: once you start, it might be hard to stop!

Charles Timmerman

Welcome to the EVERYTHING® Series!

These handy, accessible books give you all you need to tackle a difficult project, gain a new hobby, comprehend a fascinating topic, prepare for an exam, or even brush up on something you learned back in school but have since forgotten.

You can choose to read an Everything® book from cover to cover or just pick out the information you want from our four useful boxes: e-questions, e-facts, e-alerts, and e-ssentials. We give you everything you need to know on the subject, but throw in a lot of fun stuff along the way, too.

We now have more than 400 Everything® books in print, spanning such wide-ranging categories as weddings, pregnancy, cooking, music instruction, foreign language, crafts, pets, New Age, and so much more. When you're done reading them all, you can finally say you know Everything®!

PUBLISHER Karen Cooper

MANAGING EDITOR, EVERYTHING® SERIES Lisa Laing

COPY CHIEF Casey Ebert

ASSOCIATE PRODUCTION EDITOR Mary Beth Dolan

ACQUISITIONS EDITOR Lisa Laing

EVERYTHING® SERIES COVER DESIGNER Erin Alexander

THE EVERYTHING® EASY LARGE-PRINT CROSSWORDS BOOK

VOLUME V

150 easy crossword puzzles in large print

Charles Timmerman
Founder of Funster.com

Adams Media
New York London Toronto Sydney New Delhi

Adams Media
An Imprint of Simon & Schuster, Inc.
57 Littlefield Street
Avon, Massachusetts 02322

For information about special discounts for bulk purchases, please contact Simon & Schuster Special Sales at 1-866-506-1949 or business@simonandschuster.com.

The Simon & Schuster Speakers Bureau can bring authors to your live event. For more information or to book an event contact the Simon & Schuster Speakers Bureau at 1-866-248-3049 or visit our website at www.simonspeakers.com.

Manufactured in the United States of America

16 2024

ISBN 978-1-4405-5993-8

Dedicated to
Suzanne, Calla, and Meryl.

Acknowledgments

I would like to thank each and every one of the more than half a million people who have visited my website, *www.funster.com*, to play word games and puzzles. You have shown me how much fun puzzles can be and how addictive they can become!

It is a pleasure to acknowledge the folks at Adams Media who made this book possible. I particularly want to thank my editor, Lisa Laing, for so skillfully managing the many projects we have worked on together.

Contents

Introduction / 9

Puzzles / 11

Answers / 313

Introduction

What do Rosa Parks, Richard Nixon, Jesse Owens, and crossword puzzles have in common? They were all born in the year 1913. In that year, a journalist named Arthur Wynne published a "word-cross" puzzle in the *New York World*'s Sunday newspaper. Though it was diamond-shaped, it had all of the features of the crossword puzzles that we know and love today. The name evolved into *crossword* as the paper continued to publish the popular word puzzles.

It wasn't until 1924 that the first book of crossword puzzles was published. That was when the crossword craze really began. It joined other fads of the Roaring Twenties like goldfish swallowing, flagpole sitting, yo-yos, and pogo sticks. Of course, not all of these fads survived (perhaps fortunately).

Besides crossword puzzles, some really beautiful things came out of the 1920s. In music, jazz surged in popularity and George Gershwin's *Rhapsody in Blue* was performed for the first time. In literature,

F. Scott Fitzgerald published some of his most enduring novels, including *The Great Gatsby*. In design, it was the beginning of Art Deco. That's how the world was shifting when crossword puzzles came of age.

Crossword puzzles became popular closer to a time when entertainment required *active* participation. In those days, people actually played sports rather than watching them, told each other stories rather than turning on the television, and even sang songs rather than listening to an MP3. Like entertainment of yesteryear, crossword puzzles require your active participation. And this is a refreshing change for those of us who still enjoy a mental workout.

Today, nearly every major newspaper runs a crossword puzzle. Entire sections of bookstores are devoted to crossword puzzle books. (Thanks for choosing this one!) Indeed, crosswords are the most common word puzzle in the world.

Why do crossword puzzles continue to be so popular? Only you can answer that question since there are as many reasons to work a crossword puzzle as there are solvers. But perhaps it has something to do with the convenient marriage of fun and learning that crossword puzzles offer.

Puzzles

ACROSS

1. Filmmaker Spike
4. Spellbound
8. Jar tops
12. ___ and yang
13. Lifetime Oscar winner Kazan
14. Gilbert of "Roseanne"
15. Imperil
17. On
18. Letter starter
19. Stair parts
20. One of the Osmonds
23. Bottle tops
25. Writer Wiesel
26. Big name in computer games
27. "Is it a boy ___ girl?"
30. Phrase on the back of a buck
33. "The Waste Land" poet's monogram
34. Fairy tale villain
35. Christie's "Death on the ___"
36. Chinese: prefix
37. Soda bottle unit
38. Pesto herb
41. Good name for a Dalmatian
43. Taiwanese PC maker
44. Sort of
48. Outfielder's cry
49. Female horse
50. Bush 43, to Bush 41
51. Tacks on
52. Tiny hill dwellers
53. Paul Bunyan's tool

DOWN

1. Soapmaker's solution
2. Article in Der Spiegel
3. At wit's ___
4. Actress Zellweger
5. Pond plant
6. "Remington Steele" portrayer
7. Road goo
8. Exams for future attys.
9. "I can't believe ___ the whole thing!"
10. Plummet
11. Depletes, as strength
16. French farewell
19. Healthful retreats
20. Encounter
21. Austrian peaks
22. Stir up
24. Fit of fever
26. Affix one's John Hancock
27. "Don't bet ___!"
28. ___ of thumb
29. Part of N.A.
31. Agitate
32. Join
36. Horse fathers

Puzzle 1

1	2	3	■	4	5	6	7	■	8	9	10	11
12			■	13				■	14			
15			16					■	17			
■	■	■	18				■	19				
20	21	22			■	23	24			■	■	■
25				■	26				■	27	28	29
30				31					32			
33			■	34				■	35			
■	■	■	36				■	37				
38	39	40			■	41	42			■	■	■
43				■	44					45	46	47
48				■	49				■	50		
51				■	52				■	53		

37. Comes in last
38. The Crimson Tide, familiarly
39. Citric ___
40. Drop in the mail
42. Divide with a comb
44. Britney Spears's "___ Slave 4 U"
45. Top-secret org.
46. Chicago White ___
47. Opposite of WSW

Solution on Page 314

ACROSS

1. Strong wind
5. Dept. store stock
9. Battering device
12. Sale condition
13. Bridge-crossing fee
14. Memorable period
15. Restaurant valet's income
16. Medicine bottle
17. Sink, as the sun
18. "___ on Down the Road"
19. Bill the Science Guy
20. Jobs for grad students
21. Crooned
24. Originally named
26. Cartographer's concern
29. Slugging Sammy
31. Beavers' constructions
34. Fold, as paper
36. Big name in small planes
38. CAT ___
39. Put in order
41. Over there, poetically
42. Genetic initials
44. Pod contents
46. Go bad
48. Al Capp's "Daisy ___"
50. More's opposite
54. Dinghy propeller
55. Mystique
57. Hasn't ___ to stand on
58. Smelter input
59. For men only
60. Hue
61. Philosopher Lao ___
62. Middling
63. HS seniors' exams

DOWN

1. Box office take
2. Largest continent
3. "Loose ___ sink ships"
4. Double curves
5. VH1 rival
6. Happenings
7. Kill, as a dragon
8. Actress Burstyn
9. Stop worrying
10. Vicinity
11. Cushions for tumblers
22. Beast of burden
23. Turndowns
25. Mag. workers
26. Roast hosts, for short
27. Curve
28. Partridge's perch, in song
30. Farm unit
32. "L–P" filler
33. ___ Clemente
35. Raggedy ___

Puzzle 2

1	2	3	4	■	5	6	7	8	■	9	10	11
12				■	13				■	14		
15				■	16				■	17		
18				■	■	19			■	20		
■	■	■	21	22	23		■	24	25		■	■
26	27	28	■	29			30	■	31		32	33
34			35			■	36	37				
38				■	39	40			■	41		
■	■	42		43	■	44			45	■	■	■
46	47		■	48	49		■	■	50	51	52	53
54			■	55			56	■	57			
58			■	59				■	60			
61			■	62				■	63			

37. Airport posting: abbr.
40. “Falstaff” and “Fidelio”
43. Accumulate
45. Wood strips
46. Cheer (for)
47. Boat propellers
49. Car
51. Kazan who directed “On the Waterfront”
52. Shipped
53. Some noncoms: abbr.
56. In the past

Solution on Page 314

ACROSS

1. Dressed
5. Pro's opposite
8. Recipe direction
12. Townshend of The Who
13. Bikini top
14. Minuscule
15. Prepares to fire
16. Convicted criminal's punishment
18. Postpaid encl.
19. Confident
20. Maid's cloth
23. The "U" of UHF
27. Soup cracker
31. Shortly
32. Jack's preceder
33. Fencing move
36. Furniture wood
37. "___ M for Murder"
39. Front porch
41. Company with a spectacular 2001 bankruptcy
43. Food additive
44. El ___ (Pacific phenomenon)
47. "Even ___ speak"
51. Suitor's song
55. Cabbage salad
56. Bakery worker
57. "To ___ With Love"
58. "Riders of the Purple ___"
59. Puts on
60. Decimal base
61. Currier's partner in lithography

DOWN

1. IRS experts
2. Luke Skywalker's sister
3. Cash dispensers, for short
4. Gobi or Mojave
5. "60 Minutes" network
6. Loads from lodes
7. Half of Mork's goodbye
8. Braces (oneself)
9. Can material
10. Ltd., in the States
11. Cereal grass
17. Capote, familiarly
21. Feel feverish
22. Wildebeest
24. Roger Rabbit, e.g.
25. Highway
26. "Puppy Love" singer Paul
27. "West ___ Story"
28. Related (to)
29. "All in the Family" producer Norman
30. Cardholder: abbr.
34. Jewel
35. Hosp. units
38. Recluses

Puzzle 3

40. Andre of tennis
42. “Delta of Venus” author Anaïs
45. Political cartoonist Thomas
46. “Garfield” dog
48. Pole, e.g.
49. Worker’s pay
50. Lambs’ mothers
51. Caesar of comedy
52. Prefix with tourism
53. Stimpy’s cartoon pal
54. Suffix with east or west

Solution on Page 314

ACROSS

1. London's ___ Park
5. Intel product, briefly
8. What's harvested
12. "___ to Be Wild"
13. Elevation: abbr.
14. 60 minutes
15. Approved
16. Attack verbally
18. Furry "Star Wars" creature
20. Sounds of satisfaction
21. Ingenuity
23. Garbage
28. It's flipped in anger
31. Molt
33. Lotion ingredient
34. Pass, as time
36. "Michael, Row Your Boat ___"
38. Right-hand person
39. Spouse
41. Part of ITT: abbr.
42. Basil-based sauce
44. Judge-to-be
46. Wine and dine
48. Buddies
51. Japanese farewell
56. Castle protection
58. Upon
59. Sewn edge
60. Has ___ with
61. +
62. Self-proclaimed psychic Geller
63. River deposit

DOWN

1. "Entourage" network
2. Oxen connector
3. Sketched
4. Fund, as one's alma mater
5. Cool dude, in jazz
6. "The magic word"
7. Great Salt Lake's state
8. Windy City, for short
9. "Apollo 13" director Howard
10. Umpire's call
11. Con's opposite
17. "Q–U" connection
19. Smooch
22. "It's us against ___"
24. Short cheer
25. Loads
26. Achy
27. Rear of a sole
28. Vault
29. "Would ___ to you?"
30. Moms' mates
32. Go out with
35. Letterman's "Stupid ___ Tricks"
37. Ooze
40. Smitten one

Puzzle 4

1	2	3	4	■	5	6	7	■	8	9	10	11
12				■	13			■	14			
15				■	16			17				
■	18			19	■	20			■	■	■	■
■	■	■	21		22		■	23	24	25	26	27
28	29	30	■	31			32	■	33			
34			35			■	36	37				
38				■	39	40			■	41		
42				43	■	44			45	■	■	■
■	■	■	■	46	47		■	48		49	50	■
51	52	53	54				55	■	56			57
58				■	59			■	60			
61				■	62			■	63			

43. "Mind your ___ business!"
45. Papas' partners
47. Hawaiian island
49. Actress Anderson
50. Go to sea
51. Tree juice
52. Home of the Braves: abbr.
53. Last word of the golden rule
54. Photo ___ (media events)
55. "So ___!" ("Me, too!")
57. Explosive

Solution on Page 314

ACROSS

1. "Here's ___ in your eye"
4. Hit, as one's toe
8. Pack away
12. Wire service inits.
13. Alas!
14. Trillion: prefix
15. May and June: abbr.
16. Subterfuge
17. Fired
18. Univ. sports org.
20. Crime-fighting org.
22. Not that
25. What a protractor measures
29. What V-J Day ended
32. Boxer's cue
34. Eliminate
35. Go ballistic
38. GI's address
39. Memo: abbr.
40. Lawyer: abbr.
41. Basic belief
43. Drench
45. High-speed Internet inits.
47. Hair goops
50. Wind resistance
53. Scheme
56. Alert to squad cars, briefly
58. Lavish affection (on)
59. "I ___ at the office"
60. Daisy ___ of "Li'l Abner"
61. Pairs
62. Chopping tools
63. School grp.

DOWN

1. Britain's Queen ___
2. Fairy tale's second word
3. Frisbee, e.g.
4. Jazz singer Vaughan
5. Turkey Day day: abbr.
6. Sounds of hesitation
7. Hamburger meat
8. Wood finish
9. ___-Mex cuisine
10. Mine find
11. Roll of dough
19. Going ___ (fighting)
21. Indonesian island
23. Skeptic's comment
24. Religious factions
26. "True ___" (John Wayne movie)
27. Dryer residue
28. Nervously irritable
29. One of the five Ws
30. Use a dish towel
31. Lay ___ the line
33. Letterman rival
36. Milliner's supply
37. Great Salt ___

Puzzle 5

42. Borders
44. Actress Moorehead
46. Women's links org.
48. Genie's home
49. Petty quarrel
50. Banned insecticide
51. Use an oar
52. "___ Z"
54. Lenient
55. "Hail, Caesar!"
57. "Luck ___ Lady Tonight"

Solution on Page 315

ACROSS

1. PDQ
5. Grazing ground
8. Send
12. Whitish
13. Weigh-___ (boxing rituals)
14. Close by
15. Ballet movement
16. Parking place
17. Military force
18. "A Streetcar Named Desire" woman
20. Rule, for short
22. Bitterly pungent
24. Treasure hunter's aid
27. Let up
31. Teach
33. Elderly
34. "So ___ me!"
35. Yearn (for)
36. Uses logic
38. Eagle's claw
39. L.A. time
40. Tractor-maker John
42. Neptune's realm
43. Church platforms
48. Detective's assignment
51. Krazy ___
53. Milky gem
54. Wall Street inits.
55. Opposite WSW
56. Burrowing mammal
57. "___ I say more?"
58. Clear (of)
59. Hightailed it

DOWN

1. Computer programs, for short
2. Pepper's partner
3. "That's ___!" ("Not true!")
4. Rind
5. Light purple
6. Brian of ambient music
7. On both sides of
8. Glitch
9. The Beatles' "And I Love ___"
10. Sam ___ (Dr. Seuss character)
11. Use a lever
19. Young chap
21. University URL ending
23. Employ again
24. Postal delivery
25. ___ time (never)
26. Ball-shaped hammer part
27. O.K. Corral lawman
28. Gets on in years
29. Plane assignment
30. Bradley and Begley
32. Tax preparer, briefly
34. Athletic shoe

Puzzle 6

1	2	3	4	■	5	6	7	■	8	9	10	11
12				■	13			■	14			
15				■	16			■	17			
18				19		■	20	21	■	■	■	■
■	■	■	■	22		23			■	24	25	26
27	28	29	30		■	31			32			
33				■	34			■	35			
36				37			■	38				
39			■	40			41		■	■	■	■
■	■	■	42			■	43		44	45	46	47
48	49	50		■	51	52		■	53			
54				■	55			■	56			
57				■	58			■	59			

37. "___ to a Nightingale"
38. Rolodex no.
41. Put on a scale of 1 to 10
42. Gardener's spring purchase
44. "Uncle ___ Cabin"
45. Individually
46. Chest rattle
47. Iditarod vehicle
48. "Headline News" channel
49. Sailor's yes
50. NNW's reverse
52. "Wheel of Fortune" purchase

Solution on Page 315

ACROSS

1. "Bette Davis Eyes" singer Carnes
4. "Let's go!"
8. Words before arms or smoke
12. "ER" setting
13. Is under the weather
14. Completely demolish
15. Football great Dawson
16. Baby's first word, maybe
17. Expand
18. Cree or Crow
20. Marsh plants
21. Perfect world
25. Do housework
28. Penny
29. Winter bug
32. Somewhat: suffix
33. Shuts tightly
34. "___ about time!"
35. MIT or NYU
36. Prefix with graph
37. G-men
38. "Is that your final ___?"
40. Bricklayer
44. Eyeshade
48. "For ___ know . . ."
49. Monster
52. It's between Can. and Mex.
53. Matinee hero
54. Withdraw gradually
55. "The Sweetheart of Sigma ___"
56. Applies lightly
57. Liberals, with "the"
58. Holbrook or Linden

DOWN

1. Bagpipers' wear
2. Cake finisher
3. City bond, for short
4. West Pointer
5. "Mamma ___!" (Broadway musical)
6. Elderly
7. Code-cracking org.
8. Goad
9. Whittle down
10. Polo shirt brand
11. Part of CNN
19. "Thanks, ___ no thanks"
20. "Phooey!"
22. Atlantic or Pacific
23. Bosc and Bartlett
24. Acquired relative
25. Put down, in the 'hood
26. L.A. school
27. Hush!
29. "Fee, ___, foe, fum"
30. Inc., in Britain
31. ___ Enterprise
33. Cable TV's C-___
37. Sat. preceder

Puzzle 7

1	2	3	■	4	5	6	7	■	8	9	10	11
12			■	13				■	14			
15			■	16				■	17			
18			19		■	■	■	20				
■	■	■	21		22	23	24		■	■	■	■
25	26	27		■	28				■	29	30	31
32			■	33					■	34		
35			■	36				■	37			
■	■	■	■	38				39		■	■	■
40	41	42	43		■	■	■	44		45	46	47
48				■	49	50	51		■	52		
53				■	54				■	55		
56				■	57				■	58		

39. Happening
40. Housekeeper
41. Alan of "M*A*S*H"
42. Messy dresser
43. Removes a squeak from
45. ___ as it is
46. Safety org.
47. Racetrack fence
49. Hooter
50. "___ whiz!"
51. WWII fliers

Solution on Page 315

ACROSS

1. Lose traction
5. Engine additive letters
8. Second-largest Hawaiian island
12. "St. Elmo's Fire" actor Rob
13. Mai ___ cocktail
14. "Alphabet Song" start
15. Individually, on a menu
17. Game on horseback
18. Neon or freon
19. Acquire knowledge
21. Kilmer who played Batman
22. "Do ___ favor"
23. Anger, with "up"
25. On the line
28. Runs off to marry
31. Legal claim
32. Is unable to
33. Newspaper advertising piece
36. Medals and trophies, e.g.
38. Came apart at the seams
39. Blanc who was the voice of Bugs Bunny
40. Notwithstanding that, briefly
42. Took notice
44. Olive in the comics
47. Tennis champ Bjorn
49. Smoked deli beef
51. ". . . not always what they ___"
52. Poetic tribute
53. SeaWorld attraction
54. Attention-getter
55. Helpers for profs.
56. Romanov ruler

DOWN

1. Coal waste
2. Soft drink nut
3. "___ only trying to help"
4. Follower of Nov.
5. Run of luck
6. "Cheerio!"
7. South Dakota's capital
8. Atlas page
9. Better than average
10. The Bruins of the NCAA
11. False god
16. Pub offerings
20. Zilch
22. Actor Sal
24. Hometown-related
25. Muhammad ___
26. ___ Lizzie (Model T)
27. Makes as good as new
29. Conclusion
30. Urban roads: abbr.
34. Four Monopoly properties: abbr.
35. ___ Dome (Harding administration scandal)
36. Tickles the fancy

Puzzle 8

1	2	3	4	■	5	6	7	■	8	9	10	11
12				■	13			■	14			
15				16				■	17			
18			■	19				20	■	21		
■	■	■	22			■	23		24		■	■
25	26	27				■	28				29	30
31				■	■	■	■	■	32			
33				34	35	■	36	37				
■	■	38				■	39			■	■	■
40	41		■	42		43			■	44	45	46
47			48	■	49				50			
51				■	52			■	53			
54				■	55			■	56			

37. Shed some tears
40. Recipe amt.
41. Garden tools
43. Cry of success
44. Sculls
45. Family rec. facility
46. Tall tale teller
48. Clock-setting std.
50. Spoil

Solution on Page 315

ACROSS

1. Tiny branch
5. Altar vows
9. Rent out
12. "___ you don't!"
13. Big name in computers
14. "___ bin ein Berliner"
15. Refine, as flour
16. "Me, myself ___"
17. D.C. mortgage insurer
18. Silky
20. Film cutter
22. Temporary wheels
24. "For shame!"
27. Subway alternative
28. Mock words of understanding
32. Street urchin
34. "The Flying ___"
36. Campus courtyard
37. ___ mater
38. Witnessed
40. Navigational gizmo
41. Tripod topper
44. Plot
47. Girl in a Beach Boys song
52. Aye canceler
53. Machu Picchu resident
55. Remove from a mother's milk
56. Any doctrine
57. Vegas machine
58. The Swedish Nightingale
59. Skillet
60. "Fourth base"
61. Murder

DOWN

1. ___ and turn
2. Sudden impulse
3. Facts
4. Attend, as a party
5. Man from Boise
6. TV room
7. Ancient
8. It's shown on a projector
9. Boost
10. Canyon sound
11. In that direction, to a whaler
19. Special attention, for short
21. Baghdad's country
23. Mistreat
24. Bygone airline
25. "I've got a mule, her name is ___"
26. Kipling novel
29. Bear greeting?
30. Gullible person
31. Has too much of a bad thing
33. ___ off (hockey opener)
35. Provide a voice-over
39. Crib cry
42. Some of the Pennsylvania Dutch

Puzzle 9

1	2	3	4	■	5	6	7	8	■	9	10	11
12				■	13				■	14		
15				■	16				■	17		
18				19		■	20		21			
■	■	■	■	22		23				■	■	■
24	25	26	■	27			■	■	28	29	30	31
32			33	■	34		35	■	36			
37				■	■	38		39	■	40		
■	■	■	41	42	43				■	■	■	■
44	45	46				■	47		48	49	50	51
52			■	53		54		■	55			
56			■	57				■	58			
59			■	60				■	61			

43. ___ Park (Edison's lab site)
44. Barber's motion
45. Spanish house
46. "The Battle ___ of the Republic"
48. Big-eyed birds
49. Playwright Simon
50. Delany of "China Beach"
51. Rooney of "60 Minutes"
54. Common URL ender

Solution on Page 316

ACROSS

1. Picket line crosser
5. Baden-Baden and others
9. "Morning Edition" network
12. House, in Havana
13. Drawn tight
14. Nay's opposite
15. Lenin's land, for short
16. In re
17. Put into words
18. Shooting star
20. Selects from the menu
22. Liquid part of blood
24. Use a straw
27. Number of pool pockets
28. Fem. opposite
32. Chicken ___ (deep-fried dish)
34. Deadlock
36. Solid parts of orange juice
37. "Holy moly!"
38. Walk-___ (small parts)
40. Watchdog warning
41. Everyday
44. Old Testament prophet
47. Tile art
52. LP speed
53. Widespread
55. Luxuriant, as vegetation
56. ___ Jong Il
57. Letter accompanier: abbr.
58. ___ extra cost
59. ___-Cat (winter vehicle)
60. Medics
61. Betty of comics

DOWN

1. Pond gunk
2. 24 cans of beer
3. Helper: abbr.
4. Unadorned
5. Like a clear night sky
6. Mas' mates
7. Cars
8. Lightning and thunder event
9. Big Board letters
10. Bosc or Bartlett
11. Sunbathers catch them
19. Covert ___ (military assignments)
21. Subject to mildew, perhaps
23. Self-evident truth
24. Cloud's locale
25. Three, on a sundial
26. Vigor
29. Sept. preceder
30. 35 mm camera type
31. Lifesaving skill, for short
33. "___, vidi, vici" (Caesar's boast)
35. Nail and tooth coverings
39. ___-pitch softball
42. Rowed

Puzzle 10

1	2	3	4	■	5	6	7	8	■	9	10	11
12				■	13				■	14		
15				■	16				■	17		
18				19		■	20		21			
■	■	■	■	22		23				■	■	■
24	25	26	■	27			■	■	28	29	30	31
32			33	■	34		35	■	36			
37				■	■	38		39	■	40		
■	■	■	41	42	43				■	■	■	■
44	45	46				■	47		48	49	50	51
52			■	53		54		■	55			
56			■	57				■	58			
59			■	60				■	61			

43. Thick-skinned critter
44. Annoys
45. Whirl
46. Bullets and such
48. Thick piece
49. Sedan or coupe
50. "Ignorance of the law ___ excuse"
51. Karate blow
54. Airwaves regulatory gp.

Solution on Page 316

ACROSS

1. Trio before "O"
4. Imitated
8. "___ Slidin' Away"
12. Hugs, symbolically
13. Mislay
14. Exclamation with a drum roll
15. ___ mot (witticism)
16. Actor Lugosi
17. Food item served in a basket
18. Rock
20. Sounds
22. Nettle
24. Soak (up)
25. Struck by Cupid
29. Parts of British pounds
33. Bumbler
34. Not yea
36. "___ Gang"
37. Clamorous
40. Settle a score
43. Small amount
45. Actor Beatty
46. ___ valve (part of an engine)
49. Surgeon's assistant
53. Choo choo's sound
54. "Sesame Street" skills
57. Since Jan. 1
58. "Star Trek" navigator
59. Tackle box item
60. Hosp. brain readout
61. No ifs, ___ or buts
62. Walked (on)
63. 007, for one

DOWN

1. Soft throws
2. No longer worth debating
3. "___, Nanette"
4. London's Royal ___ Hall
5. "The Tell-Tale Heart" author
6. Immigrant's subj.
7. College bigwigs
8. Zebra feature
9. Neighbor of Vietnam
10. Not busy
11. Chums
19. ___picker (overly critical one)
21. Alley___
23. Documentary filmmaker Burns
25. Dad's boy
26. ___ Zedong
27. "Don't mind ___ do!"
28. Old horse
30. Election mo.
31. Feed lines to
32. White-tailed eagle
35. Craving
38. ___ quo
39. Talk, talk, talk

Puzzle 11

41. ___ up (got nervous)
42. End of some e-mail addresses
44. Handed out
46. "___ Long Way to Tipperary"
47. Verb accompanier
48. Spilled the beans
50. Deli loaves
51. Stair part
52. Tense
55. Prickly seed cover
56. ___-Magnon

Solution on Page 316

ACROSS

1. Speedometer letters
4. Chick's chirp
8. Hole-punching tools
12. Susan of "The Partridge Family"
13. ___ breve (2/2 time)
14. ___ Ness monster
15. Vermont harvest
16. Edges
17. Memorial Day race, informally
18. Beer barrels
20. ___ of war
22. 500 sheets of paper
25. Animal nose
29. Passage for Santa
32. "No ___, no foul"
34. Roswell sighting
35. Baseball's "Mr. October"
38. Sushi fish
39. Air pollution
40. Teeny, informally
41. Romantic rendezvous
43. Corrode
45. Stir-fryer
47. Southpaw's side
50. Eat fancily
53. Tennis champ Nastase
56. Captain's journal
58. The Beatles' "Let ___"
59. Amount of medicine
60. Earthlink competitor
61. Diplomat's forte
62. Tiff
63. WBA decision

DOWN

1. AMA members
2. Summit
3. Overpublicize
4. Analyze, as a sentence
5. Gin maker Whitney
6. Stately tree
7. Future's opposite
8. Set straight
9. Took the gold
10. Calc. display
11. Like a wallflower
19. Actor Kinnear
21. Mil. branch
23. "Pardon me"
24. Collegian's declaration
26. Remove from power
27. Roswell sightings
28. Crooner Bennett
29. Worry
30. Wanton look
31. Hideous
33. Prego rival
36. Words in an analogy
37. Paper-and-string flier

Puzzle 12

1	2	3	■	4	5	6	7	■	8	9	10	11
12			■	13				■	14			
15			■	16				■	17			
■	18		19	■	■	■	20	21		■	■	■
■	■	■	22		23	24	■	25		26	27	28
29	30	31		■	32		33		■	34		
35				36					37			
38			■	39				■	40			
41			42		■	43		44		■	■	■
■	■	■	45		46	■	■	47		48	49	■
50	51	52		■	53	54	55		■	56		57
58				■	59				■	60		
61				■	62				■	63		

42. Like Georgia Brown
44. Winter precipitation
46. Baby goats
48. Like a pancake
49. Borrowed without permission
50. Dah's partner
51. "Give ___ whirl"
52. "SNL" network
54. Cut (off)
55. ". . . for what ___ man . . ."
57. Day___ paints

Solution on Page 316

ACROSS

1. Cry of pain
5. Downy
9. Money for old age: abbr.
12. Leg joint
13. "T" on a test
14. "Ay, there's the ___"
15. Card game for one
17. Recede
18. Excavated
19. Forty-___ (gold rush participant)
21. ___-pea soup
24. Fashion
26. ___ the line (obey)
27. "The Simpsons" shopkeeper
28. Subj. for Milton Friedman
31. Street shaders
33. Hamelin pest
34. Scotch ___
35. Milne bear
36. Capote, to friends
37. Critic Reed
38. Gallows loop
40. Commence
42. Honeydew, e.g.
44. Revolutionary Guevara
45. Gardner of Hollywood
46. Head honcho
52. Use a Singer
53. "Garfield" canine
54. June 6, 1944
55. 60-min. periods
56. One's equal
57. Amount between all and none

DOWN

1. Authorizes
2. Popular card game
3. Disney frame
4. Supermodel Klum
5. Without women
6. "Either you do it, ___ will!"
7. PETA peeve
8. Wee
9. "Flashdance . . . What a Feeling" singer
10. Cartoonist Goldberg
11. Shortened form, in shortened form
16. Egyptian boy king
20. "Before ___ you go . . ."
21. Dance move
22. Game with mallets
23. They protect car buyers
24. Tire in the trunk
25. Ballet skirt
27. ___ and sciences
29. Phone: abbr.
30. Waiting room call
32. Word to a fly
39. "___ of Old Smoky"

Puzzle 13

1	2	3	4	■	5	6	7	8	■	9	10	11
12				■	13				■	14		
15				16					■	17		
■	■	■	18			■	■	19	20			
21	22	23			■	24	25				■	■
26			■	■	27			■	28		29	30
31			32	■	33			■	34			
35				■	36			■	■	37		
■	■	38		39			■	40	41			
42	43				■	■	44			■	■	■
45			■	46	47	48				49	50	51
52			■	53				■	54			
55			■	56				■	57			

40. Nostalgic vocal group ___ Na Na
41. Takes care of
42. Prepare potatoes, in a way
43. ". . . happily ___ after."
44. "Good buddy"
47. Poem of praise
48. Lemon meringue, for one
49. "Without further ___ . . ."
50. '60s war site
51. Affirmative vote

Solution on Page 317

ACROSS

1. Fed. property manager
4. Fri. preceder
7. Spill the beans
11. Propel a boat
12. Elvis moved his, famously
14. Peru's capital
15. Shrouded in mystery
17. Datebook entry: abbr.
18. In abundance
19. Dashboard: abbr.
21. Danson of "Cheers"
22. Vote into office
25. Citrus fruit
28. "___ Jude" (Beatles classic)
29. WC
31. Raised
32. Attila, e.g.
33. Cooking fat
34. ___ Quentin
35. Wild bunch
36. Was in the red
37. Actress Sarandon
39. Title for Walter Scott
41. Drano ingredient
42. Lump in the throat
46. Funeral fire
49. Caveman's era
51. Roadrunner's sound
52. Disneyland's Enchanted ___ Room
53. Money in Tokyo
54. NaCl
55. Black-eyed ___
56. Part of EST

DOWN

1. Diver Louganis
2. Slugger Sammy
3. Military no-show
4. "Halt! Who goes ___?"
5. Put on the payroll
6. AP rival
7. Hold responsible
8. Place for gloss
9. Stereo component
10. Dracula, at times
13. Bug barrier
16. Lugged
20. Tissue layer
23. Talon
24. Drove like mad
25. Ozs. and ozs.
26. Gershwin and others
27. Restaurant handout
28. Wheel's center
30. Like 1, 3, 5, 7, etc.
32. Like Abe
33. Michaels of "SNL"
35. Merry month
38. Caught some Z's

Puzzle 14

1	2	3	■	4	5	6	■	■	7	8	9	10
11			■	12			13	■	14			
15			16					■	17			
18					■		19	20		■	■	■
■	■	■	21			■	22			23	24	■
25	26	27		■	■	28			■	29		30
31				■	32			■	33			
34			■	35			■	■	36			
■	37		38			■	39	40		■	■	■
■	■	■	41			■	42			43	44	45
46	47	48		■	49	50						
51				■	52				■	53		
54				■	■	55			■	56		

39. Stir up, as a fire
40. Ancient Aegean land
43. Verbalizes
44. "___ a Kick Out of You"
45. Give temporarily
46. "Mystery!" network
47. Thumbs-up vote
48. Meth. or Cath.
50. Waiter's reward

Solution on Page 317

ACROSS

1. Victoria's Secret purchase
4. Exclamations of disgust
8. ___ 500
12. Disposable pen maker
13. Depilatory brand
14. Arp's art
15. Rank above Maj.
16. 007 foe
17. ABA member: abbr.
18. Toothpaste holder
20. Cry of disgust
22. Wild time
25. Sedan alternative
29. Huffed and puffed
32. Hay storage place
34. Droop
35. Ship's record
36. Fountain drinks
37. Archaeological site
38. Pull
39. Was in debt
40. Wacky
41. Got up
43. Brand of blocks
45. Rock's Fleetwood ___
47. Thoroughfare
50. Nabors role
53. Olympic gymnast Korbut
56. Sgt. ___
58. Butcher's cut
59. Chick's sound
60. To and ___
61. Burden
62. Wheel turner
63. Ryan of "When Harry Met Sally"

DOWN

1. English TV/radio inits.
2. Melee
3. Legal rights grp.
4. "___ the Boardwalk"
5. Berlin's land: abbr.
6. Egg layer
7. Cease
8. Boise's state
9. Slave Turner
10. Banned bug spray
11. "Yippee!"
19. Arrow shooter
21. ___ of the Apostles
23. Moon shine
24. Alpine call
26. Meat package letters
27. "No ___, no gain."
28. Like custard
29. Deli orders
30. Uncouth person
31. Frozen waffle brand
33. Lose color
36. Fizzy drink

Puzzle 15

40. San Diego attraction
42. Signs of things to come
44. Vineyard fruit
46. Cabana of song
48. Radio letters
49. Challenge
50. Gp. once headed by Arafat
51. Hither's partner
52. "Ally McBeal" actress Lucy
54. ___ Luthor of "Superman"
55. Toothpaste type
57. Training run

Solution on Page 317

ACROSS

1. ___ Perignon champagne
4. Avg.
7. Commotions
11. Check texts
13. Calendar abbr.
14. Prefix with legal or chute
15. Apple leftover
16. Tummy muscles
17. Have ___ with
18. Sports venues
20. Actor Mineo
22. Reverberated
24. Gardner of film
27. One of the senses
30. Monopoly quartet: abbr.
31. El ___ (Spanish hero)
32. Pub quaffs
33. Word before or after pack
34. Use Western Union, e.g.
35. April 15 payment
36. Obtain
37. First, second, third, and home
38. "___ questions?"
39. Kind of monkey
41. Barely passing grade
42. Evaluate
46. Mailing courtesy: abbr.
49. Follower of Mar.
51. Vogue competitor
52. Nastase of tennis
53. Earl Grey, e.g.
54. Bed board
55. Little lice
56. Bus term.
57. Physician's org.

DOWN

1. Ten: prefix
2. Stench
3. "No time to wallow in the ___." (Doors lyric)
4. Hide away
5. Margarine container
6. Dinner finale
7. "Be ___!" ("Help me out!")
8. Actor Aykroyd
9. You ___ (one of us)
10. ___ Jose
12. Doctrines
19. Expert
21. TV interruptions
23. Speechify
24. King beaters
25. Tarzan's transport
26. Does sums
27. Informal farewell
28. Astronaut Shepard
29. "I'm too ___ for my shirt" (Right Said Fred lyric)
33. Warms up again
34. Talks back to

Puzzle 16

1	2	3	■	■	4	5	6	■	7	8	9	10
11			12	■	13			■	14			
15				■	16			■	17			
18				19		■	20	21		■	■	■
■	■	■	22			23			■	24	25	26
27	28	29			■	30			■	31		
32				■	33			■	34			
35			■	36			■	37				
38			■	39			40			■	■	■
■	■	■	41			■	42			43	44	45
46	47	48		■	49	50		■	51			
52				■	53			■	54			
55				■	56			■	■	57		

36. Test for college srs.
37. Tour transportation
40. Brand of wrap
41. "Disco Duck" singer Rick
43. Jazzy Fitzgerald
44. ___ dunk
45. ___ record
46. Break a commandment
47. "Float like a butterfly, sting like a bee" boxer
48. Command to Fido
50. Caress

Solution on Page 317

ACROSS

1. "Slow down!"
5. Volcanic flow
9. Furry foot
12. Help for the stumped
13. Infamous Idi
14. "It's no ___!"
15. 0 on a phone: abbr.
16. Red vegetable
17. Mighty Ducks' org.
18. Edmonton hockey player
20. Detested
22. Instruction book
24. ___ and improved
25. Mushroom-cloud maker
26. Tiny village
29. Hankering
30. Where spokes meet
31. Backwoods refusal
33. Of the pre-Easter season
36. "___ Entertain You"
38. Meddle
39. Flew high
40. Make points
43. Daft
44. 90 degrees from vert.
45. Radar image
47. In that case
50. Neighbor of Scot.
51. "I ___ Ike"
52. Within a stone's throw
53. Susan of "L.A. Law"
54. Eternally
55. Precious stones

DOWN

1. Sci-fi's "Doctor ___"
2. ___-hop (music genre)
3. Mano a mano
4. Courtyard
5. File folder stick-on
6. Part of USA
7. Fight (for)
8. National song
9. Football kick
10. Tennis's Arthur
11. Fuse, as metal
19. Research room
21. Hole-making tool
22. Indy 500 month
23. Cain's brother
24. Catch, as a criminal
26. Attila the ___
27. Tournament charge
28. Not feral
30. Attention-getting shout
32. Say "I do"
34. "All Things Considered" network
35. ___ clef
36. Stephen King's "Salem's ___"

Puzzle 17

1	2	3	4	■	5	6	7	8	■	9	10	11
12				■	13				■	14		
15				■	16				■	17		
■	■	18		19			■	20	21			
22	23					■	24			■	■	■
25					■	26				27	28	■
29			■	■	30			■	■	31		32
■	33		34	35			■	36	37			
■	■	■	38			■	39					
40	41	42			■	43					■	■
44			■	45	46			■	47		48	49
50			■	51				■	52			
53			■	54				■	55			

37. Restaurant activity
39. "Great!"
40. Backyard building
41. Ice cream holder
42. Wild party
43. "Just do it." sloganeer
46. Actress Tyler of "Armageddon"
48. Detective Spade
49. Surgery sites, briefly

Solution on Page 318

ACROSS

1. Retailer's goods: abbr.
5. ___-Magnon, Upper Paleolithic man
8. Singer Irene
12. Tears
13. Rooster's mate
14. "C'mon, be ___"
15. Guitarist Clapton
16. Gardner of "On the Beach"
17. Seeks office
18. National park in Alaska
20. Omaha's state: abbr.
22. Memorial Day event
24. "X": kiss, "O": ___
27. Miser's hoarding
30. Nautical journal
31. One ___ kind
32. ___ page (newspaper part)
33. Untold centuries
34. Gun blast
35. DiCaprio, to fans
36. "Crossfire" network
37. Picked
38. "Grand Ole Opry" airer
39. "Ditto!"
41. Anatomical pouch
42. San Simeon castle builder
46. New York theater award
49. ___-night doubleheader
51. Something to whistle
52. Microwave
53. Suffix with north or south
54. Estate receiver
55. "Star ___"
56. Color changer
57. Armchair athlete's channel

DOWN

1. TV's talking horse
2. Dreadful
3. Twirl
4. Broke out
5. Committee head
6. Minister's title: abbr.
7. Endlessly
8. Low-___ diet
9. "The Simpsons" storekeeper
10. Took off
11. Capone and Pacino
19. "Now I ___ me down to sleep . . ."
21. Brain scan, for short
23. Parallel to
24. Cry from Santa
25. "X-Files" subjects
26. Fence opening
27. Shed one's skin
28. Dentist's request
29. Sign gas
33. Made into law

Puzzle 18

1	2	3	4	■	5	6	7	■	8	9	10	11
12				■	13			■	14			
15				■	16			■	17			
18				19		■	20	21		■	■	■
■	■	■	22			23			■	24	25	26
27	28	29			■	30			■	31		
32				■	33			■	34			
35			■	36			■	37				
38			■	39			40			■	■	■
■	■	■	41			■	42			43	44	45
46	47	48		■	49	50		■	51			
52				■	53			■	54			
55				■	56			■	57			

34. Put away, as a sword
36. Undercover org.
37. Middling grade
40. German wine valley
41. Hide-and-___
43. Regrets
44. Scissors cut
45. Sea swallow
46. Ottawa's prov.
47. Prickly husk
48. Eisenhower nickname
50. Twisted, as humor

Solution on Page 318

ACROSS

1. Talk show host Dr. ___
5. Taiwanese-born director Lee
8. ___ and outs
11. Make perfect
12. Taverns
14. Word after waste and want
15. Art ___ (1920s–30s style)
16. Work without ___
17. Sutcliffe of the early Beatles
18. ___ sequitur
20. Tried out
22. Ragged, as a garment
26. New pedometer reading
27. Friend's opposite
28. "Revenge of the ___"
32. Surveyor's map
34. Nope
36. Sign on for another tour
37. Blood component
39. Tofu base
41. DDT-banning agency
42. Chart-topper
45. Jolly Roger flier
48. ___ loss for words
49. Troop-entertaining grp.
50. Elvis Presley's middle name
52. Arrests
56. Hit head-on
57. Leo's symbol
58. Let fall
59. Deli loaf
60. Home loan agcy.
61. Remain

DOWN

1. Prof.'s degree
2. Clod chopper
3. Bus. name ending
4. Africa's Sierra ___
5. Leave high and dry
6. Tandoori bread
7. Miss Garbo
8. Part of RPI
9. Memo
10. Poker variety
13. Back of a boat
19. Buffoon
21. Clairvoyant
22. Bikini parts
23. Golfer's target
24. Crowd sound
25. Beauty's counterpart
29. Film spool
30. Bamboozle
31. Practice in the ring
33. Oompah instrument
35. Biblical cry of praise
38. "Heavy" music genre
40. Nevertheless

Puzzle 19

1	2	3	4	■	5	6	7	■	■	8	9	10
11				■	12			13	■	14		
15				■	16				■	17		
■	■	■	18	19		■	20		21			
22	23	24				25				■	■	■
26			■	27			■	28		29	30	31
32			33	■	34		35	■	36			
37				38	■	39		40	■	41		
■	■	■	42		43				44			
45	46	47				■	48			■	■	■
49			■	50		51		■	52	53	54	55
56			■	57				■	58			
59			■	■	60			■	61			

43. Letter flourish
44. Touches down
45. Cat or engine sound
46. "___, old chap!"
47. Italy's capital
51. Aah's partner
53. The "A" in MoMA
54. Fluffy scarf
55. Finder of secrets

Solution on Page 318

ACROSS

1. ___ Bartlet, president on "The West Wing"
4. Richard of "Pretty Woman"
8. Medical researcher's goal
12. Mimic
13. Property encumbrance
14. Wise ___ owl
15. "Who ___ that masked man?"
16. Be jealous of
17. Coin factory
18. MSNBC rival
20. Get even for
22. Rigby of song
26. Rags-to-riches author
27. Singer k.d. ___
28. Shower
30. Elect, with "for"
31. Storage container
32. Kind of pie
35. Professional org.
36. Open the mouth wide
37. Overalls material
41. Perfume
43. Titillating
45. ___ Glory
46. Taxis
47. Head covering
50. Jackie's second spouse
53. Scandinavian capital
54. "Money ___ everything!"
55. Malleable metal
56. Strong odor
57. Pie pans
58. Ambulance letters

DOWN

1. Mandible
2. Ecol. watchdog
3. Mountain climber's return
4. First American in orbit
5. German article
6. Minister: abbr.
7. "Orinoco Flow" singer
8. Oasis animal
9. Taking advantage of
10. Where the deer and the antelope play
11. Go in
19. Henpeck
21. Vehicle with sliding doors
22. "Don't Bring Me Down" band
23. Once around the track
24. Globes
25. Elevate
29. Bed-and-breakfasts
32. Authoritative order
33. Merchandise ID
34. Fiddle-de-___
35. "What ___, chopped liver?"

Puzzle 20

1	2	3	■	4	5	6	7	■	8	9	10	11
12			■	13				■	14			
15			■	16				■	17			
■	■	18	19		■	■	20	21				
22	23				24	25	■	26				
27				■	28		29		■	■	■	■
30			■	■	31			■	■	32	33	34
■	■	■	■	35				■	36			
37	38	39	40		■	41		42				
43					44	■	■	45			■	■
46				■	47	48	49		■	50	51	52
53				■	54				■	55		
56				■	57				■	58		

36. Come together
37. Interior design
38. Wipe clean
39. Barnes & ___
40. “No problem!”
42. Puts into piles
44. IOU
48. “___ was saying . . .”
49. Roadhouse
51. Edge
52. “Walk-___ welcome”

Solution on Page 318

ACROSS

1. Hoover, for one
4. Gun sound
8. Young lady
12. Critical hosp. area
13. Brother of Cain
14. Teen woe
15. Early hrs.
16. Parcel of land
17. "Little ___ of Horrors"
18. Sleep symbols
20. Service charges
22. "___ Be Seeing You"
25. Ignited again
29. Countdown of top tunes
34. "What was ___ do?"
35. From point ___ point B
36. Subject
37. It may be put out to pasture
38. Dubya's deg.
39. Shredded
41. Four-door car
43. Leary's drug
44. Silent assents
47. Sailor's mop
51. Head honcho
54. Overwhelmed
57. Gardner of "The Night of the Iguana"
58. Fairy tale starter
59. Encl. with a manuscript
60. Title for Galahad
61. Astronaut Armstrong
62. Hoopla
63. Winter clock setting in S.F.

DOWN

1. Actress Cameron
2. Pinnacle
3. Artist's inspiration
4. Bleat
5. Jackson 5 hit
6. Kid's ball material
7. ___ club (singing group)
8. En ___ (as a group)
9. I, as in Innsbruck
10. ___-Caps (candy brand)
11. Fall mo.
19. Tiny taste
21. Puts up, as a tower
23. Mexican-American, e.g.
24. Author Hubbard
26. Dog pests
27. "Love ___ leave it"
28. Pulls along behind
29. Easter roasts
30. "Can ___ true?"
31. Frog relative
32. Likely
33. Obsolescent phone feature

Puzzle 21

1	2	3	■	4	5	6	7	■	8	9	10	11
12			■	13				■	14			
15			■	16				■	17			
18			19	■	■	20		21		■	■	■
■	■	■	22	23	24	■	■	25		26	27	28
29	30	31				32	33		■	34		
35			■	36					■	37		
38			■	39					40			
41			42		■	■	43			■	■	■
■	■	■	44		45	46	■	■	47	48	49	50
51	52	53		■	54		55	56	■	57		
58				■	59				■	60		
61				■	62				■	63		

40. QB's scores
42. Photographer Adams
45. Short race
46. Influence
48. Stinging insect
49. Budget competitor
50. Lisa Simpson's brother
51. Rockers ___ Jovi
52. ___ of a kind
53. Part of BS
55. Mind reading, for short
56. Actor Billy ___ Williams

Solution on Page 319

ACROSS

1. Knights' wives
6. Finished first
9. Drs.' group
12. Nimble
13. Sailor's assent
14. X-ray dose unit
15. Simple swimming stroke
17. Neither Rep. nor Dem.
18. &
19. WWII riveter
21. San ___ Obispo, Calif.
24. ___ Harbor, Long Island
27. Slightly
28. Passion
30. Game with a jackpot
32. Expire
33. "Don't Cry for Me, Argentina" musical
35. Part of an iceberg that's visible
38. "That's the truth!"
40. Actress Shire of "Rocky"
42. Lane
44. "L–P" connection
46. Opposite of ja
47. "Ghostbusters" goo
49. Jury-___ (improvise)
51. Easy as ___
52. Some three-digit numbers
58. Pasture
59. Baseball score
60. "Well done!"
61. Actor Gibson
62. Tent pin
63. Lions' locks

DOWN

1. "Dear old" guy
2. "Four score and seven years ___. . ."
3. Russian fighter jet
4. Rio Grande city
5. Actor Connery
6. Mouthful of gum
7. Popeye's Olive
8. ___-do-well
9. Pupil of Plato
10. Craze
11. Threw in
16. Dentist's deg.
20. Grain in Cheerios
21. Young fellow
22. Geller with a psychic act
23. Like some twins
25. Extraterrestrial
26. "I ___ Rhythm"
29. Seminary subj.
31. "I tawt I taw a puddy ___"
34. ___ and vigor
36. Rightmost number on a grandfather clock
37. ___-Hellenic (like the ancient Olympics)

Puzzle 22

39. Unit of electrical resistance
41. Sweater material
42. Old Testament song
43. "The Zoo Story" playwright Edward
45. ". . . ___ reasonable facsimile"
48. Lawman Wyatt
50. Warhead weapon, for short
53. Wish it weren't so
54. Part of the U.K.
55. Dapper ___
56. New Year's ___
57. Call for help

Solution on Page 319

ACROSS

1. Entraps
7. Rock layers
13. Eagle's grabbers
14. Beaver State
15. Tarzan, for one
16. Androids
17. Test
18. Letter after zeta
19. Alaskan city where the Iditarod ends
22. Scarecrow stuffing
26. Distant finishers
30. Individually
31. Actress Myrna
32. "i" topper
33. Wintry
34. Long and lean
36. Strunk and White's "The ___ of Style"
39. Ancient Peruvians
41. Collections of anecdotes
42. Steal from
44. Kilt wearer
47. Entertain, as with stories
50. Kind of energy
52. Rhetorician
53. Loewe's partner on Broadway
54. What some scouts seek
55. Monet or Manet

DOWN

1. RR depot
2. Scruff
3. Author Haley
4. Italian cheese
5. Fill with love
6. Nine-digit ID
7. Kind of loser
8. Horses' gaits
9. Money-back offer
10. In times past
11. Rug rat
12. Response: abbr.
20. Fashioned
21. ___ Gay (WWII plane)
23. Drought relief
24. No. on a bank statement
25. Reasons
26. "___ Wanna Do" (Sheryl Crow hit)
27. The "L" in S&L
28. Harmony
29. British submachine gun
35. Sport in which belts are awarded
37. Top chess player
38. Accompany to a party
40. Wise lawgiver
43. Ernie's muppet pal
45. Prefix with potent
46. Neckwear
47. Go to waste

Puzzle 23

48. Historic period
49. “My ___ Sal”
50. Chicken ___ king
51. Monitor, for short

Solution on Page 319

ACROSS

1. Com preceder
4. Recipe amt.
7. Striped fish
11. Honest ___ (presidential moniker)
12. Skirt lines
14. Working without ___
15. Buck's mate
16. Take a load off
17. Ginger cookie
18. Terminator
20. Preferred invitees
22. ___ Moines, Iowa
23. ___ center (community facility)
24. Back talk
27. Actor with the catchphrase "I pity the fool!"
28. Toward the back of a boat
31. Jamaican music
32. Sticks around
34. Media mogul Turner
35. Candle material
36. Teachers' union, in brief
37. Honey makers
38. Swindle
39. "Make ___ double!"
41. ___ in the back (betrays)
43. Dog strap
46. Golfers' gadgets
47. New York's ___ Canal
49. "That feels good!"
51. Dryer outlet
52. Actor Penn
53. Second Amendment advocacy gp.
54. Diarist Frank
55. Hosp. workers
56. Family room

DOWN

1. Pop
2. Cousin of a bassoon
3. Adolescent
4. Number of little pigs or blind mice
5. Prophets
6. Afternoons and evenings, briefly
7. Fundamental
8. Landers and Sothern
9. Chair or sofa
10. Popular oil additive
13. Like the night sky
19. Shingle letters
21. Allows
24. NNE's opposite
25. Abbr. before an alias
26. Kenny G's instrument
27. Goat's cry
28. Consumed
29. Lawyer's charge
30. NFL scores
32. Elitist

Puzzle 24

1	2	3	■	4	5	6	■	■	7	8	9	10
11			■	12			13	■	14			
15			■	16				■	17			
■	18		19			■	20	21				■
■	■	■	22			■	23			■	■	■
24	25	26		■	■	27			■	28	29	30
31			■	32	33				■	34		
35			■	36			■	■	37			
■	■	■	38			■	39	40		■	■	■
■	41	42				■	43			44	45	■
46				■	47	48			■	49		50
51				■	52				■	53		
54				■	■	55			■	56		

33. Past, present, and future
37. Sheep's cry
38. Hindu social division
39. Trojan War epic
40. Adolescents
41. "As ___ on TV!"
42. Ky. neighbor
44. Beach composition
45. ___ Krishna
46. New Deal agcy.
48. "Losing My Religion" band
50. Solo in space

Solution on Page 319

ACROSS

1. Motor City org.
4. Lions and tigers
8. Writer/illustrator Silverstein
12. ’60s muscle car
13. Marco Polo crossed it
14. Unseat
15. Not vert.
16. Barely made, with “out”
17. Dog docs
18. Olympian ruler
20. Surrealist Salvador
22. ___ Tuesday (Mardi Gras)
24. Wobble
28. Loser
32. Europe’s “boot”
33. Actor Cariou
34. Searched for buried treasure
36. Brownies’ org.
37. Animal life
40. Big name in TV ratings
43. Makes irate
45. Day-___ colors
46. Short sketch
48. Physicians, briefly
51. Falling-out
54. Rotunda’s crown
56. Harley-Davidson, slangily
58. “___ from Muskogee”
59. Recedes
60. Lincoln, informally
61. Proof of ownership
62. Cop’s route
63. China’s Mao ___-tung

DOWN

1. “That’s disgusting!”
2. From “___” (the gamut)
3. Sported
4. Kind of salad
5. Query
6. Like a 4–4 score
7. Peace Nobelist Anwar
8. ___ Union
9. Tint
10. Approx. figure
11. Capts.’ subordinates
19. Mysterious saucer
21. Hawaiian garland
23. Little bit
25. Labels
26. “If all ___ fails . . .”
27. Pitcher Nolan
28. ___ Romeo
29. Like Jack Sprat’s diet
30. Like a bug in a rug
31. Mother Teresa, e.g.
35. Musician’s engagement
38. Fitted one within another
39. Noah’s vessel

Puzzle 25

41. Most senior
42. British john
44. Lesser-played half of a 45
47. "___ honest with you . . ."
49. Converse
50. Blubbers
51. Serling of "The Twilight Zone"
52. Tina Turner's ex
53. Old expression of disgust
55. Deg. for a corporate ladder climber
57. "Gosh!"

Solution on Page 320

ACROSS

1. Tex. neighbor
5. Food served with a ladle
9. Its capital is Boise: abbr.
12. Life stories, for short
13. Lo-cal
14. It's south of S.D.
15. Photographer's request
17. HBO competitor
18. Charged particle
19. Legitimate
21. Let in
24. "Laughing" animal
26. Tetley product
27. Justice Dept. division
28. Engrave with acid
31. Prefix meaning "trillion"
33. Diamond arbiter
34. "Hold your horses!"
35. Boats like Noah's
36. Prosecutors, briefly
37. Goof up
38. 11- or 12-year-old
40. Insertion mark
42. Cut wood
44. Animation frame
45. Thurman of "Kill Bill"
46. Privy to confidential information
52. Baseball card stat
53. Stalactite site
54. ___-European languages
55. Menacing sight in "Jaws"
56. Melt
57. Lymph bump

DOWN

1. No longer used: abbr.
2. Hyundai rival
3. "The Thin Man" actress
4. Computer character set, for short
5. Singer Campbell
6. Fib
7. Extra play periods, for short
8. "Pet" annoyance
9. All worked up
10. Moore of "G.I. Jane"
11. Introductory letters?
16. Sexy
20. Once more
21. Lead-in to girl
22. Venison source
23. Tom Sawyer's creator
24. Macho dude
25. Shrill barks
27. "___, Where's My Car?" (2000 comedy)
29. Heart
30. Lyricist Lorenz
32. "Even ___ speak . . ."
39. Decree

Puzzle 26

1	2	3	4	■	5	6	7	8	■	9	10	11
12				■	13				■	14		
15				16					■	17		
■	■	■	18			■	■	19	20			
21	22	23			■	24	25				■	■
26			■	■	27			■	28		29	30
31			32	■	33			■	34			
35				■	36			■	■	37		
■	■	38		39			■	40	41			
42	43				■	■	44			■	■	■
45			■	46	47	48				49	50	51
52			■	53				■	54			
55			■	56				■	57			

40. Middling mark
41. "___ the Family" (classic sitcom)
42. Ride the waves
43. Prefix with dextrous
44. ___ the fat
47. Slangy negative
48. Dam-building org.
49. Musician Yoko
50. ___ man out
51. "Annabel Lee" poet

Solution on Page 320

ACROSS

1. Bashful
4. Computer key
7. "Are we having fun ___?"
10. Hammer part
12. ___ contendere (court plea)
14. "How revolting!"
15. Mrs., in Munich
16. Minnesota ballplayer
17. Cow sound
18. H. S. T.'s successor
20. King with a golden touch
22. Try again, as a court case
25. Three before "E"
26. Palindromic English river
27. Anti-fray border
29. Devour
33. Meat in a can
35. Two, in Tijuana
37. ". . . golden days of ___"
38. Synagogue scroll
40. Air conditioner meas.
42. Guy's partner
43. Floor cleaner
45. Fill the lungs
47. Ross of the Supremes
49. Word with pick or wit
50. Karaoke singer's need, for short
51. Copier input: abbr.
53. Pack (down)
57. "Shame on you!"
58. Abundant
59. Sound of contentment
60. Wild blue yonder
61. Lancelot's title
62. Classic Pontiac

DOWN

1. Coppertone no.
2. Not him
3. Vote of support
4. Came in
5. Female pig
6. "___ Every Mountain"
7. Arizona city on the Colorado River
8. Self-images
9. Even if, informally
11. Naked
13. In the cooler
19. Morse code sound
21. Invasion date
22. Take a breather
23. Giant fair
24. Listen to
28. Mafia
30. Roman robe
31. Russian river
32. Brazilian booter
34. Cry from a crib
36. Wasp weapon

Puzzle 27

1	2	3	■	■	4	5	6	■	■	7	8	9
10			11	■	12			13	■	14		
15				■	16				■	17		
■	■	■	18	19		■	20		21			■
22	23	24				■	25			■	■	■
26			■	27		28	■	29		30	31	32
33			34	■	35		36	■	37			
38				39	■	40		41	■	42		
■	■	■	43		44	■	45		46			
■	47	48				■	49			■	■	■
50			■	51		52		■	53	54	55	56
57			■	58				■	59			
60			■	■	61			■	■	62		

39. Pay tribute to
41. Bi- halved
44. Eiffel Tower locale
46. Website address starter
47. "Slipped" backbone part
48. Gross
50. Range units: abbr.
52. "___ Were a Rich Man"
54. Dog days mo.
55. Chain-wearing "A-Team" actor
56. Paid player

Solution on Page 320

ACROSS

1. Onetime Jeep mfr.
4. Paddle
7. Bank no.
11. "Do ___ Diddy Diddy": 1964 song
12. Pepsi alternative
14. German three
15. Negative particle
17. Weaver's apparatus
18. "Sesame ___"
19. Espionage org.
21. One thing ___ time
22. "Hasta la vista!"
25. Uses a stool
28. Next-to-last Greek letter
29. Boar's mate
31. Clinton's #2
32. Opponent
33. Breathing sound
34. A pair
35. Cherry seed
36. Jekyll's alter ego
37. Bridal path
39. Go head to head
41. Some boxing wins, for short
42. Horn
46. ___ mater
49. Poe story, "The ___ Heart"
51. Codger
52. Tropical fever
53. Size between sm. and lge.
54. Use a Smith-Corona
55. Receive
56. Bad ___ (German spa)

DOWN

1. Bedazzles
2. ___ liquor
3. "Moonstruck" actress
4. Group of eight
5. Main artery
6. Early MGM rival
7. 1950s candidate Stevenson
8. ___-Magnon
9. Corp. boss
10. Comic Conway
13. Sheathe
16. Discontinue
20. Exiled Amin
23. Start of "The Star-Spangled Banner"
24. Auctioneer's last word
25. Certain NCO
26. Presidential caucus state
27. Enterprise counselor
28. Poker prize
30. Itsy-bitsy
32. Cinco de Mayo party
33. Scarlett's love
35. Mahmoud Abbas's grp.

Puzzle 28

38. Use Rollerblades
39. What it's worth
40. Cove
43. Weak, as an excuse
44. Grades 1–6: abbr.
45. 1981 Beatty film
46. Play part
47. Silver screen star Myrna
48. Finish, with "up"
50. "Which came first?" choice

Solution on Page 320

ACROSS

1. Early late-night host
5. "Pet" that's a plant
9. Brit. fliers
12. "All ___!" (court phrase)
13. Bring up, as children
14. "Xanadu" rock grp.
15. Miners' finds
16. Domesticated
17. EMT's skill
18. Religious faction
19. Dashed
20. CD-___
21. Filmed
24. A dog's ___ (long spell)
26. "Tip-Toe Thru' the Tulips with Me" instrument
29. Celestial bear
31. O. Henry's "The Gift of the ___"
34. Military greeting
36. Make a difference
38. Small bills
39. Central-American Indian
41. Mouse spotter's cry
42. Kilmer of "The Doors"
44. HS junior's test
46. The Sunshine State, briefly
48. Stock mkt. debut
50. Nile reptiles
54. Counterpart of long.
55. Auctioneer's closing word
57. In ___ of (instead of)
58. Had a bite
59. ___ vault
60. "The ___ of the Cave Bear"
61. "You betcha!"
62. Tortoiselike
63. Tipplers

DOWN

1. ___ and cons
2. Suffix with concession
3. "Hold on ___!"
4. Takes five
5. Computer screen, for short
6. Red card suit
7. "___ Rock" (Simon & Garfunkel hit)
8. Boxing venue
9. Bring to life again
10. Dog food brand
11. ". . . in no way, shape or ___"
22. Crude shelter
23. Utah city
25. All clocks are set by it: abbr.
26. GI show sponsor
27. Colo. neighbor
28. Raises
30. Grant and Carter
32. Beaver's exclamation
33. Rankle
35. Made in the ___

Puzzle 29

37. Org. that gets members reduced motel rates
40. Moon-landing program
43. Has speech difficulties
45. Bathroom powders
46. Whip
47. Running behind
49. Motel amenity
51. Round farm building
52. ___ moss
53. Solar-system centers
56. Morning droplets

Solution on Page 321

ACROSS

1. Guitar cousin
4. Prayer's end
8. Eastern European
12. Fish feature
13. Umpteen
14. Musical quality
15. "Cat ___ Hot Tin Roof"
16. Computer memory measure
17. Learning by memorization
18. Back tooth
20. "Peter, Peter, pumpkin ___ . . ."
21. "___ all ye faithful . . ."
23. With competence
25. "Phooey!"
26. "C'mon, be ___!"
27. Gear tooth
30. Dramatist Eugene
32. "___ Weapon" (Mel Gibson film)
34. Crimson
35. Roman love poet
37. Abhor
38. Bosom companions
39. Get up
40. Bawl out
43. Twice-seen TV show
45. Inlet
46. Hoover and Grand Coulee
47. Female sib
50. Home of Iowa State
51. "Finding ___"
52. "___ and ye shall receive"
53. Beach shades
54. Comedian King
55. Philosopher's question

DOWN

1. ET carrier
2. Relatives
3. Smitten
4. Mosey along
5. Poet Angelou
6. Snare
7. "Bill ___, the Science Guy"
8. Homeless animal
9. Booty
10. Poker payment
11. Suddenly change course
19. Old Dodge
20. Fashion magazine
21. Scent
22. Walking stick
24. Hairless
26. Thomas ___ Edison
27. Logger's tool
28. Horse feed
29. Tickled-pink feeling
31. "The ___ of the Rings"
33. "No ___ traffic"
36. Tel Aviv's land

Puzzle 30

1	2	3	■	4	5	6	7	■	8	9	10	11
12			■	13				■	14			
15			■	16				■	17			
■	■	18	19				■	20				
21	22				■	23	24			■	■	■
25				■	26				■	27	28	29
30				31		■	32		33			
34			■	35		36		■	37			
■	■	■	38				■	39				
40	41	42			■	43	44				■	■
45				■	46				■	47	48	49
50				■	51				■	52		
53				■	54				■	55		

38. “God ___ America”
39. Fire-setting crime
40. “Scram!”
41. Un-wake-able state
42. Pizzeria fixture
44. Jane Austen novel
46. Code of life
48. Relative of -esque
49. Where a telescope is aimed

Solution on Page 321

ACROSS

1. "Gotcha"
5. Soprano Gluck
9. "Killer" PC program
12. Kind of ranch
13. Touch
14. Japanese "yes"
15. Lascivious look
16. Sharp flavor
17. Sch. near Harvard
18. Borden's cow
20. Actor's representative
22. God's honest truth
26. String after "A"
29. Battering wind
30. Circle segments
34. Rosary unit
36. Mad Hatter's drink
37. Singer Celine
38. Arrive
39. Grasped
41. "The ___ and the Pussycat"
42. Spoke roughly
44. Meager
47. Oodles
52. Western omelet ingredient
53. "Goodness!"
57. Prefix with lateral
58. Venomous viper
59. Lion's hair
60. Break in the action
61. The Appalachians, e.g.: abbr.
62. Dinner from a bucket
63. Chat

DOWN

1. Doing nothing
2. Old-fashioned showdown
3. ___ of March
4. Ex Spice Girl Halliwell
5. Astern
6. "Back to the Future" actress Thompson
7. "Of Mice and ___"
8. Pond scum
9. "Alas!"
10. Aspirin target
11. Actor Brad
19. Silly Putty holder
21. "___ All Over" (Dave Clark Five hit)
23. Solemn pledges
24. Catch some Z's
25. Norman Vincent ___
26. Eng. channel
27. Corp. biggie
28. Hydroelectric project
31. Brazilian vacation spot, informally
32. Milk source
33. NBC weekend comedy

Puzzle 31

35. Bruce or Laura of Hollywood
40. Driller's deg.
43. Parts of molecules
44. Fraud
45. Players in a play
46. Electrical units
48. Irish native
49. Shade of blue
50. Uninteresting
51. Fine pajama material
54. Twain portrayer Holbrook
55. Pre–"P" three
56. "You betcha!"

Solution on Page 321

ACROSS

1. Last year of the 3rd century
4. Drains
8. Enlistees
11. Boast
13. Ninny
14. Dictator Amin
15. Song for one
16. Seized vehicle
17. Jazz job
18. Nevertheless
20. Junior naval officer
22. Soak up
25. Dem.'s foe
26. Barfly
27. Topic for Dr. Ruth
29. Actress Winger
33. Egyptian goddess
35. Back-to-school mo.
37. Cut, as nails
38. Throw out
40. Salty sauce
42. World Series mo.
43. Alternative to KS
45. Knights' weapons
47. Assert without proof
50. Letters before an alias
51. Promissory note
52. Finished
54. Jockey's whip
58. Aves.
59. Lucy's husband
60. Hawaiian feast
61. Filming site
62. Circle parts
63. Mohawk-sporting actor

DOWN

1. "Survivor" network
2. ___-Magnon (early human)
3. Baseball's Ripken
4. Flashing lights
5. Fill with wonder
6. Peter the pepper picker
7. High on something other than life
8. "Thank Heaven for Little Girls" musical
9. Beatnik's "Gotcha"
10. Omen
12. "___ jail" (Monopoly directive)
19. Day divs.
21. Design detail
22. Sale tag caution
23. Pear variety
24. Mix (up)
28. Illiterates' signatures
30. Voting group
31. Serving with chop suey
32. Bldg. units
34. "For Pete's ___!"

Puzzle 32

36. North Star
39. Chinese temple
41. Chatter
44. "And ___ the twain shall meet"
46. Table salt, to a chemist
47. Broadcasts
48. Ore deposit
49. A deadly sin
53. PC bailout key
55. Daiquiri base
56. Boat mover
57. "To ___ it mildly . . ."

Solution on Page 321

ACROSS

1. U.K. channel
4. Faucet
7. Campaign funders, for short
11. Meadow
12. Ancient Peruvian
14. Each, in pricing
15. Old salt
16. Env. notation
17. Castro's country
18. Daubs
20. '50s pres.
22. "Whoopee!"
23. Choirs may stand on them
27. "Psycho" motel name
30. Computer storage unit, informally
31. ___ goo gai pan
32. Bullfight cheers
33. Color TV pioneer
34. Pasta choice
35. '60s hallucinogen
36. "Now, where ___ I?"
37. Christmas song
38. ___ salad
40. Author Fleming or McEwan
41. Uganda's ___ Amin
42. Fashioned
46. Incinerate
49. Sediment
51. Antiquated
52. Intl. oil group
53. Dog command
54. Thurman of Hollywood
55. Wile E. Coyote's supplier
56. Numbered hwy.
57. Plaything

DOWN

1. Crunchy sandwiches, for short
2. "___ me up, Scotty"
3. Give a hoot
4. Pageant crowns
5. Unable to sit still
6. %: abbr.
7. Walks back and forth
8. Storekeeper on "The Simpsons"
9. What corn kernels attach to
10. Health resort
13. ___ Doria (ill-fated ship)
19. Nays' opposites
21. Excavate
24. Dubai dignitary
25. Prefix with tiller
26. Potting material
27. Lightning flash
28. In addition
29. Kennedy and Turner
30. Banquet hosts: abbr.
33. Salad ingredient
34. Madcap

Puzzle 33

1	2	3	■	4	5	6	■	■	7	8	9	10
11			■	12			13	■	14			
15			■	16				■	17			
18			19			■	20	21		■	■	■
■	■	■	22			■	23			24	25	26
27	28	29			■	30			■	31		
32				■	33			■	34			
35			■	36			■	37				
38			39			■	40			■	■	■
■	■	■	41			■	42			43	44	45
46	47	48		■	49	50			■	51		
52				■	53				■	54		
55				■	■	56			■	57		

36. Commit matrimony
37. Longhorns, e.g.
39. "___ you asked . . ."
40. Speck in the sea
43. Boor
44. "Tickle me" doll
45. WWII turning point
46. ___ constrictor
47. It's scanned at checkout: abbr.
48. Michael Stipe's band
50. Suffix with hotel

Solution on Page 322

ACROSS

1. Londoner, e.g.
5. Easy mark
8. Maxi's opposite
12. Piece next to a knight
13. CBS forensic drama
14. "___ just me or . . . ?"
15. Comment on, as in a margin
17. Wall Street order
18. Hitter's stat
19. Man of ___ (Superman)
20. Get the soap out
24. Peacock's pride
26. Oneness
27. West Pointers
30. Garden entrance
31. Mortgage org.
32. ___ to one's word
34. Kathmandu native
36. Romantic recitals
37. Elvis's middle name
38. Fable writer
39. Involuntary twitch
42. ___-tac-toe
44. Anderson of "WKRP in Cincinnati"
45. Wimbledon fault-caller
50. Matured
51. Mantra syllables
52. "___ kleine Nachtmusik"
53. Carry
54. Acquire
55. Stick in one's ___ (rankle)

DOWN

1. Lingerie item
2. Politico ___ Paul
3. Lithium-___ battery
4. Ring decision
5. Strikebreaker
6. Saver of nine
7. Crusty dessert
8. Christmas greenery
9. Words of comprehension
10. World's longest river
11. "___ cost you!"
16. "South Park" co-creator Parker
19. Vicious or Caesar
20. Alternative to a bare floor
21. ___ instant (quickly)
22. Nick at ___
23. Get out of the way
25. Battery size
28. Uno + dos
29. Japanese wrestling
31. Andy Capp's wife
33. Clairvoyant's claim
35. Elbow's site
36. Walk back and forth
39. Venetian-blind part
40. Kind of stick

Puzzle 34

41. Work without ___ (take risks)
43. The "I" in MIT: abbr.
45. Fireplace fuel
46. "Hold on a ___!"
47. Fallen space station
48. ___ for effort
49. Just off the assembly line

Solution on Page 322

ACROSS

1. "Casual" dress day: abbr.
4. Vex
7. Steep, as tea
11. Continental abbr.
12. "The Ghost and Mrs. ___"
14. Swedish furniture giant
15. Hawkeye Pierce portrayer
17. Realtor's favorite sign
18. Go back on one's word
19. Mop & ___: cleaning brand
21. Marry
22. Salad servers
25. Moniker
28. Smidgen
29. Ignited
31. Fuzzy image
32. Harbor vessel
33. Multinational currency
34. Cartoon frame
35. He's no gentleman
36. Marvel Comics group
37. Actor Romero
39. How some stocks are sold: abbr.
41. ThinkPad maker
42. Like better
46. Break in friendly relations
49. "Home on the Range" critter
51. "___ Ha'i" ("South Pacific" song)
52. Genesis son
53. Repartee
54. "___ a roll!"
55. Fractional amt.
56. Kind of PC monitor

DOWN

1. Phobia
2. Golden ___
3. Tehran's land
4. Spitting ___
5. Governed
6. Young goat
7. American buffalo
8. "It's a Wonderful Life" studio
9. Slippery one
10. Money roll
13. Disheveled
16. More recent
20. Soft toss
23. Down in the dumps
24. Filly's father
25. "30 Rock" network
26. Actor Guinness
27. Stubborn beast
28. Firecracker that fizzles
30. Heavy weight
32. Airport surface
33. Microsoft spreadsheet program
35. Urban ride
38. Peaceful protest

Puzzle 35

1	2	3	■	4	5	6	■	■	7	8	9	10
11			■	12			13	■	14			
15			16					■	17			
18						■	19	20		■	■	■
■	■	■	21			■	22			23	24	■
25	26	27		■	■	28			■	29		30
31				■	32			■	33			
34			■	35			■	■	36			
■	37		38			■	39	40		■	■	■
■	■	■	41			■	42			43	44	45
46	47	48		■	49	50						
51				■	52				■	53		
54				■	■	55			■	56		

39. Eye-related
40. Senator Lott
43. Chickens and turkeys
44. “Ben-Hur,” for one
45. AARP part: abbr.
46. Baseball stat
47. The Beatles’ “___ the Walrus”
48. ___-Jo (1988 Olympics star)
50. Short snooze

Solution on Page 322

ACROSS

1. ___ Gerard (Buck Rogers portrayer)
4. ET transporters
8. "___ died and made you king?"
11. Bread unit
13. City map
14. Suffix with bombard
15. "Drinks are ___!"
16. "No thanks, ___ already"
17. Small amount
18. Makes leather
20. Aids and ___
22. ___ ego
25. "Where the heart is"
27. "Charlie's Angels" costar Lucy
28. Tennis score after deuce
30. TV, slangily, with "the"
34. Trio after "K"
35. Gin's partner
37. Where to hang one's hat
38. Stitched line
40. "Leave ___ Beaver"
41. Playground game
42. Trail
44. ___ Lodge (motel chain)
46. Former Iranian rulers
49. "___, meeny, miney, mo"
51. Novelist Deighton
52. Mafia boss
54. Display
58. Ash holder
59. ___ empty stomach
60. Drop from the eye
61. Calendar pgs.
62. Cookie containers
63. Cook, as onion rings

DOWN

1. Day-___ (fluorescent paint brand)
2. "Am ___ time?"
3. On the ___ (fleeing)
4. ___ arms (angry)
5. One-hit wonder, e.g.
6. Mare's morsel
7. Sauna feature
8. Not narrow
9. Furnace output
10. Spheres
12. Celebration
19. "I smell ___!"
21. Gamble
22. Cure-___ (panaceas)
23. Green shade
24. Sandwich fish
26. Step ___ (hurry)
29. "Just ___" (Nike slogan)
31. ___ no good
32. Legume
33. Breakfast brand

Puzzle 36

36. Joel or Ethan of film
39. Speed limit abbr.
43. High-class tie
45. Abnormal sac
46. Urban renewal target
47. Submarine sandwich
48. Raggedy ___ (dolls)
50. Many millennia
53. Folk singer DiFranco
55. "Playboy" mogul, to pals
56. Boat propeller
57. Lopsided, as a grin

Solution on Page 322

ACROSS

1. "Good Will Hunting" school
4. Lima's land
8. Clarinetist Artie
12. Winning tic-tac-toe row
13. ___ the Terrible
14. Large volume
15. Scheduled to arrive
16. Kudrow of "Friends"
17. Sluggers' stats
18. Police informer
21. Canadian prov.
22. Morning moisture
23. "That's all there ___ it!"
25. Badminton court divider
26. Tach. reading
29. Pleasantly brief
33. Half a laugh
34. Hwy.
35. Armed conflicts
36. Row's opp.
37. U.S. soldiers
38. Twists and turns in a bowling alley
43. Impoverished
44. Atmosphere
45. Actress Thurman
47. Classic clown
48. Hits the slopes
49. Letters after CD
50. ___ cell research
51. Column next to the ones
52. Computer key: abbr.

DOWN

1. Chic, to Austin Powers
2. Bettors' promises, e.g.
3. In direct confrontation
4. Aviator
5. Demonic
6. Coarse file
7. Without assistance
8. Spread, as seed
9. Boxcar rider
10. Despot Idi ___
11. Film director Craven
19. ___ about (circa)
20. "Smoke ___ in Your Eyes"
23. Sort of: suffix
24. "Steady as ___ goes"
25. SSW's reverse
26. Give comforting words to
27. Price ___ pound
28. McKinley, Hood, et al.: abbr.
30. "Iliad" setting
31. If nothing else
32. Axis vs. Allies conflict
36. PC storage medium
37. Windshield material
38. Cowboy's footwear
39. Move like molasses

Puzzle 37

1	2	3	■	4	5	6	7	■	8	9	10	11
12			■	13				■	14			
15			■	16				■	17			
■	18		19					20				■
■	■	21			■	■	22			■	■	■
23	24			■	■	25			■	26	27	28
29				30	31				32			
33			■	34			■	■	35			
■	■	■	36			■	■	37			■	■
■	38	39				40	41				42	■
43				■	44				■	45		46
47				■	48				■	49		
50				■	51				■	52		

40. Cook in the microwave
41. Smile
42. Med. care options
43. "Frontline" airer
46. "Mad Men" network

Solution on Page 323

ACROSS

1. Gives in to gravity
5. Light knock
8. Vipers
12. Location
13. $ dispenser
14. Thick carpet
15. Biblical garden
16. Prefix meaning "wrong"
17. Exterminator's target
18. Hit, as a fly
20. Shopping aids
21. See eye to eye
24. Knight's title
25. Renter's paper
26. Web-footed mammals
29. ___ bygones be bygones
30. Country rtes.
31. Mornings, briefly
33. Hand-holding, spirit-raising get-together
36. Fortune-teller's card
38. Na Na lead-in
39. Alpha's opposite
40. Escargot
43. Teen affliction
45. Volcano output
46. Ginger ___ (Canada Dry product)
47. March Madness org.
51. Deuce follower, in tennis
52. N.Y.C.'s ___ of the Americas
53. Johnny of "Pirates of the Caribbean"
54. Writing tablets
55. "My dog ___ fleas"
56. Campbell's product

DOWN

1. Opposite of NNW
2. Word with first or foreign
3. Communications conglomerate
4. Perceives
5. Avatar of Vishnu
6. Going ___ tooth and nail
7. U.K. leaders
8. Have ambitions
9. "___ a Lady" (Tom Jones hit)
10. Proust's "Remembrance of Things ___"
11. Ones ranked above cpls.
19. Itty-bitty
20. Set fire to
21. "___ in the Family"
22. Pop music's Bee ___
23. Evaluate
24. Blvds.
26. "___ to Billy Joe"
27. Pink, as a steak
28. Urban haze
30. Sony rival
32. RR stop
34. Chinese, e.g.

Puzzle 38

1	2	3	4	■	5	6	7	■	8	9	10	11
12				■	13			■	14			
15				■	16			■	17			
■	■	■	18	19			■	20				
21	22	23			■	■	24			■	■	■
25					■	26				27	28	■
29			■	■	30			■	■	31		32
■	33		34	35			■	36	37			
■	■	■	38			■	■	39				
40	41	42			■	43	44			■	■	■
45				■	46			■	47	48	49	50
51				■	52			■	53			
54				■	55			■	56			

35. Gretzky's org.
36. "This weighs a ___!"
37. Changes, as the Constitution
40. Hockey shot
41. Zilch
42. Enthusiastic
43. Thomas Edison's middle name
44. Middling grades
46. "Say ___" (doctor's order)
48. Corporate VIP
49. Kwik-E-Mart clerk on "The Simpsons"
50. PC program, briefly

Solution on Page 323

ACROSS

1. Leaning Tower city
5. NBC show since 1975
8. Some PCs
12. Part of a home entertainment system
13. "Once upon a midnight dreary" writer
14. Egg ___ soup
15. Eat well
16. "Monsters, ___"
17. "Toodle-oo"
18. After expenses
20. "I don't care" feeling
22. Magnetism
25. Medium size: abbr.
26. Short-straw drawer
27. Sea eagle
28. Scoreboard nos.
31. ___ double take (show surprise)
32. Tim of "Home Improvement"
34. "Skip to My ___"
35. Fitting
36. Tiny ___, Dickens character
37. Less than 90 degrees
39. Battleship score
40. Pictures on a screen
41. "Dennis the ___"
44. N.J. neighbor
45. Observer
46. Fam. member
48. Scientologist Hubbard
52. A ___ pittance
53. Whiz
54. Incantation start
55. Bookie's quote
56. Rock's ___ Lobos
57. "The King and I" setting

DOWN

1. High degree
2. Uganda's Amin
3. Greyhound stop: abbr.
4. Park or Fifth, say
5. "Cut off your nose to ___ your face"
6. Persona ___ grata
7. Spy novelist John
8. Luggage attachment
9. Spoiled kid
10. One drawn to a flame
11. Fix, at the vet's
19. Inconsistent
21. Mark Twain, for Samuel Clemens
22. Actor Alan
23. Roller coaster feature
24. Future DA's exam
27. "A Nightmare on ___ Street"
28. Outlet insert
29. Kind of bag
30. Litigates

Puzzle 39

1	2	3	4	■	5	6	7	■	8	9	10	11
12				■	13			■	14			
15				■	16			■	17			
■	■	■	18	19		■	20	21				
22	23	24				■	25			■	■	■
26				■	27				■	28	29	30
31			■	32	33				■	34		
35			■	36			■	37	38			
■	■	■	39			■	40					
41	42	43				■	44			■	■	■
45				■	46	47		■	48	49	50	51
52				■	53			■	54			
55				■	56			■	57			

33. Reproduced word for word
38. Diva Maria
39. Rabbit relatives
40. Runs in neutral
41. Office note
42. Ogled
43. Dweeb
47. "Green" prefix
49. Baseball hitting stat
50. ". . . good witch ___ bad witch?" (Glinda's query)
51. Viet ___

Solution on Page 323

ACROSS

1. Spelling contest
4. From "___ Z"
7. Playing with a full deck
11. Singer Grant
12. Daughters' counterparts
14. Singer Turner
15. Even score
16. Bandwagon joiner
18. Mall units
20. London lavatory
21. Frost or Burns
22. Wankel or diesel
26. Nods off
28. Teeter-totter
29. Charged atom
30. Put ___ show
31. Sisters' daughters
35. Spring or summer
38. Physicist Fermi
39. Speed skater Heiden
40. "Smoking or ___?"
41. Stroke lovingly
44. Estranges
48. "Anna Karenina" author Tolstoy
49. Rich soil
50. "Ticket to ___"
51. Directional suffix
52. "___ and the King of Siam"
53. "Waking ___ Devine" (1998 film)
54. Utter

DOWN

1. Flying mammals
2. Discharge
3. Startling revelation
4. In dreamland
5. Raises one's glass to
6. Toronto's prov.
7. Curly or Moe
8. Intention
9. Opposite of SSW
10. Big part of an elephant
13. Tennis champ Monica
17. Volcano shape
19. Fish eggs
23. Having two equal sides
24. One billionth: prefix
25. McGregor of "Star Wars" films
26. Trig function
27. Cut of meat
32. Movie theater
33. Supply-and-demand subj.
34. Submarine detector
35. Withdraw (from)
36. Rubbed out
37. Balloon filler
42. Word sung twice after "Que"

Puzzle 40

1	2	3	■	4	5	6	■	■	7	8	9	10
11			■	12			13	■	14			
15			■	16				17				
18			19			■	20			■	■	■
■	■	21				■	22			23	24	25
26	27					■	28					
29			■	■	■	■	■	■	■	30		
31			32	33	34	■	35	36	37			
38						■	39				■	■
■	■	■	40			■	41				42	43
44	45	46				47			■	48		
49				■	50				■	51		
52				■	■	53			■	54		

43. Walkman maker
44. Pie ___ mode
45. “Man of a Thousand Faces” Chaney
46. Bond creator Fleming
47. Sn, chemically speaking

Solution on Page 323

ACROSS

1. Thurs. follower
4. Bohemian
8. Flexible, electrically
12. Not pro
13. "___ my day!"
14. Sightseeing trip
15. Barracks bed
16. TV's "American ___"
17. Small whirlpool
18. Old Glory, for one
20. Comic Costello
22. Lane of the Daily Planet
25. Separately
29. Five-and-___
32. Part of a bottle
34. Civil ___
35. Big-screen format
36. Loving murmur
37. Hence
38. Manta ___ (large fish)
39. Ostracize
40. Dermatologist's concern
41. Food-poisoning bacteria
43. Poland's Walesa
45. Printer's need
47. "___ of the Flies"
50. Cougar
53. "For ___ us a child is born . . ."
56. Nurse
58. Lion's den
59. Parade spoiler
60. Remote control abbr.
61. Wise birds
62. Use a keyboard
63. Snoop

DOWN

1. Broadcast-regulating gp.
2. It's over your head
3. The "I" in IHOP: abbr.
4. Friend in a sombrero
5. "Cool!"
6. Bout stopper, for short
7. Holler
8. Devoured
9. $-due mail
10. It doesn't detonate
11. Boo-hoo
19. Trebek of "Jeopardy!"
21. "Mighty" fine home for a squirrel?
23. 1/36 of a yard
24. Capital of South Korea
26. Out of kilter
27. ___ to riches
28. Gait between walk and canter
29. In ___ straits
30. Apple computer
31. Cinco de ___
33. Dunce cap, geometrically

Puzzle 41

37. Reverberate
39. Moral no-no
42. Fibbers
44. Genetic duplicate
46. Actor Russell
48. Invitation letters
49. Designer Christian
50. Gaza Strip gp.
51. Detroit labor org.
52. Wire measure
54. Aye's opposite
55. Gratuity
57. Carry on, as a trade

Solution on Page 324

ACROSS

1. Keeps out
5. Wastes, in mob slang
9. Crow's call
12. James of "The Godfather"
13. Cotton bundle
14. Have bills
15. Notre ___
16. Repeated
18. Pres. Lincoln
20. Morse code click
21. Fire sign
24. Baldwin and Guinness
28. Cargo weight
29. Artist's stand
33. Bush spokesman Fleischer
34. Like some stocks: abbr.
35. Thing to play with
36. Label
37. Letters of debt
38. "___ and the Wolf"
40. ___ Arbor, Mich.
41. Thin pancake
43. Writer Joyce Carol ___
45. Lunch meat
47. Dieters' units: abbr.
48. Grand Prix, e.g.
52. Playbill listing
56. Fine
57. Scientologist ___ Hubbard
58. Declare openly
59. Dean's list fig.
60. Aberdeen native
61. Mexican moolah

DOWN

1. "A–E" connection
2. Auto org.
3. Computer capacity, for short
4. Kind of preview
5. Theater award
6. Budgetary excess
7. Skipped town
8. Story that's "to be continued"
9. Camp bed
10. Leave dumbstruck
11. Join in holy matrimony
17. Capital of Ga.
19. Honey maker
21. Stiff-upper-lip type
22. Engine
23. Perfectly timed
25. "___ Joe's" (restaurant sign)
26. Whooping ___
27. Omens
30. Chowed down
31. Drunkard
32. Ogle
38. Bits of wisdom?
39. Hold up

Puzzle 42

1	2	3	4	■	5	6	7	8	■	9	10	11
12				■	13				■	14		
15				■	16				17			
■	■	■	18	19		■	20			■	■	■
21	22	23			■	■	■	24		25	26	27
28			■	29	30	31	32		■	33		
34			■	■	35			■	■	36		
37			■	38				39	■	40		
41			42		■	■	■	43	44			
■	■	■	45		46	■	47			■	■	■
48	49	50				51		■	52	53	54	55
56			■	57				■	58			
59			■	60				■	61			

42. Dissertation writer's prize
44. Songwriters' grp.
46. Painter Chagall
47. Gave temporarily
48. Cleaning cloth
49. "Alley ___!"
50. Wanted poster abbr.
51. Whisper sweet nothings
53. N.Y.C.'s Park or Madison
54. Distress signal
55. Toddler's age

Solution on Page 324

ACROSS

1. Encl. for a reply
5. "I didn't know that!"
8. Cries from creative people
12. Unrestrained revelry
13. Roll-___ (some deodorants)
14. Cummerbund
15. Quick snack
16. Takes too much of a drug
17. Do in
18. Gives some lip
20. Chow down
22. Vast amounts
24. Antonym's antonym: abbr.
27. Houston baseballer
30. Jr. high, e.g.
31. Duracell size
32. Folk tales and such
33. Enemy
34. Cheerful tune
35. It's north of Calif.
36. Isle of ___
37. Red-tag events
38. Golf ball prop
39. Retort to "Am too!"
41. "Get it?"
42. Met productions
46. "Smooth Operator" singer
49. Amazement
51. Restaurant freebie
52. Leeds's river
53. Mineo of "Rebel Without a Cause"
54. Intro for boy or girl
55. Veep's superior
56. NFL six-pointers
57. Swag

DOWN

1. Cries convulsively
2. Song for a diva
3. Bilko and Pepper: abbr.
4. Blight on the landscape
5. Barnyard honker
6. Wrap up
7. Gist
8. Aide: abbr.
9. Computer in "2001"
10. Cool ___ cucumber
11. Like a shrinking violet
19. "The Name of the Rose" author Umberto
21. Baseball bat wood
23. Together
24. Leave port
25. Harvard rival
26. King Cole and Turner
27. Very much
28. Tender
29. Squirrel's home
33. Orient

Puzzle 43

1	2	3	4		5	6	7		8	9	10	11
12					13				14			
15					16				17			
18				19			20	21				
			22			23				24	25	26
27	28	29				30				31		
32					33				34			
35				36				37				
38				39			40					
			41				42			43	44	45
46	47	48			49	50			51			
52					53				54			
55					56				57			

34. Sideways throw
36. West of "My Little Chickadee"
37. Soak up, as gravy
40. Christmas carols
41. Understands
43. ___-Rooter
44. Choir voice
45. Wood strip used as a bed support
46. Maple fluid
47. Lungful
48. Dr. of hip-hop
50. Bankroll

Solution on Page 324

ACROSS

1. Like Mother Hubbard's cupboard
5. Flower holders
9. Regret
12. Thumbs-up votes
13. "I cannot tell ___"
14. Happy ___ clam
15. Mailed
16. Adolescent
18. Hosp. areas
20. Get handed a bum ___
21. Stock unit
24. Snares
28. Weighty weight
29. Kindergarten adhesive
33. Spigot
34. Onassis nickname
35. Pod occupant
36. Entertainer Zadora
37. Shoo-___ (sure things)
38. Numerical data
40. Common conjunction
41. Witherspoon of "Walk the Line"
43. Buying binge
45. Look at
47. Ends with cone or -Cat
48. Ferrari rival
52. Cole ___
56. Literary collection
57. Level
58. Trillion: prefix
59. Comic Caesar
60. ___ Xiaoping
61. Comprehends

DOWN

1. Some coll. degrees
2. Sailor's affirmative
3. Stimpy's canine pal
4. Fragrant compound
5. ___ down (frisks)
6. Cheer for a matador
7. Wedding cake layer
8. 100-member group
9. Scott Joplin piece
10. "___ only as directed"
11. Unit of corn
17. Tax mo.
19. Not Dem.
21. Flight of steps
22. Songstress Lena
23. Licorice flavoring
25. Face-valued, as stocks
26. Revolutionary pamphleteer Thomas
27. Digging tool
30. Suitable
31. ___ of Galilee
32. Tit for ___
38. Become enraged
39. Tax form ID

Puzzle 44

1	2	3	4	■	5	6	7	8	■	9	10	11
12				■	13				■	14		
15				■	16				17			
■	■	■	18	19		■	20			■	■	■
21	22	23			■	■	■	24		25	26	27
28			■	29	30	31	32		■	33		
34			■	■	35			■	■	36		
37			■	38				39	■	40		
41			42		■	■	■	43	44			
■	■	■	45		46	■	47			■	■	■
48	49	50				51		■	52	53	54	55
56			■	57				■	58			
59			■	60				■	61			

42. Reverse of NNW
44. Blog entries
46. Roof overhang
47. Serenade
48. Pas' mates
49. "I'd like to buy ___"
50. Down in the dumps
51. Hamilton's bill
53. Attorney F. ___ Bailey
54. "___ you kidding?"
55. "___ it something I said?"

Solution on Page 324

ACROSS

1. Green Bay Packers' org.
4. J. F. K.'s predecessor
7. Bring to 212 degrees
11. Bullfight cries
13. Summer mo.
14. The "I" of "The King and I"
15. Litter's littlest
16. Eggy drink
17. Went off, as a bell
18. Like grams and liters
20. Wane
22. Frozen potato brand
24. Cardinals' home: abbr.
27. Spills the beans
30. Doze (off)
31. "Either he goes ___ go!"
32. Delinquent GI
33. Million ___ March
34. Was sorry about
35. Dorm monitors: abbr.
36. Motor City labor org.
37. Yawn inducers
38. Reply to a ques.
39. Squinted
41. Battleship letters
42. Standards of perfection
46. German mister
49. "The Joy Luck Club" author
51. Track shape
52. Stuntman Knievel
53. Get ___ of (toss out)
54. ___ qua non
55. Fly traps
56. Meditative sounds
57. Drops on the grass

DOWN

1. Standard
2. Chimney passage
3. Mardi Gras follower
4. Rumba or samba
5. Half a quartet
6. Incited
7. Fishhook's end
8. Stop ___ dime
9. Bed-and-breakfast
10. Hang back
12. Leisurely walk
19. Tax org.
21. Michael Jackson album
23. Thunderstruck
24. Like a lemon
25. Genealogy chart
26. Box tops
27. Scarlett's estate
28. McGregor of "Trainspotting"
29. Profit's opposite
33. Eminent conductor
34. Cowboy contests

Puzzle 45

36. Brown truck co.
37. Four-poster, e.g.
40. Orange covers
41. Web addresses, for short
43. Gung-ho
44. Country road
45. Triple Crown winner Seattle ___
46. Chop
47. Adam's madam
48. Johnny ___
50. Order between "ready" and "fire"

Solution on Page 325

ACROSS

1. "Sock ___ me!"
5. Doctors' org.
8. Number cruncher, for short
11. Pork serving
12. Stylish, in the '60s
13. Give the cold shoulder
14. Unembellished
15. "___ baby makes three"
16. "___ it the truth!"
17. Jackie Gleason role in "The Hustler"
20. "Send help!"
21. "Put ___ Happy Face"
22. Heat meas.
25. Flanders of "The Simpsons"
27. Notre Dame's Fighting ___
31. Entice
33. Uno + uno
35. Early Peruvian
36. Tithe amount
38. El ___ (Heston role)
40. "Here's looking at you, ___"
41. Cool
43. Kook
45. Kids' party game
52. Auricular
53. Once known as
54. Castle defense
55. Gives under pressure
56. Breathable stuff
57. Big cat
58. "Quiet!"
59. Screen siren West
60. Org.

DOWN

1. Part of a nuclear arsenal, for short
2. Bangkok native
3. Shredded
4. Big tournaments
5. Piled up
6. Pre-stereo
7. Supplement
8. Pet that grows on you?
9. Fourth-down option
10. Picnic pests
13. African adventure
18. Years and years
19. "Gimme ___!" (start of an Iowa State cheer)
22. Crunchy sandwich
23. Wed. preceder
24. Vase
26. Bandleader Severinsen
28. Squid's defense
29. Biol. or chem.
30. "It ___ to Be You"
32. Moral principles
34. Heartfelt

Puzzle 46

1	2	3	4	■	5	6	7	■	■	8	9	10
11				■	12			■	13			
14				■	15			■	16			
17				18				19				
■	■	■	20			■	21			■	■	■
22	23	24	■	25		26	■	27		28	29	30
31			32	■	33		34	■	35			
36				37	■	38		39	■	40		
■	■	■	41		42	■	43		44	■	■	■
45	46	47				48				49	50	51
52				■	53			■	54			
55				■	56			■	57			
58			■	■	59			■	60			

37. Drunk's sound
39. "Well, that's obvious!"
42. Former TWA rival
44. Home of the NFL's Buccaneers
45. It grows on trees
46. Mormon state
47. Sound of relief
48. "Star Wars" princess
49. Promissory notes
50. Ewes' mates
51. Baseball's ___ the Man

Solution on Page 325

ACROSS

1. Place to play darts
4. Chew the fat
8. "I've been ___!"
11. Snatch
13. "The ___ of Greenwich Village" (1984 movie)
14. Slippery, as winter sidewalks
15. Seaweed
16. Shortened wd.
17. Compete (for)
18. "Should that be the case"
20. Outbuildings
22. Desert plants
25. Last letter
26. Unit of resistance
27. U2 lead singer
30. Hawaiian dance
34. Gunk
35. Holy one
37. ___'easter
38. In ___ (together)
40. Went by plane
41. Comedian DeLuise
42. Mac alternatives
44. Computer symbols
46. Based on eight
49. Mercedes-___
51. Center of activity
52. "Stronger than dirt!" sloganeer
54. Pound sounds
58. "The Ghost and ___ Muir"
59. Rice wine
60. Country music's McEntire
61. Slangy assent
62. JFK or LBJ
63. eBay action

DOWN

1. Ernie Els org.
2. WWW address
3. Word with punching or sleeping
4. Bean counters, for short
5. Vagrant
6. Police alert, for short
7. Brief and to the point
8. Bees' home
9. Etching liquid
10. Henna and others
12. Angler's need
19. Little lies
21. Sneaky laugh sound
22. Mechanical teeth
23. Popeye's greeting
24. "Get the lead out!"
25. The "Z" of DMZ
28. Blockheads
29. Nada
31. Loosen, as laces
32. Diving bird
33. Hug givers
36. Exact duplicate

Puzzle 47

1	2	3	■	4	5	6	7	■	8	9	10
11			12	13				■	14		
15				16				■	17		
■	■	■	18	19		■	20	21			
22	23	24		■	■	25			■	■	■
26			■	27	28	29		■	30	31	32	33
34			■	35			36	■	37		
38			39	■	40			■	41		
■	■	■	42	43		■	■	44	45		
46	47	48		■	49	50			■	■	■
51			■	52	53			■	54	55	56	57
58			■	59				■	60		
61			■	62				■	■	63		

39. Tax pro, for short
43. Necklace fastener
45. Old Russian autocrat
46. "Lions and tigers and bears" follower
47. Remedy
48. Recipe abbr.
49. Use the oven
50. Alimony recipients
53. Cookie holder
55. Confederate soldier, for short
56. "Ten Most Wanted" agcy.
57. Depressed

Solution on Page 325

ACROSS

1. Winter mo.
4. Piercing tool
7. Face-off
11. Self-image
12. Broadway's "Five Guys Named ___"
13. Humorist Bombeck
14. "My gal" of song
15. Pigs' digs
17. Powerful punch
18. Church donation
20. Bag
22. Look of disdain
23. Big bother
27. Avis offering
30. Country singer Ritter
31. Lane of "Superman"
34. Continent north of Afr.
35. Bigger than big
36. E-file receiver
37. Jewish mystical doctrine
39. Come-on
41. Voices above tenors
45. Jury member
47. Walk proudly
48. Munch
51. Decomposes
53. Dined
54. Clearasil target
55. "___ Hear a Waltz?"
56. Neighbor of Wyo.
57. Take care of
58. Visualize
59. Online "ha ha"

DOWN

1. Jokes
2. "Here we go ___!"
3. Actor Nick
4. Electric current unit
5. "___ is me!"
6. Microscope part
7. Office furniture
8. Dot-com's address
9. Cousin of an ostrich
10. Fall behind
16. African desert
19. His and ___
21. Ariz. neighbor
24. "R–V" connection
25. Relay segment
26. Computer file extension
28. "___, My God, to Thee"
29. Place for a bath
31. Put a match to
32. Lode load
33. "This ___ fine how-do-you-do!"
35. Sentry's command
37. Middle grade

Puzzle 48

38. TV collie
40. Swiftness
42. Hiker's path
43. Surpass
44. Pilfer
46. Fishing poles
48. Mammal that sleeps upside down
49. Rink surface
50. Former C&W station
52. It may test the waters

Solution on Page 325

ACROSS

1. Bearded beast of Africa
4. Torture device
8. Gymnast Korbut
12. Neither here ___ there
13. Fed. workplace watchdog
14. Struggle for air
15. Young ___ (tots)
16. Rob Reiner's mock rock band
18. Roebuck's partner
20. Relinquish
21. Sty resident
23. Dentist's tool
27. Reunion attendee, for short
30. '60s hairdo
33. Casino cube
34. The "N" in NCO
35. Collect bit by bit
36. Time delay
37. "___ have to?"
38. Catches
39. Exercise establishments
40. Opening bars
42. Letters on a tire
44. Radiate
47. Skirt fold
51. Lincoln's hat
55. Canine warning
56. Drive-___ window
57. Elliptical
58. Mop & ___ (floor cleaner)
59. Olympic sled
60. Cabbage Patch Kid, e.g.
61. Hither and ___

DOWN

1. African antelopes
2. All's opposite
3. ___ Major (constellation)
4. Martini & ___ vermouth
5. Nile viper
6. "Blondie" cartoonist Young
7. Welles role
8. Girl watcher, perhaps
9. Back muscle, briefly
10. Govt. property overseer
11. Computer program, for short
17. Supplementary feature
19. Engine speed, for short
22. Grand party
24. Without purpose
25. "Schindler's List" star Neeson
26. Table supports
27. "___ Love Her" (Beatles song)
28. Crazy as a ___
29. The "U" of CPU
31. Jan. follower
32. Hoarse voice
35. Garden statuette
39. Old Dodger great Hodges

Puzzle 49

1	2	3	■	4	5	6	7	■	8	9	10	11
12			■	13				■	14			
15			■	16				17				
18			19		■	20				■	■	■
■	■	■	21		22	■	■	23		24	25	26
27	28	29		■	30	31	32		■	33		
34			■	35					■	36		
37			■	38				■	39			
40			41		■	■	42	43		■	■	■
■	■	■	44		45	46	■	47		48	49	50
51	52	53					54		■	55		
56				■	57				■	58		
59				■	60				■	61		

41. Variety show
43. Compete in a bee
45. Digital music player
46. DVR pioneer
48. Like quiche or custard
49. Folkie Guthrie
50. 1982 Disney sci-fi film
51. Home of the NFL's Rams
52. Calendar column: abbr.
53. Alternative to .com or .edu
54. "Be a ___!"

Solution on Page 326

ACROSS

1. Douglas ___
4. Out ___ limb
7. Golfer's goal
10. "Auntie" in a play
11. Writing implement
12. Sailor's greeting
14. MP's quarry
15. Delta rival
16. File menu option
17. Perfectly pitched
19. Dangerous African flies
21. Put two and two together
23. Coffee alternative
24. Like Mozart's music
28. Tint
31. Practice, as skills
32. Hip-hop's ___ Def
33. Painful
34. Supermodel Carol
35. Espresso cup
37. Payroll ID
38. Assistance
39. King Arthur's home
43. Tangle
47. Abbr. on a contour map
48. Tennessee athlete, for short
50. Household power: abbr.
51. Come-on
52. When a plane is due in: abbr.
53. Transmit
54. Guys
55. Nearing depletion
56. Friday's rank: abbr.

DOWN

1. Young Bambi
2. "Don't worry about me!"
3. Let go
4. Select, with "for"
5. Small salamander
6. "Cinderella" stepsister
7. Noodles
8. Solvers' shouts
9. Wander about
10. China's Chairman ___
13. "Absolutely!"
18. Football gains: abbr.
20. Snakelike fish
22. Trashy paperback
24. When repeated, a Latin dance
25. Chat room chuckle
26. Six-legged worker
27. End of many URLs
28. Windows predecessor
29. Decade divs.
30. Extra-wide, at the shoe store
33. Unhappy state
35. Dial-up alternative
36. "My country, ___ of thee . . ."

Puzzle 50

37. Deadly sins number
39. Animation unit
40. Homecoming attendee, for short
41. Nothing more than
42. In ___ (completely)
44. Words after shake or break
45. Landlord's check
46. Digital readout, for short
49. Perry Mason's field

Solution on Page 326

ACROSS

1. Slightly open
5. "How was ___ know?"
8. Feeling no pain
12. "Newsweek" rival
13. "___ la la!"
14. "___ Karenina"
15. "The Art of Love" poet
16. Sci-fi vehicle
17. Geezer
18. Waiter's handout
19. "This looks bad"
21. Soup order
24. Pause indicator
28. Prohibited
32. Business as ___
33. Narc's agcy.
34. Ring-shaped island
36. Fuel additive
37. Dine at home
39. Squirrels away
41. Save alternative
42. Dehydrated
43. Votes against
46. Sprint
50. Rim
53. Worker in Santa's workshop
55. Microwave, slangily
56. Yep's opposite
57. "Put a ___ on it!"
58. Idle of "Monty Python"
59. Lifeless
60. "Harper Valley ___"
61. Pull sharply

DOWN

1. Molecule part
2. "___ Talkin'" (Bee Gees hit)
3. Dictator Idi
4. Decrease
5. Commitment to pay
6. Bean curd
7. "Oops!"
8. Mexican snacks
9. Half of dos
10. Letters after "L"
11. Louisville Slugger
20. Of the eye
22. Idi Amin's land
23. Butter serving
25. Sled dog command
26. Chess finale
27. Swiss peaks
28. Mid-month date
29. Spring
30. Tardy
31. ___ Alamos, NM
35. Inc., in London
38. Wanting
40. Australia's largest city

Puzzle 51

1	2	3	4	■	5	6	7	■	8	9	10	11
12				■	13			■	14			
15				■	16			■	17			
18				■	■	19		20		■	■	■
■	■	■	21	22	23	■	■	24		25	26	27
28	29	30				31	■	32				
33			■	34			35		■	36		
37			38		■	39			40			
41					■	■	42			■	■	■
■	■	■	43		44	45	■	■	46	47	48	49
50	51	52		■	53		54	■	55			
56				■	57			■	58			
59				■	60			■	61			

44. Kennel cry
45. Skirt opening
47. Surrounding glow
48. Onion covering
49. "What the ___?"
50. Finish
51. Female deer
52. Transcript fig.
54. Pharmaceutical watchdog grp.

Solution on Page 326

ACROSS

1. Travel far and wide
5. Current units
9. Ryder Cup org.
12. "Ali ___ and the 40 Thieves"
13. Sir's counterpart
14. "Play It Again, ___"
15. "___ never fly!"
16. Race driver Yarborough
17. TV's "Judging ___"
18. Luster
20. Poker-pot starters
22. Hold in high regard
26. Opposite of ant.
29. Quarterback's option
30. ___ and feathers
34. Cousin of an onion
36. Byways: abbr.
37. Ladder rung
38. "Dedicated to the ___ Love"
39. Talk up
41. Put down
42. "Children of a ___ God"
44. Reads, as a bar code
47. Writer Asimov
52. Game show host Sajak
53. Nothing special
57. Rights grp.
58. Slot machine part
59. Ever and ___
60. Radio host Don
61. Moms
62. Hankerings
63. Reps.' foes

DOWN

1. Hitting stats
2. ___ of office
3. Up to the task
4. Stag party attender
5. Car co. bought by Chrysler
6. Barnyard bleat
7. Chum
8. Dirty campaign tactic
9. HS junior's exam
10. Hearts or darts
11. Carter and Grant
19. Short sleep
21. New Jersey hoopsters
23. Pub game
24. Windows predecessor
25. Debate topic
26. Traffic caution
27. Desire
28. Born as
31. U.S./U.K. divider
32. Actor Stephen
33. "The ___ Who Loved Me"
35. Pottery oven
40. The first "T" of TNT

Puzzle 52

1	2	3	4	■	5	6	7	8	■	9	10	11
12				■	13				■	14		
15				■	16				■	17		
18				19	■	■	■	20	21			
■	■	■	■	22	23	24	25			■	■	■
26	27	28	■	29				■	30	31	32	33
34			35	■	36			■	37			
38				■	39			40	■	41		
■	■	■	42	43					■	■	■	■
44	45	46			■	■	■	47	48	49	50	51
52			■	53	54	55	56	■	57			
58			■	59				■	60			
61			■	62				■	63			

43. Opinion piece
44. Unwanted e-mail
45. Irene of "Fame"
46. $20 bill dispensers
48. Uttered
49. High point
50. Graduate, for short
51. Swear
54. Singleton
55. Michael Douglas, to Kirk
56. Carry-___ (some luggage)

Solution on Page 326

ACROSS

1. Kuwaiti ruler
5. Leatherworker's tool
8. Irate
11. Challenged
13. ___ rally (school event)
14. Bobby of hockey
15. Big mess
16. Daddies
17. Capote's nickname
18. Raggedy Ann, e.g.
20. Actor Selleck
21. Queue before "U"
24. Boeing 747, e.g.
25. "Holy cow!"
26. Hangmen's needs
29. Half a laugh
31. Thread holder
32. Feudal workers
36. Son ___ gun
38. Sheep's coat
39. Large container
41. Work wk. ender
43. Junk-bond rating
44. Help
45. McNally's partner
47. CD follower
48. Body art, for short
49. New York Harbor's ___ Island
54. State south of Ga.
55. Med. group
56. Bakers get a rise out of it
57. ___ Francisco
58. Longing for Japanese money?
59. Some PCs

DOWN

1. Mag. staffers
2. "___ overboard!"
3. George Gershwin's brother
4. Ump
5. Macintosh maker
6. Riches
7. Turntable turners, briefly
8. Words to live by
9. Cupid's projectile
10. Percussion instrument
12. Bad firecracker
19. Breakfast drinks, for short
21. Hosp. workers
22. ___ up (absorb)
23. "Not a moment ___ soon!"
25. Cry on a roller coaster
27. Chimney buildup
28. Santa's little helper
30. Class for U.S. immigrants
33. ___ room
34. TV watchdog: abbr.
35. $1/60$ of a min.
37. Steep-roofed house

Puzzle 53

1	2	3	4	■	■	5	6	7	■	8	9	10
11				12	■	13			■	14		
15					■	16			■	17		
■	■	■	■	18	19			■	■	20		
21	22	23	■	■	24			■	25			■
26			27	28		■	29	30		■	■	■
31					■	■	■	32		33	34	35
■	■	■	36		37	■	38					
■	39	40		■	41	42		■	■	43		
44			■	■	45			46	■	■	■	■
47			■	48			■	49	50	51	52	53
54			■	55			■	56				
57			■	58			■	■	59			

38. Snorkeling accessory
39. String quartet member
40. Madison Avenue worker
42. Boca ___, FL
44. Sandy's barks
46. TV actress Susan
48. "Love ___ neighbor . . ."
50. Kauai keepsake
51. Chem. room
52. Theory suffix
53. Kin of aves.

Solution on Page 327

ACROSS

1. "___ Lama Ding Dong" (1961 hit)
5. Some Caribbean music
8. Resort
11. Author Wiesel
12. First-down yardage
13. Walk heavily
14. "Hey . . . , over here!"
15. London's locale: abbr.
16. It may be drawn in the sand
17. Eventually
20. October brew
21. "You ain't seen nothin' ___!"
22. ER workers
25. "Hi ___!" (fan's message)
27. Flat-topped hills
31. Cash substitutes
33. Amniotic ___
35. Second-year student, for short
36. Christmas visitor
38. ___-Man (arcade game)
40. Edgar Allan ___
41. Frequently, to Frost
43. Feathered stole
45. Certain look-alike
52. Cheese on crackers
53. Neither fish ___ fowl
54. Military installation
55. Rustic lodgings
56. Tic-tac-___
57. "And pretty maids all in ___"
58. ___ and don'ts
59. Fast flier
60. Camper's shelter

DOWN

1. House members, for short
2. As well
3. Japanese soup
4. Prudential rival
5. Hi-fis
6. Vegas numbers game
7. Furious
8. Narrow cut
9. Johnnycake
10. Golden ___ (senior citizen)
13. Candidate lists
18. Shade maker
19. Moon vehicle, for short
22. Prefix with place or print
23. ___ good deed
24. Snow melter
26. Glove compartment item
28. Apply bread to gravy
29. Sgt.'s mail drop
30. "That's all ___ wrote"
32. Gems
34. Club with a floor show
37. Not fore
39. Newspaper div.

Puzzle 54

42. Shades
44. Up, in baseball
45. As before, in footnotes
46. Ian Fleming villain
47. German one
48. Dove sounds
49. Suffix with silver or glass
50. “Help ___ the way!”
51. Former Speaker Gingrich

Solution on Page 327

ACROSS

1. Big bash
5. Has too much
8. Nimble
12. Trash bag closers
13. Seek the affection of
14. Warty hopper
15. Change for a five
16. Blazed the trail
17. Inquires
18. Get undressed
20. Relieve
22. Shoot the breeze
24. Hosp. scanner
25. Middle of the ocean
29. "Git!"
33. Opener for two tins?
34. Bust a ___ (laugh hard)
36. Prefix with cycle
37. Spreads unchecked
40. Like some traits
43. Nut on a wheel
45. Mingle
46. Whooping birds
49. Piano part
53. Parcel of land
54. Actor Robbins
56. Spy
57. Scrabble piece
58. Infamous Amin
59. Mexican money
60. Went fast
61. ___ Aviv, Israel
62. 1982 Disney film starring Jeff Bridges

DOWN

1. Classic Pontiacs
2. "___ Misbehavin'"
3. Lecherous look
4. Give, as homework
5. Bird that gives a hoot
6. Bucks' mates
7. Gomorrah's sister city
8. Kind of electricity
9. Ritzy
10. Autumn tool
11. Fabric amts.
19. Joad and Kettle
21. Surgeons' workplaces, for short
23. Panhandle
25. Hockey's Bobby
26. Zadora of "Butterfly"
27. High school subj.
28. Mo. with no holidays
30. Dirt road feature
31. "Gimme ___!" (Indiana cheerleaders' cry)
32. Open ___ night
35. Chairman pro ___
38. On cloud nine

Puzzle 55

39. "Here Comes the ___"
41. ___ in the bud
42. Tax-___ (like municipal bonds)
44. "Dig?"
46. Cut out, as coupons
47. Auditioner's quest
48. One of six for a hexagon
50. Active one
51. "The Sun ___ Rises"
52. Trotsky or Uris
53. Qt. halves
55. $1,000,000, for short

Solution on Page 327

ACROSS

1. Misfortunes
5. Educ. institution
8. Pants parts
12. Tidy
13. "Bali ___"
14. ___ vera
15. Emulate Greg Louganis
16. "___ away we go!"
17. Big top
18. Steals, with "off"
20. December 24 and 31
21. Batter's position
24. "Mad ___" (Mel Gibson movie)
26. Tippy craft
27. "___ to worry"
28. Homer Simpson exclamation
31. Star pitcher
32. Unaccompanied
34. Friend in France
35. Stranded motorist's need
36. Exxon product
37. Taxpayer's dread
39. Moon lander, for short
40. Liabilities' opposites
41. Pet adoption org.
44. Dog's annoyance
45. Whoppers
46. Soccer Hall of Famer Hamm
47. ___ cheese dressing
51. "___ It Romantic?"
52. Writer Fleming
53. Temperature extremes
54. Butter squares
55. USN officers
56. Peepers

DOWN

1. Not Dem. or Rep.
2. Hawaiian wreath
3. Water closet, informally
4. Canned heat
5. Mold
6. Some soda containers
7. Went underground
8. Material for a doctor's glove
9. Height: abbr.
10. "Going, going, ___!"
11. Movie locations
19. Freezing period
21. "Shoo!"
22. Stuffed tortilla
23. All over again
24. Calendar abbr.
25. "Relax, soldier!"
27. Turndowns
28. Florida's Miami-___ County
29. Leave out
30. Chart toppers
33. On the ___ (at large)

Puzzle 56

38. In working order
39. Endures
40. Arkin and Alda
41. Woman's undergarment
42. Tilting-tower town
43. "Red" coin
44. Decree
46. .001 inch
48. Myrna of "The Thin Man"
49. She sheep
50. Ship letters

Solution on Page 327

ACROSS

1. To ___ (perfectly)
5. ___ room (play area)
8. Pillow filler
12. Put blacktop on
13. Something to lend or bend
14. Buffalo's lake
15. Birds of ___
16. "R–V" link
17. Disorder
18. Took long steps
20. Nosy people
22. Stimpy's pal
23. Frequently, in poetry
24. Bemoan
27. Votes into office
31. "___ been had!"
32. Noah's boat
33. Surface layer
37. Saudi ___
40. Science guy Bill
41. Buck Rogers player Gerard
42. Speechifies
45. Join the military
49. Bob of "Road" films
50. Light brown
52. "What's gotten ___ you?"
53. "Like ___ not"
54. "C'___ la vie!"
55. Paradise
56. Butterfingers' cry
57. Insult, slangily
58. Scatters, as seed

DOWN

1. PC programs
2. Pucker-producing
3. Always
4. Pooh's donkey friend
5. Take offense at
6. Dine
7. "Robinson ___"
8. Take down a notch
9. Nabisco cookie
10. Bit of smoke
11. Loch ___ monster
19. Room with an easy chair
21. Super Bowl org.
24. Ullmann or Tyler
25. Blvd.
26. "A Few Good ___"
28. Part of a semi
29. Prefix meaning "three"
30. Reggae relative
34. Goes in
35. Needle part
36. Took a breather
37. Insurance sellers
38. ___ Tin Tin (heroic dog of 1950s TV)

Puzzle 57

39. Axis foes
42. Akron's home
43. ___-Rooter
44. Each
46. Prefix with European or China
47. Meal in a pot
48. A lot
51. "Just ___ thought!"

Solution on Page 328

ACROSS

1. Showman Ziegfeld
4. Curtain holder
7. It's grown in ears
11. Mustache site
12. Fix up, as text
14. Hawaiian cookout
15. Baseball arbiter, for short
16. Refusals
17. Sports cable channel
18. Alternative to briefs
21. Unused
22. It's kept in a pen
23. Enemies
25. "In Cold Blood" writer, to pals
26. ___-fi
29. Attila, for one
30. Trousers
32. Alley in the comics
33. "Wherefore ___ thou Romeo?"
34. Big coffee holder
35. Martial art
36. Rainbow's shape
37. ___ Joey
38. Agree
43. "To Sir With Love" singer
44. "___ out?" (pet's choice)
45. Spring mo.
47. "Trinity" author
48. Zoo fixture
49. Datebook abbr.
50. Heredity unit
51. Rejections
52. Letter holder: abbr.

DOWN

1. Kind of shot
2. An arm or a leg
3. Foe
4. Extend, as a subscription
5. Aroma
6. Goes kaput
7. Office worker
8. Evict
9. Emulates Eminem
10. Woman of habit?
13. Souvenir garment
19. Ballot marks
20. Responsibility
23. Agcy. for homeowners
24. Lord's Prayer start
25. Spike TV, formerly
26. Life partner
27. Massachusetts's Cape ___
28. Nasdaq debut: abbr.
30. Like the driven snow
31. Polar bear's domain
35. "The Bell ___" (Sylvia Plath book)
36. Entertain
37. Israel's Shimon

Puzzle 58

1	2	3	■	4	5	6	■	■	7	8	9	10
11			■	12			13	■	14			
15			■	16				■	17			
■	18		19					20				■
■	■	21			■	■	22			■	■	■
23	24			■	■	25			■	26	27	28
29			■	30	31				■	32		
33			■	34			■	■	35			
■	■	■	36		■	■	■	37			■	■
■	38	39				40	41				42	■
43				■	44				■	45		46
47				■	48				■	49		
50				■	■	51			■	52		

38. Heal
39. Ken of "Thirtysomething"
40. "Chestnuts roasting ___ open fire"
41. Not for here
42. Whirled
43. Carry with effort
46. Race, as an engine

Solution on Page 328

ACROSS

1. Colorless
5. ". . . life is ___ a dream"
8. ___ Beauty (apple variety)
12. Not naughty
13. Military address: abbr.
14. Wide-eyed
15. Help in a heist
16. Opposite NNE
17. Trudge
18. Six-pointers, for short
20. Overage
22. Globe or ball
25. Stephen of "Michael Collins"
26. Baseball's Gehrig
27. Engine additive brand
29. What italics do
33. Young ___ (kids)
34. Dine
36. "Norma ___" (Sally Field film)
37. Get-well program
40. Pampering, for short
42. Historical period
43. Truck track
45. Opinion pieces
47. Few and far between
50. Feel under the weather
51. Employ
52. Road curve
54. Austen heroine
58. Invites
59. Golf ball support
60. Money owed
61. Ship pole
62. "This ___ better be good!"
63. Did laps in a pool

DOWN

1. Genetic letters
2. Tease
3. King topper
4. Singer Midler
5. Droopy-eared hounds
6. FedEx competitor
7. Pisa landmark
8. Scalawag
9. Eye amorously
10. Cattle calls
11. Omelet ingredients
19. ER workers
21. Crosses (out)
22. Speak drunkenly
23. Corn bread
24. Silence
28. "___ Your Head on My Shoulder"
30. Neighborhood
31. ___ a one
32. Oolong and pekoe
35. Made happy
38. Slap the cuffs on

Puzzle 59

39. Clear tables
41. "___: Miami"
44. Pearly whites
46. Toboggans
47. Counterfeit
48. Leaning-tower site
49. Torah holders
53. Poseidon's domain
55. Kitten's cry
56. Wharton deg.
57. 24-hr. banking convenience

Solution on Page 328

ACROSS

1. Ave. crossers
4. Opposed to
8. Grocery carrier
12. "___ Got You Under My Skin"
13. Do one of the three R's
14. Nobelist Wiesel
15. ___ King Cole
16. Kite part
17. King of the jungle
18. Part of TGIF: abbr.
20. Throws out
22. U2's "Where the ___ Have No Name"
26. More than fat
27. ___ the line (obeyed)
28. "Must've been something ___"
30. TV's "Science Guy"
31. Pair
32. Gorilla
35. Newcastle's river
36. Tractor attachment
37. ___ Doone cookies
41. "Top Hat" star Fred
43. One-celled organism
45. Lyricist Gershwin
46. Siestas
47. Fibber
50. Fill-in
53. Guitarist Atkins
54. Ill at ___
55. Freud subject
56. Hearing organs
57. Dec. 25
58. Oldies group ___ Na Na

DOWN

1. One of a deadly septet
2. New Deal proj.
3. Emancipate
4. Bandleader Shaw
5. Cultural grant giver, for short
6. Mai ___
7. Inactive
8. Star
9. Wonderland girl
10. They're a laugh a minute
11. Uptight
19. Sunburned
21. Baseball's DiMaggio
22. Depot: abbr.
23. ___ with (tease)
24. Neat
25. Steam bath
29. On one's ___ (alert)
32. Assumed names
33. ___ favor (please, in Spanish)
34. Lamb's mother
35. Bar bill
36. Bogey beater

Puzzle 60

1	2	3	■	4	5	6	7	■	8	9	10	11
12			■	13				■	14			
15			■	16				■	17			
■	■	18	19		■	■	20	21				
22	23				24	25	■	26				
27				■	28		29		■	■	■	■
30			■	■	31			■	■	32	33	34
■	■	■	■	35				■	36			
37	38	39	40		■	41		42				
43					44	■	■	45			■	■
46				■	47	48	49		■	50	51	52
53				■	54				■	55		
56				■	57				■	58		

37. Knight's weapon
38. Mutual of ___
39. Rodeo performer
40. Hatchlings' homes
42. Whitewalls
44. "Jeopardy!" host Trebek
48. "___ so sorry!"
49. Naked ___ jaybird
51. "Yecch!"
52. Constrictor

Solution on Page 328

ACROSS

1. Meowers
5. Irish actor Stephen
8. Snead and Spade
12. Smell ___ (be suspicious)
13. Louse-to-be
14. Hawkeye portrayer
15. Tick off
16. Least gradual
18. Over hill and ___
19. The Pointer Sisters' "___ So Shy"
20. Mechanical learning
23. Exams
28. Fire
31. Seniors' org.
33. Beget
34. Adjusts to fit
36. Aviator Earhart
38. Teri of "Tootsie"
39. Not crazy
41. ___ Altos, Calif.
42. Host
44. Hitchcock's "___ Window"
46. Female sheep
48. Landed
52. Kind of pregame party
57. Bargain hunter's delight
58. Merlot, for one
59. Chaney of old films
60. ___ bargain
61. Persia, now
62. London lav.
63. Pre-coll. exams

DOWN

1. Check the age of
2. Opera highlight
3. Like skyscrapers
4. Have the wheel of a car
5. They may administer IVs
6. ___-or situation
7. To ___ (precisely)
8. Maple output
9. Pub pint
10. Rx prescribers
11. Took a load off
17. Superlative ending
21. Granola grain
22. Former Soviet news agency
24. Suffix with Canton
25. Pie-cooling spot
26. Threesome
27. Caribbean and Mediterranean
28. Actor Nicolas of "The Rock"
29. Economist Smith
30. DEA agent
32. Window section
35. ___-K (before kindergarten)
37. "Give ___ break!"
40. "Am not!" rejoinder

Puzzle 61

1	2	3	4	■	5	6	7	■	8	9	10	11
12				■	13			■	14			
15				■	16			17				
18				■	■	19			■	■	■	■
■	■	■	20	21	22		■	23	24	25	26	27
28	29	30	■	31			32	■	33			
34			35			■	36	37				
38				■	39	40			■	41		
42				43	■	44			45	■	■	■
■	■	■	■	46	47		■	■	48	49	50	51
52	53	54	55				56	■	57			
58				■	59			■	60			
61				■	62			■	63			

43. Head lines?
45. Talks hoarsely
47. China has a Great one
49. Singsong syllables
50. "Okay if ___ myself out?"
51. Afternoon socials
52. Light opening?
53. Tire filler
54. ___ nutshell
55. Spy novelist Deighton
56. Musician Brian

Solution on Page 329

ACROSS

1. Jolson and Jarreau
4. The "A" in ETA: abbr.
7. Rodeo rope
12. Warmed the bench
13. Tee-___
14. Cockeyed
15. Wedding vow
16. Kangaroo pouch
17. Hawker's pitch
18. The whole shebang
19. Business attire
21. Nair rival
23. Nonprofit's URL ending
24. Ho of Hawaii
27. Hostel
29. Bargain-hunter's favorite words
32. Oodles
35. Bamboo eater
36. Pants measurement
38. Sophs., two years later
39. "Yikes!"
40. Pied Piper follower
42. "Bonanza" brother
46. Mah-jongg piece
47. Decay
48. The Jetsons' dog
52. Former California fort
54. "Gimme ___!" (Alabama cheerleader's cry)
55. Camp shelters
56. Finder's ___
57. "___ Abner"
58. Spouses
59. Male turkey
60. Erie Canal mule

DOWN

1. From the East
2. Soup server
3. Ripped off
4. Cries at fireworks
5. Justification
6. Happen again
7. Bringing up the rear
8. Nile biter
9. Go down a slippery slope
10. Observe
11. "Wise" bird
20. "Where did ___ wrong?"
22. Ocean motion
24. Quarterback Marino
25. Getting on in years
26. Teachers' org.
28. CIA relative
30. "Fresh Air" airer
31. Window frame
32. Tell a whopper
33. Long-distance number starter
34. Inquire

Puzzle 62

37. Med. scan
38. Not mono
41. Skyward
43. Face-to-face exams
44. Actress Braga
45. Play for time
46. Fling
48. Place to enter a PIN
49. Caribbean, e.g.
50. Blasting stuff
51. Numbered rd.
53. Rep.'s rival

Solution on Page 329

ACROSS

1. Final inning, usually
6. Three-strikes result
9. Dell products
12. Worship
13. Type of test on "CSI"
14. Same old, same old
15. Sum
16. Use a shovel
17. 401(k) alternative
18. Pecan and pumpkin
20. Lower, as the lights
21. Cook in hot oil
24. To's opposite
25. "Read 'em and ___!"
26. Gets smart
29. The highest degree
31. Higher of two
32. Shelf
36. Industrial container
38. Seas
39. Chest muscles, briefly
42. Chicago airport code
44. Have dinner
45. Electric fish
46. Lone Ranger attire
48. Have a go at
49. Alfred E. Neuman's magazine
50. Basement's opposite
55. First ___ kit
56. Sporty Pontiac
57. Have the throne
58. Golfer Trevino
59. Work wk. start
60. Furniture polish scent

DOWN

1. Rebellious Turner
2. "___ solemnly swear . . ."
3. Forget-me-___
4. "La la" preceder
5. Lend a hand
6. More peculiar
7. In ___ (together)
8. "Guten ___" (German greeting)
9. Group of lions
10. Physics Nobelist Marie
11. Post office purchase
19. Conditions
21. Winter ailment
22. Bench press unit
23. Big fat mouth
25. Amusement park shout
27. Guns, as an engine
28. Pro-gun org.
30. RN's touch
33. Karl Marx's "___ Kapital"
34. Bearded antelope
35. Paranormal letters
37. Beefsteak or cherry

Puzzle 63

1	2	3	4	5	■	6	7	8	■	9	10	11
12					■	13			■	14		
15					■	16			■	17		
■	■	■	■	18	19			■	■	20		
21	22	23	■	■	24			■	25			
26			27	28		■	29	30		■	■	■
31					■	■	■	32		33	34	35
■	■	■	36		37	■	38					
39	40	41		■	42	43		■	■	44		
45			■	■	46			47	■	■	■	■
48			■	49			■	50	51	52	53	54
55			■	56			■	57				
58			■	59			■	60				

38. ER drug disasters
39. Flower part
40. Spine-tingling
41. Bonnie's partner in crime
43. Hazardous gas
47. Bush adviser Rove
49. Famed movie studio
51. Golf peg
52. Director Burton
53. "May ___ now?"
54. Atlanta's ___ Center

Solution on Page 329

ACROSS

1. Wild guess
5. Robe for Caesar
9. Antlered animal
12. Computer input
13. "Are you ___ out?"
14. Contend (for)
15. "___ See Clearly Now"
16. "Go, ___!"
17. Squeeze (out)
18. "You've got mail" co.
20. Hardy's partner
22. Immediately
25. Printers' needs
26. Gem units
27. Refrain in "Old MacDonald"
29. Prefix with cycle
30. At once
32. Old photo tint
36. "Fort ___, the Bronx"
39. Henpecks
40. Most reasonable
41. Prepare to go
43. Prefix with night or light
44. Actress Gardner
45. See-___ (transparent)
47. Weapons of ___ destruction
51. Belfry denizen
52. "Haven't ___ you somewhere before?"
53. Not at home
54. 180 degrees from NNW
55. Story
56. Ponce de ___

DOWN

1. Anti-ICBM plan
2. Middle "X" of "X-X-X"
3. ___ glance
4. ___ split
5. Knight, dame, etc.
6. Last number in a countdown
7. Net defender
8. Fashion designer Giorgio
9. From then on
10. Take a shine to
11. Ship's backbone
19. Halloween mo.
21. Tiny Tim's instrument
22. Play a role
23. Old salts
24. Get one's bearings
28. ___ and aahs
31. ___ behind the ears
33. Dads
34. "Aha!"
35. Respiratory disorder
36. Shrewd
37. Fido's foot
38. Orwell's "___ Farm"

Puzzle 64

1	2	3	4	■	5	6	7	8	■	9	10	11
12				■	13				■	14		
15				■	16				■	17		
■	■	■	18	19		■	20		21			
22	23	24				■	25				■	■
26						■	27				28	■
29			■	■	■	■	■	■	■	30		31
■	32		33	34	35	■	36	37	38			
■	■	39				■	40					
41	42					■	43			■	■	■
44			■	45		46		■	47	48	49	50
51			■	52				■	53			
54			■	55				■	56			

41. Chews the fat
42. Gabor and Peron
46. Fam. reunion attendee
48. Wonderment
49. ___ Paulo, Brazil
50. Roget wd.

Solution on Page 329

ACROSS

1. Sleeve filler
4. Long-range weapon, for short
8. Snake's sound
12. ___ de Janeiro
13. Respiratory sound
14. Forever ___ day
15. Contingencies
16. Singer Kristofferson
17. Take some off the top
18. Lemon peel
20. Excellent, in modern slang
22. Indian bread
25. Raises, as children
29. Free as a bird
34. Spy org.
35. "Citizen Kane" studio
36. Stanford-___ test
37. Omelet ingredient
38. "That feels so-o-o good!"
39. Old name for a locomotive
41. Boxer Mike
43. IRS payment
44. Average
47. Klutzes
51. Israeli guns
54. Muck
57. Bon ___ (witty saying)
58. Pie a la ___
59. Old TV host Jack
60. To's partner
61. Blog entry
62. Tech. sch. grad
63. Rand McNally product

DOWN

1. Phoenix's home: abbr.
2. Prevalent
3. Velvety flora
4. Annoy
5. Train unit
6. Radar signal
7. Fishnet stocking material
8. Waste maker
9. Squid's squirt
10. "Star Wars" mil. project
11. Walmart founder Walton
19. Explosive initials
21. Franklin known as the Queen of Soul
23. Lacking pigment
24. Roulette color
26. Excellent server
27. Fixes, as a fight
28. Wise one
29. "Animal House" grp.
30. Approve
31. Cries at fireworks
32. Lennon's widow
33. Transmitted

Puzzle 65

40. Tic-tac-toe non-winner
42. Beginning
45. You can skip it
46. Sound of discomfort
48. Radio switch
49. ___ song (cheaply)
50. "That's enough!"
51. "Steee-rike!" caller
52. Dr. Seuss' "If I Ran the ___"
53. Bouncers check them
55. Zig's opposite
56. Flub

Solution on Page 330

ACROSS

1. "Sesame Street" network
4. Adjoin
8. ___ of measure
12. In great shape
13. Window framework
14. Fountain drink
15. Winter malady
16. Helen of ___
17. Nose-in-the-air type
18. Professor's security blanket
20. Attire
21. Moody
24. Infield covers
27. Convent dweller
28. Glacial
31. Places for holsters
32. Hit with a stun gun
33. Apple MP3 player
34. Dutch ___ disease
35. I. M. ___
36. Adored ones
37. Infuriate
39. TV show that had its Dey in court?
43. "I'll be right there!"
47. Giant-screen film format
48. Generic pooch
50. Tic-tac-toe loser
51. Dole (out)
52. Cake decorator
53. FedEx rival
54. Pitcher Hershiser
55. Stratagem
56. Auction unit

DOWN

1. "All gone!" sound
2. Rancor
3. Phaser setting
4. Houston team
5. Less furnished
6. Grp. that entertains troops
7. "Honor ___ father and . . ."
8. The Beatles' "Back in the ___"
9. Zero
10. Wedding vows
11. Keep ___ on (watch)
19. Strike callers
20. Cub Scout group
22. TV studio light
23. Break bread
24. "___ end"
25. Be sick
26. Meas. of engine speed
28. NYSE debut
29. Maj.'s superior
30. NFL gains
32. Buddhist sect
33. Thought
35. Sunday seat

Puzzle 66

36. Pay no heed to
38. Helpers
39. Prom night transportation
40. New World abbr.
41. Overdue
42. Skating jump
44. James Brown's genre
45. Montreal ballplayer
46. Purchase price
48. Tree with needles
49. Post-op area

Solution on Page 330

ACROSS

1. Use an ax
4. Like steak tartare
7. Not out
11. "The Little Red Book" chairman
12. Lincoln and Vigoda
14. Continental money
15. Hockey great Bobby
16. IRA variety
17. Genesis garden
18. Persevere
21. Actor Carney
22. Cowboy Rogers
23. "The heat ___!"
26. Prefix with day or night
27. "Some Like It ___"
30. No middle ground, successwise
34. Letters on a Coppertone bottle
35. Prefix with dermal
36. Part of a molecule
37. Egyptian viper
38. ___-fi (book genre)
40. Carnival confection
45. Formal dance
46. Salty seven
47. "___, though I walk through the valley . . ."
49. Fed. food inspectors
50. Jazz's Fitzgerald
51. Have a meal
52. "___ Gotta Have It" (Spike Lee film)
53. CD predecessors
54. Alternate to dial-up, for short

DOWN

1. Med. cost-saving plan
2. Bring home the bacon
3. Had on
4. Harder to find
5. Cancel the launch
6. Soaks
7. Run-down
8. BMW competitor
9. Gratis
10. Ages and ages
13. Actor Omar
19. Movers' trucks
20. Luke Skywalker's mentor
23. No ___, ands, or buts
24. Aug. follower
25. Big galoot
26. Hosp. scan
27. Flop's opposite
28. Singer Yoko
29. President pro ___
31. The "T" of S.A.T.
32. Be against
33. Central street name
37. Book of maps

Puzzle 67

38. Where hair roots grow
39. Spanish houses
40. Bills and coins
41. Merrie ___ England
42. "Little" Dickens girl
43. ___-in-the-wool
44. Affirmative votes
45. School transport
48. The "A" in NATO: abbr.

Solution on Page 330

ACROSS

1. Cable station from Tenn.
4. ___ up (come clean)
8. Dad
11. Sedona maker
12. Egg-shaped
13. Yogi or Smokey
14. Fall mo.
15. Antitoxins
16. Beer choice
17. Millions of years
19. Start of a magician's cry
21. Mideast export
23. Actress Spacek
26. Major inconveniences
30. "On the ___ hand . . ."
32. Shade of blond
33. Bit of resistance
35. "Grand ___ Opry"
36. At large
39. Harrison Ford's "Star Wars" role
42. False move
44. Feb. preceder
45. Defeat
47. Drunkards
50. "I see," facetiously
53. Actor Baldwin
55. Old TV knob abbr.
57. Degrees held by many CEOs
58. Hindu deity
59. Sternward
60. Pea holder
61. Thing on a cowboy's boot
62. Norma ___ (Sally Field role)

DOWN

1. Ring result, briefly
2. Pleasant
3. Defense org. since 1949
4. Paleontologist's find
5. Holiday preceder
6. ___ Lee cakes
7. Thick slices
8. I. M. the architect
9. ___ bran
10. Before: prefix
13. "___ from the Past"
18. Denials
20. "Blame It on ___" (Caine film)
22. Sign before Virgo
24. "Scat!"
25. Rebel ___ (Confederate battle cry)
26. Linden of "Barney Miller"
27. Beginning on
28. Nursery-rhyme residence
29. Library admonition
31. Rock's ___ Speedwagon
34. Like some chords: abbr.
37. Farm storage structures
38. Rocker Brian

Puzzle 68

40. Winston Cup org.
41. ___-Cat (off-road vehicle)
43. Romanov rulers
46. High-five sound
48. "There's gold in them ___ hills!"
49. Couch
50. Current unit, for short
51. Cable movie channel
52. Feeling blue
54. Australian bird
56. Rd. or hwy.

Solution on Page 330

ACROSS

1. Accessory for Miss America
5. DSL provider
8. Advantage
12. Air freshener scent
13. "I ___ Rock" (Simon & Garfunkel hit)
14. Once around the sun
15. ". . . and to ___ good night!"
16. Spring month
17. "A Day without Rain" singer
18. "Don't touch that ___!"
20. Carries
21. Knight's protection
24. Fall faller
26. Throw with effort
27. Angel hair and penne
30. "If it's all the ___ to you . . ."
31. Foldaway bed
32. Med. care choices
34. Repeat
36. Swarms (with)
37. "Mary ___ little lamb"
38. Liability's opposite
39. Fireplace residue
42. Small pie
44. Pump or loafer
45. Pull along
46. Eight: prefix
50. "Ask me no questions and I'll ___ . . ."
51. Wide shoe spec.
52. Genuine
53. Bullring cries
54. Double curve
55. Clothing store department

DOWN

1. Where you might get into hot water?
2. Feel sick
3. Lorne Michaels show
4. One way to fall in love
5. "___ lineman for the county . . ."
6. Something of trivial importance
7. Salary
8. Cyclonic center
9. Fender-bender result
10. Marvin of Motown
11. Historic periods
19. Fury
20. Prof.'s helpers
21. Sighing sounds
22. Gather, as grain
23. Papa's partner
25. Sup
28. Ed of "Daniel Boone"
29. "___ Like It Hot"
31. Atlantic food fish

Puzzle 69

33. Concorde, e.g.
35. Dorm overseers, for short
36. Tobacco smoke component
39. Regarding
40. Author Silverstein
41. Doughnut's middle
43. Fills with wonder
45. ___ time (golf course slot)
47. So-so grade
48. Sunbathe
49. Capp and Gore

Solution on Page 331

ACROSS

1. Nile slitherers
5. Shoestring
9. Fedora or fez
12. "The Andy Griffith Show" boy
13. Soon
14. "Who ___ to argue?"
15. Grandmother, affectionately
16. Part of a Dracula costume
17. Last of 26
18. Some are bitter or sworn
20. Egg layers
21. Ques. counterpart
22. "It's c-c-cold!"
24. Farm buildings
27. Goes ballistic
31. Slalom curve
32. Draw ___ in the sand
34. Mrs. Peron
35. Ill-fated liner
37. Vaults
39. "Golly!"
40. The "p" in r.p.m.
41. "___ closed!"
44. Least difficult
48. Imitate
49. Simon ___
51. Old sayings
52. Put in stitches
53. Lumberjacks' tools
54. Excursion
55. TV commercials
56. "Those ___ the Days"
57. Charity

DOWN

1. First-rate
2. Stretch over
3. Knotty wood
4. Sailor
5. Shoestrings
6. Santa ___ (hot California winds)
7. Officer of the peace
8. WSW's reverse
9. "Purple ___" (Jimi Hendrix song)
10. "You said it, brother!"
11. What extra innings break
19. Completely cuckoo
20. Mins. and mins.
22. Oscar winner Kingsley
23. ___ Peanut Butter Cups
24. Wager
25. "___ live and breathe!"
26. Queue after "Q"
27. "___ 'em, Rover!"
28. NBA official
29. Night before a holiday
30. Prosecutors, for short
33. More than stretch the truth
36. Get older

Puzzle 70

38. Popular record label
40. So last year
41. House in Spain
42. Copied
43. Uses needle and thread
44. Beholder
45. Husband of a countess
46. Sink's alternative
47. Dosage amts.
49. Lumberjack's tool
50. Give the boot to

Solution on Page 331

ACROSS

1. Be inquisitive
4. ___ Law (basic law of current flow)
8. Tater
12. Pigeon's sound
13. Low in fat
14. Cape Canaveral org.
15. Sink in the middle
16. Retro art style
17. St. Louis landmark
18. Actress Rogers who was once married to Tom Cruise
20. Stir-fry pan
22. Mended
25. Two of cards
29. Fake coin
32. Broke new ground?
34. Machine tooth
35. Flattens in the ring, for short
36. Alphas' followers
37. Table support
38. "Big Blue"
39. Caustic cleaners
40. Rolls of bills
41. Muhammad's birthplace
43. Hair colorer
45. Resistance unit
47. Legendary story
50. Confesses, with "up"
53. Killer whale
56. Ebenezer's exclamation
58. Pedal pushers
59. Classic soft drink
60. Take to court
61. Government agents
62. Skater's jump
63. Two-___ paper towels

DOWN

1. Dell or Toshiba products, for short
2. ". . . where the buffalo ___"
3. Bear or Berra
4. Hit from Grandpa's day
5. "___ Haw"
6. PC alternative
7. Winter blanket
8. Viper, for one
9. Duffer's goal
10. L.A. campus
11. "Zip-A-Dee-Doo-___"
19. Chinese-food additive
21. Ten to one, e.g.
23. Curds and ___
24. Famous
26. West Coast sch.
27. Like some dorms
28. Breakfast order
29. Glance through quickly
30. Place for an earring
31. Gomer Pyle's org.
33. "___ does it"
36. Ho-hum

Puzzle 71

40. Dryly humorous
42. Expenses
44. Online correspondence
46. Homer Simpson's mother
48. Recipe meas.
49. Transport, as a load
50. Popular insect repellent
51. Pint-sized
52. Homer Simpson's neighbor
54. "Oedipus ___"
55. ___ Guevara
57. The Say ___ Kid (Willie Mays)

Solution on Page 331

ACROSS

1. Devotees
5. Blubber
8. It must go on
12. Cafe au ___
13. Auto
14. Choice for Hamlet
15. Ivy League school
16. Alias
17. Touched down
18. Pro Bowl org.
20. Dark loaves
21. "One more time!"
24. Tavern
26. Bullwinkle, for one
27. Warm embrace
28. U-turn from NNE
31. Russian fighter plane
32. "Stars and Stripes Forever" composer
34. "Say what?"
35. 52-wk. periods
36. Negative prefix
37. Steakhouse order
39. Animal park
40. Pick
41. Soft, white cheese
44. "The Eagle ___ Landed"
45. Mary's pet
46. Expected to arrive
48. Thailand, once
52. Ivan or Nicholas
53. Meditation syllables
54. Repeat
55. Pet lovers' org.
56. Burro
57. Fake

DOWN

1. Spider's prey
2. Auto club letters
3. Nonexistent
4. Dictation takers
5. Postal device
6. Durable wood
7. Playtex product
8. Bart or Brenda
9. Sacred
10. Annual theater award
11. Dampens
19. California raisin city
21. TV award
22. Pinot ___ (wine)
23. Gear teeth
24. Greyhound vehicle
25. Christie of mystery
27. Barbarian
28. "Scram!"
29. Phoenix hoopsters
30. "This ride is great!"

Puzzle 72

1	2	3	4	■	5	6	7	■	8	9	10	11
12				■	13			■	14			
15				■	16			■	17			
■	■	■	18	19		■	■	■	20			
21	22	23				■	24	25		■	■	■
26					■	27			■	28	29	30
31			■	32	33				■	34		
35			■	36			■	37	38			
■	■	■	39			■	40					
41	42	43		■	■	■	44			■	■	■
45				■	46	47		■	48	49	50	51
52				■	53			■	54			
55				■	56			■	57			

33. “Hollywood Squares” win
38. Supervisors
39. Striped equine
40. Kasparov’s game
41. Diner sandwiches
42. Sound gravelly
43. Apple product
46. Arrived lifeless, briefly
47. Verbal stumbles
49. “___ liebe dich”
50. “I get it!”
51. Popular tattoo

Solution on Page 331

ACROSS

1. Doctrines
5. No longer working: abbr.
9. Gave dinner
12. Trendy
13. Gumbo ingredient
14. Israeli weapon
15. ___ and now
16. Submissive
17. Hospital trauma ctrs.
18. Intel org.
20. Simoleons
22. Film director's cry
25. Needing no prescription: abbr.
26. Stretches of land
27. 3:1 or 7:2, e.g.
30. Superman foe Luthor
31. Bean counter, for short
33. Oscar who wrote "The Picture of Dorian Gray"
37. Confer holy orders on
40. It's charged in physics
41. ___ out (postponed, in a way)
42. Literary postscript
45. Definite article
46. Happened upon
47. Letterman, to friends
49. Stay away from
53. Young ___ (tykes)
54. Bug-eyed
55. Continental currency
56. Hogs' home
57. Creme ___ creme
58. Give for a while

DOWN

1. Marlene Dietrich's "___ Bin Die Fesche Lola"
2. "___ Drives Me Crazy" (Fine Young Cannibals hit)
3. Russian space station
4. Eye-pleasing, as a view
5. "Friends, ___, countrymen"
6. Barely make, with "out"
7. Aftershock
8. End of two state names
9. Gas or oil
10. Book before Nehemiah
11. Plate
19. Boozer
21. Tenth mo.
22. City in GA
23. Rowing team
24. Cab
28. Words of confidence
29. Mayberry lad
32. ". . . ___ a bottle of rum"
34. "___ ol' me?"
35. Thingamajig
36. Hire

Puzzle 73

1	2	3	4	■	5	6	7	8	■	9	10	11
12				■	13				■	14		
15				■	16				■	17		
■	■	■	18	19		■	20		21			
22	23	24				■	25			■	■	■
26						■	27			28	29	■
30			■	■	■	■	■	■	■	31		32
■	33		34	35	36	■	37	38	39			
■	■	■	40			■	41					
42	43	44				■	45			■	■	■
46			■	47		48		■	49	50	51	52
53			■	54				■	55			
56			■	57				■	58			

37. Daniel of Nicaragua
38. "Go team!"
39. Engine type
42. Ostrich cousins
43. ___-up rage
44. ___-bitsy
48. Encyclopedia bk.
50. ___ and cry
51. Coffee server
52. Silent assent

Solution on Page 332

ACROSS

1. Brokaw's network
4. Parts of a min.
8. Hunk
12. Response to a bad call
13. Lower-left key on many keyboards
14. Rain gutter site
15. "All systems go"
16. Bi-, quadrupled
17. Checked out
18. Second to none
20. "___ kingdom come . . ."
22. Letter carriers' grp.
25. Home run king Hank
29. It ebbs and flows
32. Sounds of amazement
34. Flightless bird
35. Unwanted possession
38. "XXX" counterpart
39. Molecule component
40. Van Gogh flower
41. Nursery rhyme Jack
43. Tie fabric
45. Naughty
47. Prefix with dynamic
50. Cafeteria carrier
53. Springsteen's "___ Fire"
56. Gives a thumbs-up
58. Breaks bread
59. Barn topper
60. Assn.
61. Hides the gray
62. Fusses
63. Wrestling surface

DOWN

1. Lakers' org.
2. Doofus
3. Pepsi rival
4. Glasgow residents
5. And so forth
6. PC component
7. Opening for a coin
8. "Later!"
9. ___ an egg (flop)
10. "___ Maria"
11. Bon Jovi's "___ of Roses"
19. Tallow source
21. Hinged fastener
23. Verse writer
24. Flies alone
26. Backside
27. All: prefix
28. Loony
29. Deuces
30. Restaurant chain acronym
31. Fashionable Christian
33. Prefix meaning "half"
36. "___ Peach" (Allman Brothers album)

Puzzle 74

1	2	3	■	4	5	6	7	■	8	9	10	11
12			■	13				■	14			
15			■	16				■	17			
■	18		19		■	■	20	21		■	■	■
■	■	■	22		23	24	■	25		26	27	28
29	30	31		■	32		33		■	34		
35				36					37			
38			■	39				■	40			
41			42		■	43		44		■	■	■
■	■	■	45		46	■	■	47		48	49	■
50	51	52		■	53	54	55		■	56		57
58				■	59				■	60		
61				■	62				■	63		

37. Nature walk
42. Bottomless pit
44. Bowling alley divisions
46. Prima donna
48. ___ and board
49. Gumbo vegetable
50. Slugger Williams
51. Beam of light
52. Gobbled up
54. "What, me worry?" magazine
55. Plastic ___ Band
57. ___ Pepper

Solution on Page 332

ACROSS

1. Some early PCs
5. "Nova" network
8. Drill a hole
12. It follows 11
13. Actress Remick
14. Figure skater's jump
15. Birdbrain
16. Big Detroit inits.
17. Ukraine's capital
18. Radiation unit
20. Compass part
22. Do-nothing
25. Reporters
26. Lucy of "Charlie's Angels," 2000
27. Raw fish dish
31. Pants part
32. Ewe's mate
33. Comic's bit
36. Single-masted boat
38. Genetic stuff
39. ___ acid
43. Prayer enders
45. Maple leaf land
47. Medicine-approving org.
48. Trampled
49. EPCOT's home
51. Spaghetti sauce brand
55. German "a"
56. Perform
57. Worked like Rumpelstiltskin
58. Active person
59. Hwys. and byways
60. "Gilligan's Island" dwellings

DOWN

1. Ill. neighbor
2. Halloween cry
3. "The ___ Squad"
4. Snoozer's sound
5. Prune, formerly
6. "Don't ___ stranger"
7. ___ up (in the bag)
8. Bread maker
9. Nitrous ___ (laughing gas)
10. Film vault collection
11. Santa's helpers
19. Speech stumbles
21. Prefix with center or dermis
22. Sick
23. Conk out
24. Big galoot
28. Web address: abbr.
29. ___ Paulo
30. Patient care grp.
33. Test for coll. seniors
34. Late columnist Landers
35. Tank filler
36. Lawn base
37. Hippie's home

Puzzle 75

1	2	3	4	■	5	6	7	■	8	9	10	11
12				■	13			■	14			
15				■	16			■	17			
■	■	■	18	19		■	20	21				
22	23	24			■	■	■	25				
26			■	27	28	29	30		■	■	■	■
31			■	■	32			■	■	33	34	35
■	■	■	■	36				37	■	38		
39	40	41	42		■	■	■	43	44			
45					46	■	47			■	■	■
48				■	49	50		■	51	52	53	54
55				■	56			■	57			
58				■	59			■	60			

39. Performed on stage
40. Novelist Puzo
41. Hole ___ (golfer's dream)
42. Consumerist Ralph
44. Wetland
46. Come from ___
47. Minnesota ___
50. Watch display, for short
52. "The Simpsons" clerk
53. Belly
54. Little ___ (tots)

Solution on Page 332

ACROSS

1. Kind of camera: abbr.
4. Stare open-mouthed
8. Company whose mascot is Sonic the Hedgehog
12. Up ___ point
13. Face-to-face exam
14. Has dinner
15. "A League of Their ___"
16. Yearn
17. Old Pontiacs
18. Smaller than small, in dress sizes
20. Crossword hint
22. Part of B&B
23. In layers
26. Free-for-all
29. Fast-paced jazz style
30. Boise's home: abbr.
31. In ___ (going nowhere)
32. Remote
33. Comedian Foxx
34. Take a load off
35. Biomedical research org.
36. High mark with low effort
37. Iran's capital
39. "Singin' in the Rain" studio
40. "I could ___ horse!"
41. Parentless child
45. Pop singer Amos
47. Al or Tipper
49. One ___ million
50. Graceful bird
51. Endure
52. Ex-GI
53. Griffey and Kesey
54. Barely makes, with "out"
55. Meadow mother

DOWN

1. Halt
2. Rob of "The West Wing"
3. ___ and rave
4. Pointed beard
5. Curved
6. Oom-___ (tuba sound)
7. "College" member who votes for president
8. Gently shift to a new topic
9. Lunch joints
10. Classic muscle car
11. Donkey
19. "Yeah, right!"
21. Sass
24. Singer Arnold
25. Early baby word
26. Sail holder
27. Cleveland's lake
28. Follower of a German Protestant
29. "Phooey!"
32. Achieve through trickery

Puzzle 76

1	2	3		4	5	6	7		8	9	10	11
12				13					14			
15				16					17			
18			19				20	21				
			22				23				24	25
26	27	28				29				30		
31					32				33			
34				35				36				
37			38				39					
		40					41			42	43	44
45	46				47	48				49		
50					51					52		
53					54					55		

33. Freeway access
35. Singer ___ King Cole
36. Marsh birds
38. Showers
39. Samuel with a code
42. Honey factory
43. From the top
44. Basketball's Archibald
45. Sound of disappointment
46. Be in the hole
48. Acorn's source

Solution on Page 332

ACROSS

1. Jack Horner's find
5. Slice (off)
8. Retained
12. Ready for harvest
13. Pig ___ poke
14. ___ out (barely made)
15. Computer symbol
16. Students
18. High-IQ group
20. Desertlike
21. Run for exercise
23. Put into law
28. Chiang ___ (Thai city)
31. Gave the boot
33. Perfect server
34. Bill Clinton's veep
36. Hold back
38. Perched on
39. Canceled, as a launch
41. "L.A. Law" actress
42. Lusterless finish
44. GI entertainers
45. "You've ___ Mail"
47. Leopard features
52. Europe, Asia, and Africa
57. Mob scene
58. Become bushed
59. ___ Miguel (largest of the Azores)
60. "I'm ___ you!"
61. Prompts
62. Have title to
63. Twist

DOWN

1. ___ and proper
2. Children's head pests
3. "Once ___ a midnight dreary . . ."
4. Restroom door word
5. Rapper ___ Wayne
6. Jittery
7. Carson's predecessor
8. Baseball's Griffey
9. ___ out a living
10. The "p" in m.p.g.
11. Super Bowl stats
17. Bread for a ham sandwich
19. Barely open
22. Yoked beasts
24. Siesta
25. Served well
26. Hand over
27. Card with three pips
28. Sir's partner
29. ___Vista (search engine)
30. Jim Croce's "___ a Name"
32. Uses a shovel
35. Choose
37. Dairy farm sounds
40. "The ___ Josey Wales"

Puzzle 77

1	2	3	4	■	5	6	7	■	8	9	10	11
12				■	13			■	14			
15				■	16			17				
18				19	■	20			■	■	■	■
■	■	■	■	21	22		■	23	24	25	26	27
28	29	30	■	31			32	■	33			
34			35			■	36	37				
38				■	39	40			■	41		
42				43	■	44			■	■	■	■
■	■	■	■	45	46		■	47	48	49	50	51
52	53	54	55				56	■	57			
58				■	59			■	60			
61				■	62			■	63			

43. Swelled head
46. Approximately
48. Paid players
49. Pigpen cry
50. Lug
51. Stash away
52. Like some stocks, for short
53. Lucy of "Kill Bill"
54. Dr. of rap
55. "Scream" director Craven
56. Mafia boss

Solution on Page 333

ACROSS

1. "Doggone it!"
5. Trojans' sch.
8. Nightclub in a Manilow song
12. Sup
13. Signal approval
14. The Bard of ___ (Shakespeare)
15. Playthings
16. Some univ. instructors
17. Job benefit
18. Car roof with removable panels
20. Seoul's home
21. Very, very thin
24. "The ___ and the Pendulum"
25. Four: prefix
26. Abhor
29. Bit of butter
30. Move one's tail
31. Tape rec. jack
33. Wiggle room
36. Mrs. Bush
38. Fishing pole
39. ___ up (paid)
40. Beauty parlor
43. ___ Ruth
45. Trudge (along)
46. Lobbying org.
47. Auntie of Broadway
51. "What'll ___?" (bartender's question)
52. "Gnarly!"
53. De-wrinkle
54. Russia's Itar-___ news agency
55. Emergency PC key
56. Scored 100 on

DOWN

1. Banned insecticide, for short
2. ___ Grande
3. "Pick a card, ___ card"
4. Examiner
5. "Do ___ others . . ."
6. Cleansing agent
7. Record store purchases
8. Truman who wrote "Breakfast at Tiffany's"
9. "Roger, ___ and out!"
10. Read (over)
11. Paul who wrote "My Way"
19. "La-la" lead-in
20. Caboodle's partner
21. Motor oil additive
22. "Physician, ___ thyself"
23. Suffix with cigar
24. Cribbage board insert
26. 24 hours
27. Pornography
28. Michelin product
30. Roll of bills
32. Philanderer
34. Wears away
35. Took the blue ribbon

Puzzle 78

1	2	3	4	■	5	6	7	■	8	9	10	11
12				■	13			■	14			
15				■	16			■	17			
■	■	■	18	19			■	20				
21	22	23			■	■	24			■	■	■
25					■	26				27	28	■
29			■	■	30			■	■	31		32
■	33		34	35			■	36	37			
■	■	■	38			■	■	39				
40	41	42			■	43	44			■	■	■
45				■	46			■	47	48	49	50
51				■	52			■	53			
54				■	55			■	56			

36. Chemist's workplace
37. Deficiency of red blood cells
40. Roasting rod
41. Claudia ___ Taylor (Lady Bird Johnson)
42. Lofty tennis shots
43. Sheep cries
44. "Back in Black" band
46. Opposite of post-
48. Arrow's path
49. One of the Stooges
50. Finale

Solution on Page 333

ACROSS

1. Hgt.
4. Suit ___ tee
7. Heavenly hunter
12. ___ tai (rum drink)
13. City reg.
14. San Diego baseballer
15. And so on, for short
16. "Jimmy Crack Corn" sentiment
18. Prickly plant
20. WNW's reverse
21. Sketch
22. "Let 'er ___!"
24. Open-and-___ case
28. Spending limit
30. Yup's opposite
32. A feast ___ famine
33. Industrious insect
35. Two under par
37. Bellhop's expectation
38. You-know-___
39. "Here ___ again!"
40. Quick swim
42. Basic util.
44. The "I" in TGIF
46. Typeface
49. "K" followers
51. Congregation leader
53. "Say what?"
57. Faulkner's "___ Lay Dying"
58. Curse
59. X-ray alternative
60. Golf bag item
61. Nonsensical
62. Over there, old-style
63. Not even

DOWN

1. Change, as the Constitution
2. Procrastinator's word
3. Game of X's and O's
4. Work hard
5. Opposite of chaos
6. "Much ___ about Nothing"
7. Chooses, with "for"
8. Indy 500 and others
9. State west of Mont.
10. Hockey legend Bobby
11. Jacqueline Kennedy ___ Bouvier
17. Kathmandu's land
19. Bygone carrier
23. Gold bar
25. Something dropped
26. Spoon-bender Geller
27. Do some soft-shoe
29. Louvre Pyramid architect
31. Tie the knot
33. Shock's partner
34. Rink org.
36. Growing older

Puzzle 79

41. Uncertainties
43. Spotless
45. Former veep Agnew
47. Snooped (around)
48. ___ and true
50. Stable female
52. Have ___ (be connected)
53. Popular TV police drama
54. "To thine ___ self . . ."
55. "Cry ___ River"
56. Poehler of "Parks and Recreation"

Solution on Page 333

ACROSS

1. Toupee, slangily
4. ___-cone (summer treat)
7. Cousin of Calypso
10. Employs
12. One ___ customer
13. Trade
14. Damon of "Good Will Hunting"
15. Wilder's "___ Town"
16. Stack
17. Make, as money
19. Senate gofers
20. Connected to the Internet
23. ___ and cheese
24. Save for a ___ day
25. "Do unto ___ . . ."
28. College transcript no.
29. Actress Ullmann
30. "Take me as ___"
32. Lagasse of the Food Network
35. Pilotless plane
37. Disencumber
38. Speechified
39. Bit of parsley
42. Intense craving
43. Hint
44. Jazz guitarist Montgomery
45. Office fill-in
49. Helps out
50. Stetson, e.g.
51. "___, right!" ("I bet!")
52. The ___ Gees
53. Mos. and mos.
54. Deity

DOWN

1. Captain Morgan's drink
2. Springsteen's "Born in the ___"
3. Grasp
4. Mall unit
5. Part of speech
6. Rower's need
7. Gulp down
8. Curly cabbage
9. Mimics
11. Beer mug
13. "The final frontier"
18. "___ day now . . ."
19. Oom-___ band
20. Part of NATO
21. Back of the neck
22. Author O'Flaherty
23. Station that uses veejays
25. Kuwaiti export
26. Urban unrest
27. Of sound mind
29. Pot top
31. Club ___ (resort)
33. Great Lakes Indians
34. 18-wheeler

Puzzle 80

35. Hosp. workers
36. Shabby
38. Evicts
39. Wound crust
40. Ballet bend
41. Boorish
42. Shakespearean king
44. "___ me?"
46. Brain wave reading: abbr.
47. China's ___ Zedong
48. Degree held by many univ. professors

Solution on Page 333

ACROSS

1. Airline watchdog grp.
4. Moon goddess
8. Blast furnace byproduct
12. Morning hrs.
13. "___ out?" (dealer's query)
14. "I did it!"
15. Jan. and Feb.
16. Popeye's tooter
17. Artist Warhol
18. ___ Park, Colo.
20. "Piece of cake!"
22. Paved the way
24. Stockholm native
27. Waldorf-___ Hotel
31. Archie Bunker's wife
33. "Oh, give ___ home . . ."
34. Sonnets and such
36. Pilot's prediction, for short
37. Singer Page
39. Monticello and Mount Vernon, e.g.
41. Respond to a stimulus
43. Triumph
44. Views
46. Lightens up
50. Rams' mates
53. Leave ___ (act gratuitously?)
55. Submachine gun
56. Zero, in tennis
57. Sitarist Shankar
58. Time in history
59. Close tightly
60. Eye problem
61. "Cheers" bartender

DOWN

1. Celebrity
2. Andy's partner in old radio
3. Like some profs.
4. Insincere support
5. Prefix for corn or verse
6. Slangy denial
7. Regions
8. Hung around
9. PC linkup
10. Build (on)
11. Like old Paree
19. "Turn to Stone" band
21. Term of endearment
23. Six-sided game piece
25. Weight-loss plan
26. Suffix with kitchen
27. Concert stage item
28. Char
29. London's ___ Gallery
30. "Roses ___ red . . ."
32. Possesses
35. 180 degrees from NNE
38. Mortarboard attachment
40. "I'd like to buy ___, Pat!"

Puzzle 81

42. Eye drops?
45. Immediately, to a surgeon
47. Takes to court
48. Book after II Chronicles
49. Where Anna met the king
50. Overhead trains
51. Misfortune
52. One of the Gabors
54. Climbing vine

Solution on Page 334

ACROSS

1. PC connection
4. ___-bodied seaman
8. Drinks slowly
12. Cause for overtime
13. Enthusiasm
14. "Now ___ this!"
15. Cavity filler's deg.
16. Job to do
17. Weaponry
18. Eyelid problem
20. Grassy clump
22. Play parts
25. Electrical pioneer Nikola
29. Canvas cover
32. Squeezes (out)
34. Napkin's place
35. Elevator pioneer
36. Narc's org.
37. Unaccompanied
38. Downing St. VIPs
39. Not an abstainer
40. Has debts
41. Watermelon throwaways
43. Tongue-clicking sounds
45. Jabber
47. Loch ___
50. ___ or less (approximately)
53. Feed the kitty
56. Frank McCourt's follow-up to "Angela's Ashes"
58. Way off
59. White as a ghost
60. Everything
61. Crow calls
62. Fundamentals
63. Something in Santa's bag

DOWN

1. Inc., in England
2. Lends a hand
3. Cozy place
4. Ancient Mexican
5. Arthur of "Maude"
6. "Leaving ___ Vegas"
7. Fraternal group
8. Shelter from the sun
9. Occupational suffix
10. Popular cooking spray
11. 12th graders: abbr.
19. Kennel cries
21. NFL tiebreakers
23. "Bill & ___ Excellent Adventure"
24. Trapshooting
26. Like molasses
27. Lois of the "Daily Planet"
28. "Planet of the ___"
29. Best toys in the whirl?
30. "Don't look ___ like that!"
31. Get up
33. "I'm all ___"
37. Misplace

Puzzle 82

39. The Beach Boys' "Surfin' ___"
42. Color changers
44. Leg joints
46. Mama's partner
48. Number on a baseball card
49. Fodder storage site
50. Apple computer, for short
51. Birds ___ feather
52. Uncooked
54. Arrest
55. That special touch, briefly
57. Wily

Solution on Page 334

ACROSS

1. ___ tai
4. McDonald's arches, e.g.
8. Org. for those 50+
12. Stanford-Binet nos.
13. "Excuse me . . ."
14. ___ laughing (cracks up)
15. "The word," to secret keepers
16. ___ Club (discount chain)
17. "I had no ___!"
18. Spring holiday
20. Prepared to propose
21. Ultimatum words
24. Mexican moolah
27. ___ nut (wheel fastener)
28. Sign, as a deal
31. Losing tic-tac-toe line
32. Liu Pang's dynasty
33. Korean automaker
34. Film critic Reed
35. Wrigley's product
36. Skilled
38. California peak
40. Milan's La ___
44. Cornell's home
48. ___ contendere
49. Roll call response
51. "Platoon" setting
52. Bullets
53. Frosts, as a cake
54. Rapper Dr. ___
55. Shocked reaction
56. "Stop it!"
57. Gender

DOWN

1. Silent performer
2. Water color
3. Beliefs
4. Cutting rays
5. Chicago airport
6. Precious stone
7. Meditation sounds
8. Tennis score
9. Assistant
10. Fishing rod attachment
11. Exam for teens
19. "___ many cooks spoil the broth"
20. Beer barrel
22. Andean animal
23. Solar-system center
24. "___ favor"
25. Common filename extension
26. Boston Red ___
28. ___ & Tina Turner Revue
29. Puppy's bite
30. Kit ___ bar
32. "Come again?"
35. Cookie-selling gp.
36. Swear (to)

Puzzle 83

37. Lah-di-___
39. Ambulance sound
40. Fly in the ointment
41. Unconscious state
42. Money for the poor
43. Airplane maneuver
45. "No ifs, ___, or buts!"
46. Give a darn
47. "Don't leave home without it" card
49. Stayed out of sight
50. Prefix with system or sphere

Solution on Page 334

ACROSS

1. Noose material
5. "___ your age!"
8. Ring decisions, for short
12. Pinnacle
13. Lamb's cry
14. Powerful D.C. lobby
15. Boston cager, informally
16. Larry King's channel
17. Nickname for Ford's Jones portrayal
18. Deep ___ bend
19. Pass over
21. "Peacock" network
24. Poor
28. Flat part of a chart line
32. Part of TNT
33. "Cannery ___"
34. Omega's opposite
36. Black goo
37. All thumbs
39. Put in place
41. Olympic award
42. Two hours before noon
43. Depend (on)
46. Family group
50. "Les Miserables" author Victor
53. Fine and dandy
55. "Mona ___"
56. Iridescent gem
57. Payable on demand
58. Nights before
59. Dry dishes
60. Lacking moisture
61. Splinter group

DOWN

1. ___ of lamb
2. Ready for business
3. Brazilian soccer legend
4. Scope
5. "Dancing with the Stars" network
6. Trash holders
7. Combat vehicle
8. Taiwan's capital
9. It's north of Okla.
10. Run-of-the-mill: abbr.
11. Secret agent
20. Natural
22. John, Paul, George, or Ringo
23. ___ Poly (West Coast school)
25. Kett of old comics
26. "Phooey!"
27. Time past
28. Stiffly neat
29. Solitary
30. Wowed
31. Downs' opposite
35. Batter's goal
38. Conditional release

Puzzle 84

1	2	3	4	■	5	6	7	■	8	9	10	11
12				■	13			■	14			
15				■	16			■	17			
18				■	■	19		20		■	■	■
■	■	■	21	22	23	■	■	24		25	26	27
28	29	30				31	■	32				
33			■	34			35		■	36		
37			38		■	39			40			
41					■	■	42			■	■	■
■	■	■	43		44	45	■	■	46	47	48	49
50	51	52		■	53		54	■	55			
56				■	57			■	58			
59				■	60			■	61			

40. Dad's brothers
44. Actor Alan
45. Part of BYOB
47. Not prerecorded
48. "Wait ___!"
49. Cartoonist Thomas
50. "___ about that?!"
51. News agcy.
52. Opening
54. ___ Largo

Solution on Page 334

ACROSS

1. Kills, in mob slang
5. Sheltered bay
9. Sauté
12. Masculine
13. Farewells
14. Owing
15. Falling flakes
16. Republican symbol
18. Ger. continent
20. In favor of
21. Deprive of weapons
24. Furious
28. Disreputable newspaper
29. Bloodhound's clue
33. Old Japanese coin
34. Feathery wrap
35. Tiller's tool
36. Small rug
37. Hi-fi component
38. Fender flaws
40. "To ___ is human . . ."
41. Nephew's sister
43. NBC morning show
45. UCLA rival
47. Burger roll
48. Put through hell night
52. Larger ___ life
56. Tanning lotion letters
57. Scrape, as a knee
58. "Dear" advice columnist
59. CAT scan alternative
60. Exam
61. Sit

DOWN

1. Mantra sounds
2. Enthusiast
3. "Alice" spin-off
4. Underground conduit
5. Trucker with a transmitter
6. Olive ___
7. Prez's #2
8. ___ de corps
9. Pharm. watchdog
10. Sprint
11. "The best is ___ to come!"
17. Opposite of vert.
19. Hesitation sounds
21. Rural's opposite
22. Supermodel Campbell
23. Open-mouthed
25. ___ and dangerous
26. Pageant crown
27. Contest submission
30. Friend of Fidel
31. Seemingly forever
32. What's left after deductions
38. Partner of cease
39. Trio after R

Puzzle 85

1	2	3	4	■	5	6	7	8	■	9	10	11
12				■	13				■	14		
15				■	16				17			
■	■	■	18	19		■	20			■	■	■
21	22	23			■	■	■	24		25	26	27
28			■	29	30	31	32		■	33		
34			■	■	35			■	■	36		
37			■	38				39	■	40		
41			42		■	■	■	43	44			
■	■	■	45		46	■	47			■	■	■
48	49	50				51		■	52	53	54	55
56			■	57				■	58			
59			■	60				■	61			

42. Slice
44. Like draft beer
46. Wedding reception centerpiece
47. Not straight
48. Ideology
49. Radio's PBS
50. "See ___ care!"
51. "___ the season to be jolly"
53. Premium cable channel
54. Stomach muscles, for short
55. TV's "Science Guy" Bill

Solution on Page 335

ACROSS

1. Flavor enhancer
6. Hue's partner
9. Baden-Baden, e.g.
12. Voice below alto
13. Shade
14. Sphere
15. Al of Indy
16. TLC givers
17. Ghost's cry
18. Test-driver's car
20. Repair
21. PC's "brain"
24. Not Rep. or Ind.
25. Mississippi River transport
26. "___ master's voice"
27. Archaeological find
29. Slanted printing style
32. Shoe part
36. Bird-related
38. Haw's partner
39. Beetle Bailey's boss
42. Savings acct. alternatives
44. Gives the go-ahead
45. Managed care gps.
46. Baby bovine
48. Out-of-date: abbr.
49. Dove's sound
51. Planet's path
55. "Rubber Ball" singer Bobby
56. Mo. before May
57. War's opposite
58. Hesitation sounds
59. "Acid"
60. Lucy's landlady

DOWN

1. Disco ___ of "The Simpsons"
2. Mont Blanc, e.g.
3. Walk-___ (clients without appointments)
4. For both sexes
5. Flubbed
6. Auto trim
7. "Walk, don't ___!"
8. Aye
9. Like the designated driver
10. Tine
11. Dwelling
19. Parisian thanks
20. Alternatives to PCs
21. Letter before psi
22. Peach center
23. ___ Today (newspaper)
25. "Ich ___ ein Berliner"
28. Singer Ronstadt
30. Falls behind
31. "Now ___ seen everything!"
33. Howe'er
34. Comics shriek

Puzzle 86

1	2	3	4	5	■	6	7	8	■	9	10	11
12					■	13			■	14		
15					■	16			■	17		
■	■	■	18		19		■	■	20			
21	22	23	■	24			■	25				
26			■	■	27		28			■	■	■
29			30	31		■	32			33	34	35
■	■	■	36			37		■	■	38		
39	40	41			■	42		43	■	44		
45				■	■	46			47	■	■	■
48			■	49	50		■	51		52	53	54
55			■	56			■	57				
58			■	59			■	60				

35. Parliament VIPs
37. Popular Honda
39. Push roughly
40. Yellowish brown
41. Valentine's Day bouquet
43. It can be slippery
47. Fingerboard ridge
49. Ore. neighbor
50. Co-___ (condo relatives)
52. Scrooge's cry
53. Drink cooler
54. No. on a business card

Solution on Page 336

ACROSS

1. Afternoon hrs.
4. USC rival
8. Degree held by many a CEO
11. Something you might lend
13. Screwdriver, for one
14. Blunder
15. Boxer Oscar ___ Hoya
16. Des Moines is its capital
17. Sharpshooter's asset
18. Somersault
20. Contest specifications
22. "The Taming of the ___"
25. Units of resistance
27. Singer Zadora
28. Three's opposite on a clock face
30. Young horse
34. Magazine revenue source
35. Beach souvenir
37. "How ___ love thee?"
38. Classic grape soda
40. Nobel Peace Prize city
41. Fleming who created 007
42. Frosh, next year
44. Requires
46. John or John Quincy
49. Like an omelet
51. Mechanical tooth
52. "Fargo" director
54. As a result
58. Groundbreaking tool
59. "It was ___ mistake!"
60. Volvo rival
61. Many mos.
62. Take five
63. Family MDs

DOWN

1. Advanced degree: abbr.
2. Fannie ___
3. NBC sketch show
4. Gas or elec.
5. Be kept waiting
6. Daily temperature extreme
7. Car security device
8. Breakfast, lunch, or dinner
9. French cheese
10. Second Amendment subject
12. Truth or ___ (slumber party game)
19. Holds the title to
21. The Trojans of the NCAA
22. Bridge section
23. Conceal
24. Poison ivy woe
26. "War is ___"
29. Denny's alternative
31. Garfield's canine pal
32. Dump truckful
33. Sardine containers
36. Like a hippie's hair

Puzzle 87

1	2	3	■	■	4	5	6	7	■	8	9	10
11			12	■	13				■	14		
15				■	16				■	17		
■	■	■	18	19			■	20	21			
22	23	24			■	25	26			■	■	■
27			■	28	29			■	30	31	32	33
34			■	35				36	■	37		
38			39	■	40				■	41		
■	■	■	42	43			■	44	45			
46	47	48			■	49	50			■	■	■
51			■	52	53			■	54	55	56	57
58			■	59				■	60			
61			■	62				■	■	63		

39. Suffix with patriot or manner
43. Academy Award
45. Looks at
46. Sore
47. "Let's Make a Deal" choice
48. Gets older
50. Tiny pest
53. Bullring cheer
55. Old cloth
56. Mountain pass
57. Delivery docs, for short

Solution on Page 335

ACROSS

1. Uses a powder puff
5. Swamp critter
9. Half a Latin dance
12. Cincinnati's home
13. Glowing review
14. Sombrero, e.g.
15. Kitchen gadget that turns
17. Slippery ___
18. Museum-funding org.
19. Secondhand transaction
21. Dormant
24. Pub missile
25. ___ to (not in favor of)
26. Football Hall-of-Famer Merlin
28. Bro's sib
29. "___ Boot" (1981 war film)
31. Rise from a chair
35. Author Louisa May
38. "Bye"
39. "60 Minutes" pundit Andy
40. Bound by routine
42. Billy Joel's "___ to Extremes"
43. Mobil product
44. Lacking meaning
49. WNW's opposite
50. "So what ___ is new?"
51. On a grand scale
52. Some grad students
53. "Too bad!"
54. Rolling in dough

DOWN

1. Med. school grad
2. "Now I get it!"
3. Coal container
4. Oklahoman
5. Dream up
6. Sought office
7. Exaggerate
8. Breakfast fare
9. Was unfaithful to
10. Room connector
11. "Don't look ___!"
16. Ballpoints, e.g.
20. Soon-to-be grads: abbr.
21. Part of UNLV
22. Hertz rival
23. Likely legal precedents
27. Thurmond of NBA fame
30. Pig's digs
32. Broadcast
33. Queasy feeling
34. "I want to hear all the details"
35. Comes up
36. Theater section
37. Beverage chest
40. The Beach Boys' "___ Around"

Puzzle 88

1	2	3	4	■	5	6	7	8	■	9	10	11
12				■	13				■	14		
15				16					■	17		
■	■	■	18			■	19		20			
21	22	23				■	24				■	■
25						■	26				27	■
28			■	■	■	■	■	■	■	29		30
■	31		32	33	34	■	35	36	37			
■	■	38				■	39					
40	41					■	42			■	■	■
43			■	44		45				46	47	48
49			■	50				■	51			
52			■	53				■	54			

41. Shuttle org.
45. Hush-hush govt. org.
46. Prefix with gram or center
47. “Not my error” notation
48. Coll. or univ.

Solution on Page 335

ACROSS

1. On the ___ (furtively)
4. Kind of radio
8. Aviated
12. Fall mo.
13. Dinghy or dory
14. Miner's strike
15. Wrath
16. Bawls
17. Roe
18. Annoy
20. Put back to 000
21. "Bless you" preceder
24. Take as one's own
27. Trip segment
28. Descriptive wd.
31. Striped shirt wearer
32. Tonic's partner
33. Ms. Zadora
34. Battle of Britain grp.
35. "___ Doubtfire"
36. ". . . happily ever ___"
38. Magician's word
40. Break into smithereens
44. Defeat soundly
48. Burt's ex
49. "From ___ to Eternity"
51. Moo ___ gai pan
52. Part of IBM
53. Alda of "M*A*S*H"
54. Consume
55. Load for Jack and Jill
56. Puppy bites
57. They have Xings

DOWN

1. Quick cut
2. Traditional knowledge
3. Designer ___ Saint Laurent
4. Not in class
5. Demi or Dudley
6. "Groovy!"
7. Peaks: abbr.
8. Run away
9. Captains' records
10. Upper hand
11. Sunset direction
19. Sugar amt.
20. Gas pump choice: abbr.
22. Beethoven's "Für ___"
23. "___ and the Art of Motorcycle Maintenance"
24. Airport abbr.
25. Narcs' org.
26. "They're ___!" (racetrack cry)
28. Prone
29. Go kaput
30. Peanut butter holder
32. Dog's warning
35. Speedometer abbr.

Puzzle 89

1	2	3	■	4	5	6	7	■	8	9	10	11
12			■	13				■	14			
15			■	16				■	17			
18			19			■	■	20				
■	■	■	21			22	23		■	■	■	■
24	25	26			■	27			■	28	29	30
31			■	■	32			■	■	33		
34			■	35			■	36	37			
■	■	■	■	38			39			■	■	■
40	41	42	43		■	■	44			45	46	47
48				■	49	50			■	51		
52				■	53				■	54		
55				■	56				■	57		

36. 2004 Olympics site
37. In favor of
39. Subway handhold
40. Freudian ___
41. Novelist Simpson
42. Against
43. Window ledge
45. Finish for teen or golden
46. Fly like an eagle
47. Red ___ (cinnamon candies)
49. Leia's love
50. Pharmaceutical giant ___ Lilly

Solution on Page 336

ACROSS

1. Corn units
5. Barbell abbr.
8. Plant part
12. Eyelid woe
13. Bullfight cheer
14. "Gone with the Wind" plantation
15. Prophet
16. Not at home
17. Working hard
18. Mozart's "a"
20. Alder and elder
21. 747, e.g.
24. Like ___ not
26. Former Houston footballer
27. "___ on your life!"
28. Series of scenes
31. Recent immigrant's class: abbr.
32. Road map abbr.
33. Ford or Lincoln
34. ___ tai (drink)
35. Back rub response
36. "Inferno" writer
38. Daly of "Judging Amy"
39. Gown
40. Motorized shop tool
43. It may be tempted
45. Skin soother
46. "___ chance!"
47. Mission Control org.
51. Hawaiian neckwear
52. One-spot
53. Lawyer Dershowitz
54. Car bar
55. Hillary Clinton, ___ Rodham
56. "___ in the Clowns"

DOWN

1. Feminine suffix
2. Had lunch
3. Bread with seeds
4. Tranquil
5. Nut
6. Arguer's state?
7. Complete collection
8. Ringo on drums
9. London art gallery
10. Toledo's lake
11. Wrestling surfaces
19. Suffix with cash
20. Wee one
21. Frost lines
22. Bart Simpson's brainy sister
23. "___ want for Christmas . . ."
25. Little piggy
28. Adolescent outbreak
29. Tabbies
30. Very, in Paris
32. Did a marathon
35. Certain vote

Puzzle 90

36. Banned spray
37. Stadiums
38. “We hold ___ truths . . .”
40. Tra-___
41. “Roots” author Haley
42. “Double, double, ___, and trouble . . .”
44. Suit to ___
46. Ceiling fixture
48. Pub draught
49. ___ Diego
50. In addition

Solution on Page 336

ACROSS

1. Take a chair
4. Not a copy: abbr.
8. Pleased
12. Major leaguer
13. Ill temper
14. "O ___ Night"
15. ___ a plea
16. Realtor's showing
18. Tennis's Agassi
20. Golf pegs
21. ___ Tafari
22. Agenda details
26. Anthem starter
28. Low voice
31. Eye the bull's-eye
32. Word with down or key
33. ___ badge
34. Bearded grazer
35. Expected
36. Hardwood trees
37. Dart about
38. Mistake
40. Sandra of "Gidget"
41. Trot or canter
44. Country singer Buck
47. Precision marching group
51. "Shut yer ___!"
52. Winning margin, sometimes
53. 3M product
54. Univ. e-mail ending
55. Concert equipment
56. Heavenly bodies
57. Mom's mate

DOWN

1. Org. that safeguards pets
2. Press
3. First-rate
4. Woodwind instruments
5. Tombstone letters
6. "Sorry if ___ you down"
7. Trait carrier
8. Apparition
9. Singer Rawls
10. Gore and Green
11. Recolor
17. Bank robber's job
19. Sunbeam
23. Keen of sight
24. Short skirt
25. Dirty reading
26. Ye follower
27. Acerbic
28. Arthur of "The Golden Girls"
29. "Raiders of the Lost ___"
30. Lisa, to Bart
33. Ethical
37. ___ and far between
39. Makes eyes at

Puzzle 91

40. Hemispherical roofs
42. "What's ___ you?"
43. Rip
45. Nothin'
46. Potato
47. Paternity identifier
48. CD-___ (computer insert)
49. EarthLink, e.g.
50. Police radio alert, briefly

Solution on Page 336

ACROSS

1. Ballpark arbiters
5. Bloke
9. Letter before omega
12. One and only
13. Decant
14. "Just a ___!" ("Hold on!")
15. Dire prophecy
16. Was a passenger
17. Tibetan ox
18. Shenanigan
20. Mincemeat dessert
21. Weep
22. Web address, for short
24. Extreme degree
26. ___ Plaines
29. Swedish auto
31. Genie's offering
34. Hot dog topper
36. Frozen spear
38. Playlet
39. Missile housing
41. Thesaurus listing: abbr.
42. L.A. clock setting
44. Wyo. neighbor
45. Prefix with demeanor or direction
47. ___ and Coke (mixed drink)
49. Copper-zinc alloy
54. ___ Wednesday
55. Melville captain
57. Garage occupant
58. Slime
59. Adorable
60. Extended family
61. Hoosier st.
62. Every now and ___
63. On pins and needles

DOWN

1. Beef-rating org.
2. Apollo 11 destination
3. Scheme
4. Big rig
5. Life-saving skill, for short
6. Hype
7. German auto
8. Primp
9. Mind readers
10. Scorch
11. Disgusting
19. Say "%@&#!"
23. Stadium cheers
25. Prefix for light
26. AMA members
27. Hair-raising cry
28. Sloppy
30. Liver secretion
32. Leader of the Family Stone
33. Biddy
35. For what ___ worth

Puzzle 92

1	2	3	4	■	5	6	7	8	■	9	10	11
12				■	13				■	14		
15				■	16				■	17		
18				19	■	20			■	21		
■	■	■	■	22	23		■	24	25		■	■
26	27	28	■	29			30	■	31		32	33
34			35			■	36	37				
38				■	39	40			■	41		
■	■	42		43	■	44			■	■	■	■
45	46		■	47	48		■	49	50	51	52	53
54			■	55			56	■	57			
58			■	59				■	60			
61			■	62				■	63			

37. Irvin or Ty
40. Prisoner
43. Piece of land
45. Biblical gift bearers
46. The Rolling Stones' "Time ___ My Side"
48. "Not gonna happen"
50. Marathon, e.g.
51. "___ Lang Syne"
52. Doe's mate
53. PlayStation maker
56. Jerry's partner

Solution on Page 336

ACROSS

1. Lost traction
5. Murders, mob-style
9. "It's freezing!"
12. Mexican coin
13. Froth
14. "I kid ___ not"
15. The "U" in ICU
16. Big party
17. Wee bit
18. Sniffers
20. Suspicious
22. Soothsayer
26. London hrs.
29. Banjo virtuoso Fleck
30. Film ___ (movie genre)
34. Harvest
36. Sis or bro
37. George W. Bush's alma mater
38. ___ Against the Machine
39. Footnote abbreviation
41. Airline to Holland
42. Pacific weather phenomenon
44. Vampire vanquisher
47. Lip application
52. Tavern
53. Wanes
57. Quadri- times two
58. Kind of tide
59. Learning method
60. A/C measures
61. "This means ___!"
62. Progresso product
63. "My Three ___"

DOWN

1. Made a web
2. Carson's successor
3. Egyptian fertility goddess
4. Shower affection (on)
5. Switch position
6. Adversary
7. Corpulent
8. Aroma
9. Computer unit
10. Jungle warning
11. Former mayor Giuliani
19. Cry loudly
21. Counting-out word
23. Pine exudation
24. Excuse
25. Log home
26. Weimaraner's warning
27. "Culpa" starter
28. Chasing game
31. ___ Ridge Boys
32. Under the weather
33. Sleep stage
35. Sneak a look
40. "Man's best friend"

Puzzle 93

43. Lascivious looks
44. Gush forth
45. Big brass instrument
46. E.g., e.g.
48. Arcing shots
49. Eight: prefix
50. Shock
51. Impudent talk
54. Halloween greeting
55. Approx. 252 calories
56. Calendar abbr.

Solution on Page 337

ACROSS

1. Coll. senior's test
4. Gridiron official, for short
7. Agile
11. Sun. follower
12. Has a tab
14. "Not guilty," e.g.
15. Harbor boat
16. Mideast's ___ Strip
17. ___ and file
18. Frost's "The Road Not ___"
20. Gregorian music style
22. "___ lost!"
23. Appeal to God
24. Naval lockup
26. Dress's bottom
27. Sleepwear, briefly
30. Yang's counterpart
31. Frog relatives
33. Cheerleader's cheer
34. Bird-to-be
35. MD's associates
36. Declare untrue
37. "The Way We ___"
38. Meower
39. 17-syllable poem
41. Stratum
43. Brought into the world
44. Cowboy boot attachment
46. "Believe It or ___!"
48. Fashionable
49. "Stop right there!"
50. Bro's counterpart
51. Nod off
52. Actor's prompt
53. Lodge member

DOWN

1. Prime meridian hrs.
2. Defeat decisively
3. Attractive
4. Thesaurus compiler
5. Actor McGregor
6. Casbah headgear
7. Aerosol output
8. Blueprint
9. Lease
10. Jabber
13. Like the word of God
19. Beer container
21. Radio operators
23. Moon stage
24. "See you later"
25. Fix, as a fight
27. False appearance
28. Dean's singing partner
29. Timid
31. Long journey
32. Surge
36. Calendar square

Puzzle 94

1	2	3	■	4	5	6	■	■	7	8	9	10
11			■	12			13	■	14			
15			■	16				■	17			
■	18		19			■	20	21				■
■	■	22			■	23				■	■	■
24	25			■	■	26			■	27	28	29
30			■	31	32				■	33		
34			■	35			■	■	36			
■	■	■	37				■	38			■	■
■	39	40				■	41				42	■
43				■	44	45			■	46		47
48				■	49				■	50		
51				■	■	52			■	53		

37. Flinch
38. ___ blanche
39. Sounds from Santa
40. NM neighbor
41. Humdinger
42. Stir up
43. Queue after "A"
45. Cal.'s ocean
47. Sound of disapproval

Solution on Page 337

ACROSS

1. Cyclotron particles
5. Work at, as a trade
8. Border on
12. Photographed
13. Debtor's note
14. Nightclub of song
15. ___ care in the world
16. Hair goop
17. Branch offshoot
18. "And ___ There Were None"
19. Boyfriend
21. Morse bit
24. Diamond weight
28. Soft shade
31. Barton of the Red Cross
32. Baby's bawl
33. "One of ___ days . . ."
35. Roman 300
36. Arcade game maker
38. Debate topics
40. James Dean persona
41. Recipe meas.
42. Anatomical pouches
45. Pyramid scheme, e.g.
49. Gondola propeller
52. Miss. neighbor
54. Hockey legend Gordie
55. Animal with a beard
56. Column's counterpart
57. Sign of things to come
58. iPhone downloads
59. Gateway Arch city: abbr.
60. Mary ___ Lincoln

DOWN

1. Stevie Wonder's "___ She Lovely"
2. Words of surprise
3. Post-it, e.g.
4. Bleachers
5. ___ out (overeat)
6. Leopold's partner in crime
7. Christmas season
8. Real
9. Gift decoration
10. Wire service
11. "You're it!" game
20. What passwords provide
22. Famous Hun
23. "Beavis and Butt-head" laugh
25. Speed contest
26. Rainbows
27. Between tic and toe
28. Cracker spread
29. "Moby-Dick" captain
30. Floral necklace
32. ___ of 1812
34. Mach 1 breaker
37. Turns back to zero
39. Result

Puzzle 95

43. Autos
44. Piggy bank opening
46. Crooner Perry
47. Thunderstruck
48. Darn, as socks
49. Nicklaus's org.
50. Comics caveman Alley ___
51. In the ___ of luxury
53. Cobbler's tool

Solution on Page 337

ACROSS

1. G-man's org.
4. Spanish hero El ___
7. Heavy book
11. PC linking system
12. Spoken
14. Lendl of tennis
15. Citrus drinks, for short
16. Johnny-___-lately
17. Small dent on a fender
18. Benefactor
20. ___ Vic's (restaurant chain)
22. "That's great news!"
23. Business card no.
24. Journalist Ernie
27. Bad spell
28. Gridiron org.
31. Hawaiian garlands
32. Switz. neighbor
33. Go easy on the calories
34. From Jan. 1 until now, in accounting
35. Bride's new title
36. Newspaper page
37. Election day: abbr.
38. ___-Atlantic
40. Harangue
43. Consecrate with oil
47. City near Provo
48. Slender
50. Never-before-seen
51. Lose brightness
52. Trig ratio
53. Greek "X"
54. Gorbachev was its last leader: abbr.
55. Pay-___-view
56. Chart topper

DOWN

1. Dud
2. ___ California
3. "Meet Me ___ Louis"
4. Drink served with marshmallows
5. Humor with a twist
6. Beaver's construction
7. ___ wave
8. "Metamorphoses" poet
9. Horse hair
10. MIT grad
13. A, B, or C
19. Some whiskeys
21. Harrison or Reed
24. Layer
25. "Are we there ___?"
26. Container cover
27. The Chiffons' "___ So Fine"
28. Small bite
29. Service charge
30. Inc., abroad

Puzzle 96

1	2	3	■	4	5	6	■	■	7	8	9	10
11			■	12			13	■	14			
15			■	16				■	17			
18			19			■	20	21				
■	■	■	22			■	23			■	■	■
24	25	26		■	■	27			■	28	29	30
31				■	32			■	33			
34			■	35			■	■	36			
■	■	■	37			■	38	39		■	■	■
40	41	42				■	43			44	45	46
47				■	48	49			■	50		
51				■	52				■	53		
54				■	■	55			■	56		

32. Says hello to
33. Extinct bird
35. Dirt + water
37. Circus star with a whip
38. Stephen King's state
39. ___ tube
40. Soybean product
41. Some nest eggs
42. Cincinnati baseball team
44. Ruler unit
45. Classic soda brand
46. Pinhead
49. Place to shoot from

Solution on Page 337

ACROSS

1. Clumsy sort
4. PC screen
7. Complain
11. Is sick
13. Gun, as an engine
14. "That's clear"
15. On bended ___
16. Stomach muscles
17. Spring event
18. Backs of boats
20. "What ___ to be the problem?"
21. Relent
24. Informal language
27. Arid
28. Telly network
31. Ready to pick
32. Square root of IX
33. Surprise attack
34. Sizable sandwich
35. BBC clock setting
36. Leases
37. Uses glue
39. Male deer
43. Puts forth, as effort
47. Folk singer Guthrie
48. Exec's degree
50. "Peek___!"
51. High wind
52. Tiebreakers, briefly
53. Stadium level
54. Tan and Irving
55. Mon. follower
56. Mach + jet

DOWN

1. Acorn producers
2. "___ We Got Fun?"
3. Turn tail
4. Unrefined
5. Dixie soldier
6. Household sets
7. Refer to
8. Tennis great Arthur
9. Paper quantity
10. Church benches
12. Calm
19. Remind too often
20. Snoop (on)
22. Reviews and corrects
23. Mentalist Geller
24. Last year's jrs.
25. Actress Lucy
26. LAPD alert
28. Make illegal
29. Took the bait
30. LP successors
32. "___ Loser" (Beatles song)
33. Return to office
35. Fam. doctors

Puzzle 97

1	2	3	■	■	4	5	6	■	7	8	9	10
11			12	■	13			■	14			
15				■	16			■	17			
18				19		■	■	20				
■	■	■	21			22	23		■	■	■	■
24	25	26			■	27			■	28	29	30
31				■	32			■	33			
34			■	35			■	36				
■	■	■	■	37			38			■	■	■
39	40	41	42		■	■	43			44	45	46
47				■	48	49		■	50			
51				■	52			■	53			
54				■	55			■	■	56		

36. Tyrannosaurus ___
38. Make fun of
39. Adventure story
40. Cable car
41. Party to a defense pact
42. Travels
44. Baseball stats
45. Tips of socks
46. Alphabetize, e.g.
48. Bon ___ (witty remark)
49. A/C measure

Solution on Page 338

ACROSS

1. Wee
5. Anti-attacker spray
9. Chinese tea
12. Buckeye State
13. Alka-Seltzer sound
14. ___ Vegas
15. Something to break into
16. Saintly glow
17. Biblical boat
18. Break one's silence
20. Min. fraction
21. Barnum and 109, e.g.
22. Caribou cousin
24. Derby or bowler
26. Señor Guevara
29. Wander
31. Streetcar
34. Andy Warhol genre
36. Fleet of warships
38. Literary Leon
39. ___-Soviet relations
41. Bedwear, briefly
42. Emulate Picabo Street
44. Opposite of SSE
45. "The Sopranos" network
47. Kind of school
49. Smooths wood
54. Aged
55. Straitlaced
57. Not imaginary
58. Misery
59. Waffle brand
60. Actress Irene of "Fame"
61. Sgt.'s superiors
62. Weaving machine
63. Internet address opener

DOWN

1. Light throw
2. Breakfast restaurant chain
3. Supreme Court count
4. Lotus position discipline
5. Speedometer meas.
6. Juneau's state
7. ___ slaw
8. Historical period
9. Nonsense
10. Male deer
11. Questions
19. Deborah of "The King and I"
23. Oodles
25. $20 bill dispenser
26. "Brain" of a PC
27. Opposite of vertical: abbr.
28. Sitcom segments
30. Educator Horace
32. Modifying word: abbr.
33. Postgrad. degs.
35. Invite

Puzzle 98

1	2	3	4	■	5	6	7	8	■	9	10	11
12				■	13				■	14		
15				■	16				■	17		
18				19	■	20			■	21		
■	■	■	■	22	23		■	24	25		■	■
26	27	28	■	29			30	■	31		32	33
34		35				■	36	37				
38				■	39	40			■	41		
■	■	42		43	■	44			■	■	■	■
45	46		■	47	48		■	49	50	51	52	53
54			■	55			56	■	57			
58			■	59				■	60			
61			■	62				■	63			

37. Columns' counterparts
40. Deep blue
43. Urge
45. Wolf's sound
46. Ink stain
48. Therefore
50. Part of a foot
51. Spick-and-span
52. Feathered missile
53. Open-handed blow
56. Pop's partner

Solution on Page 338

ACROSS

1. ___ one's time (wait)
5. It's right under your nose
8. Oil grp.
12. Line-___ veto
13. "___ had it!"
14. Dolt
15. Quickly, in memos
16. Soap ingredient
17. Oodles
18. Soundness of mind
20. Alex Haley saga
22. Eminem's genre
23. Absorb, with "up"
24. Weapons stash
28. Worshiper of Brahma
32. Pasture sound
33. Vice president Quayle
35. Tick off
36. Go by bike
39. Name on a slate
42. Driver's lic. and such
44. Vehicle
45. Ab strengthener
47. Cherished
51. Alternative to suspenders
52. Possess
54. ___ Scotia
55. "___ be a cold day in hell . . ."
56. Lightning attractor
57. "How much am ___?" (auction query)
58. First, second, or third, on a diamond
59. Fight stopper, briefly
60. Disney collectibles

DOWN

1. Leaning
2. "___ small world!"
3. Campus bigwig
4. "The ___ Strikes Back"
5. Frog's perch
6. ___ League
7. Equals
8. Eight-armed creatures
9. "The ___ thickens"
10. Ages and ages
11. PC inserts
19. Catch some rays
21. ___ and aah
24. Cable film channel
25. "The Illustrated Man" author Bradbury
26. Cul-de-___
27. Linked-computers acronym
29. "Henry & June" diarist
30. Dr. of gangsta rap
31. Hawaiian instrument, for short
34. "Ain't gonna happen"

Puzzle 99

37. Wee
38. End of a student's e-mail address
40. Insane
41. Humorously sarcastic
43. Athletic activity
45. ___ precedent
46. Troubles
48. Choir attire
49. Wicked
50. Fathers
51. Baby's dinner-wear
53. Chinese frying pan

Solution on Page 338

ACROSS

1. Bother
4. Reagan-era mil. program
7. Serb or Croat
11. Generous ___ fault
12. Animal hide
14. ___-deaf
15. Aardvark's morsel
16. Socially uncomfortable
18. Name of Tennessee's streetcar
20. Restroom, informally
21. Took a chair
22. Upper crusts
26. Paper clip alternative
29. Magician's hiding place
30. Hawaiian Punch alternative
31. Tennis do-over
32. Highway access
36. Drags one's feet
39. Kitchen gadget
40. Billy Joel's "Tell ___ about It"
41. Judge Lance ___
42. Printed mistakes
46. Volunteer State
50. Swift boat vets.' war
51. Words of understanding
52. Sups
53. Rapping Dr.
54. Teachers' favorites
55. Fed. property overseer
56. Bill Clinton's instrument

DOWN

1. Just slightly
2. Fully cooked
3. Cereal grains
4. Staircase shape
5. Wipe out electronically
6. Running a temperature, say
7. Musical Wonder
8. Mauna ___ (brand of macadamia nuts)
9. Part of Q&A
10. Flying geese formation
13. "The Canterbury ___"
17. Towering
19. AOL, e.g.: abbr.
23. Be a snitch
24. First name in stunts
25. Complete collections
26. Boutique
27. Prong
28. Land measure
33. Flared skirts
34. Apportion, with "out"
35. Nonpoetic writing
36. Some linens
37. Mother ___

Puzzle 100

38. Airport monitor abbr.
43. & & &
44. "Gone with the Wind" estate
45. Nasdaq alternative
46. Bit of advice
47. 180 degrees from WNW
48. Butterfly catcher
49. Give in to gravity

Solution on Page 338

ACROSS

1. Noun modifier: abbr.
4. Walk through water
8. Short hit, in baseball
12. Average grade
13. Breezy
14. Region
15. Owns
16. Apple or maple
17. Walk with a hitch
18. Main course
20. Rodeo ropes
22. California's Fort ___
23. Smart ___ whip
24. Tops
27. Cigarette's end
28. Concealed
31. Extremely exasperated
35. ___-mo
36. Corp. honcho
37. Flightless flock
38. Unknown John
39. On, as a lamp
41. Go to
44. Passes, as a law
48. Midday
49. Minstrel's instrument
51. "Wow!"
52. Heaps
53. Civil or elec. expert
54. President Lincoln
55. Eye sore
56. Chimney grime
57. Koppel or Kennedy

DOWN

1. Result of overexercise
2. University VIP
3. "Surely you ___!"
4. H2O
5. Broadcast
6. Rap's Dr. ___
7. Mascara site
8. Model airplane wood
9. "Exodus" author
10. Jules Verne captain
11. Bugler's evening call
19. Thorny flower
21. Arthur of tennis
24. Abbr. on a dumbbell
25. "___ Be Home for Christmas"
26. Simon & Garfunkel, once
27. From "___ Z" (completely): 2 wds.
28. Amateur radio-er
29. Hosp. area for acute conditions
30. ___ Plaines, Ill.
32. It's clicked on a computer
33. Christmas tree shedding
34. Greek cheese
38. Thick

Puzzle 101

1	2	3	■	4	5	6	7	■	8	9	10	11
12			■	13				■	14			
15			■	16				■	17			
18		19				■	20	21				
■	■	■	22			■	23			■	■	■
24	25	26		■	■	27			■	28	29	30
31				32	33				34			
35			■	36			■	■	37			
■	■	■	38			■	39	40		■	■	■
41	42	43				■	44			45	46	47
48				■	49	50			■	51		
52				■	53				■	54		
55				■	56				■	57		

39. Release
40. Motionless
41. Aardvark's diet
42. Tugboat sound
43. Broadway award
45. Jacket
46. Fit ___ tied
47. Cast off
50. One, to Juan

Solution on Page 339

ACROSS

1. Basketball's Larry
5. Unruly crowds
9. Strike lightly
12. Chills and fever
13. Pesky flier
14. Favorable vote
15. Specks
16. Flat-topped hill
17. Get-up-and-go
18. Moral precept
20. Gaggle members
22. Out of bed
26. Tue. preceder
29. Pub measure
30. Study hard at the last minute
34. Bumpkin
36. Batman and Robin, e.g.
37. Jiffy ___
38. Command to Fido
39. "SportsCenter" channel
41. "I ___ your pardon"
42. Most uncommon
44. Modern surgical tool
47. Emcees
52. Easy letters?
53. Current choice
57. "Hold it right there!"
58. Ghostly greeting
59. Wild hog
60. Cheryl of "Charlie's Angels"
61. Boozehound
62. Electronics giant
63. "If the ___ fits . . ."

DOWN

1. Wished
2. Gershwin's "___ Rhythm"
3. Babe with a bat
4. Arnaz of "I Love Lucy"
5. "Ben-Hur" studio
6. "We're number ___!"
7. Undergrad. degs.
8. Thespian's platform
9. VCR insert
10. Affirmative votes
11. ___ Le Pew
19. Toy gun noisemaker
21. Abbr. on a business letter
23. Bill attachment
24. Occupied
25. Halts
26. "___ Miniver"
27. ___ of bounds
28. 76ers' org.
31. Cause friction
32. Penny prez
33. Ryan or Tilly
35. "Jane ___"
40. To the ___ degree

Puzzle 102

43. Saudis, e.g.
44. Places for experiments
45. "Peek-___"
46. Edinburgh native
48. Barn birds
49. Former Iranian ruler
50. Heading on a list of errands
51. Marquis de ___
54. Amorous murmur
55. Newsman Rather
56. Have a bawl

Solution on Page 339

ACROSS

1. Marcel Marceau, e.g.
5. Health club
8. Utah ski resort
12. "We try harder" company
13. "___ Howdy Doody time!"
14. Wart causer, in legend
15. Egg holder
16. Univ. dorm supervisors
17. Business phone button
18. Break out
20. Makes amends
22. Beachgoer's shade
23. Doctrine: suffix
24. White sale items
27. Looked lecherously
31. ___ forma
32. From Jan. 1 to now
33. One thing after another
37. Choose
40. Actor Torn
41. U-turn from WSW
42. Like seawater
45. Beethoven's "Moonlight ___"
49. Freudian topics
50. Antipollution org.
52. Feed, as pigs
53. After-bath-wear
54. Grand Coulee, e.g.
55. Mozart's "___ kleine Nachtmusik"
56. Matures
57. "Murder, ___ Wrote"
58. River of Hades

DOWN

1. Lion's locks
2. Currier's partner
3. Catchall abbr.
4. Subject of a will
5. Warning devices
6. School org.
7. Attack
8. Where telecommuters work
9. "Crazy" bird
10. A fisherman may spin one
11. Opposite of subtracts
19. Pie holder
21. Mao ___-tung
24. CD forerunners
25. Anger
26. ". . . see hide ___ hair of"
28. "The Catcher in the ___"
29. And so forth: abbr.
30. Banned pesticide
34. Van Gogh subjects
35. "Ich Bin ___ Berliner": JFK
36. Goes over the limit
37. Flavorful seed

Puzzle 103

38. Rock producer Brian
39. Telescope parts
42. Blood fluids
43. Eager
44. Earring site
46. Landed (on)
47. Theater award
48. Peak
51. Oom-___

Solution on Page 339

ACROSS

1. Farrow of "Broadway Danny Rose"
4. School grps.
8. Jenny "The Swedish Nightingale"
12. S&L offerings
13. "I get it," humorously
14. Data
15. Dog command
16. Misprint
17. Soothing ointment
18. Mongolian desert
20. "Car Talk" network
22. Klutz's cry
25. Home planet
29. Norway's capital
32. Cellist Ma
34. "___ and Me Against the World"
35. Cold War symbol
38. 007 creator Fleming
39. Jump
40. Time ___ half
41. Gorge
43. Stink to high heaven
45. Thumbs-up response
47. Sleeveless garment
50. "___ a Teenage Werewolf"
53. Film part
56. Lobbying grp.
58. Nonverbal OKs
59. Plow pullers
60. Luau instrument, informally
61. Prying
62. Camp beds
63. Tierra ___ Fuego

DOWN

1. Roast hosts, briefly
2. "Cool, man!"
3. Concerning
4. Place for a barbecue
5. Iron Maiden's "Hallowed Be ___ Name"
6. Egyptian cobra
7. "Coming ___ to a theater near you"
8. The Scales, astrologically
9. "___ pig's eye!"
10. Steelers' org.
11. Joe DiMaggio's brother
19. ___ tube (television set)
21. Lowly worker
23. Combustible heap
24. Renewable energy type
26. Tatum's dad
27. "I ___ you so!"
28. Luau dance
29. Of the ear
30. Ayatollah's predecessor
31. Chanteuse Horne
33. "Holy cow!"
36. "St. ___'s Fire"

Puzzle 104

37. Rouse from slumber
42. Fresh-mouthed
44. ___ the score (gets revenge)
46. McDonald's founder Ray
48. Potato, informally
49. ___ five (rest)
50. Holiday ___
51. Try to win the hand of
52. Internet pop-ups, e.g.
54. Tic-tac-toe line
55. Permit
57. "Fantasia" frame

Solution on Page 339

ACROSS

1. Bout enders, briefly
4. Put ___ words
8. "Star Wars" sage
12. Scratch (out)
13. Glowing gas
14. Help in crime
15. Potato chip accompaniment
16. Wood-cutting tools
17. Court plea, for short
18. Hunting dog
20. Coil of yarn
21. On the line
24. Track events
27. Familiarizes with new surroundings
31. Raven's call
32. Crumb carrier
33. ___ City Rollers
34. Church topper
37. Prepare for a bout
39. Under debate
41. Practices in the ring
44. Scents
48. Actor Sean
49. Baseball glove
51. Appropriate
52. Suffix with major
53. Diabolical
54. "The Crying Game" star Stephen
55. Garden invader
56. Newcastle-upon-___, England
57. Tax ID

DOWN

1. Popular sneakers
2. Merle Haggard's "___ from Muskogee"
3. Aug. follower
4. Maps within maps
5. Approaches
6. AAA offering
7. Add-___ (extras)
8. Union member
9. Slender woodwind
10. Sandwich shop
11. Lots and lots
19. Make lace
20. Hit the slopes
22. Musical sounds
23. Gallery display
24. Show hosts, for short
25. ___ one's words
26. Ram's mate
28. Hoops grp.
29. ___ chi (martial art)
30. Prefix for thesis
32. Actress MacGraw
35. Brought in, as a salary
36. Mtge. units

Puzzle 105

1	2	3	■	4	5	6	7	■	8	9	10	11
12			■	13				■	14			
15			■	16				■	17			
18			19			■	■	20				
■	■	■	21			22	23			■	■	■
24	25	26			■	27				28	29	30
31			■	■	32			■	■	33		
34			35	36			■	37	38			
■	■	■	39				40			■	■	■
41	42	43			■	■	44			45	46	47
48				■	49	50			■	51		
52				■	53				■	54		
55				■	56				■	57		

37. Aquarium reptile
38. ___ Speed Wagon (old vehicle)
40. Glossy fabric
41. Erupt
42. Singer Seeger
43. Poker stake
45. Red planet
46. King Kong's kin
47. Ollie's partner
49. Bumped into
50. Campus climber

Solution on Page 340

ACROSS

1. Fish-and-chips fish
4. PTA meeting place
7. Prod
11. ___-inspiring
12. Colored part of the eye
14. Christmas carol
15. Lessen
17. Nobleman
18. Poultry product
19. TV's "___ and Greg"
21. "Mack the ___"
24. New Mexico art community
25. "In 25 words or ___ . . ."
26. Unsophisticated
29. Singer Tillis
30. Kennel club classification
31. "Black gold"
33. Removes
35. Fizzling-out sound
36. Mayberry's town drunk
37. Does an usher's job
38. Down's opposite
41. Zig's partner
42. "Little piggies"
43. Sudden and precipitous downturn
48. Beach washer
49. Takes a chair
50. "Give ___ rest!"
51. Shortly
52. Actress Farrow
53. At this moment

DOWN

1. Contemptible fellow
2. Be in the red
3. Last mo.
4. Prolonged attack
5. Rugged rock
6. ___ and hers
7. Nervousness
8. Lion's sound
9. Microbe
10. Singer Fitzgerald
13. Tranquilizes
16. Football officials
20. Grasp
21. Carrier to Amsterdam
22. "All You ___ Is Love"
23. ___ of Wight
24. Shade providers
26. Manet and Monet
27. Davenport
28. Separate, as flour or ashes
30. "All ___ are off!"
32. Mil. officers
34. Give some slack
35. Cribbage markers
37. Chip dip
38. "___ girl!"

Puzzle 106

1	2	3	■	4	5	6	■	■	7	8	9	10
11			■	12			13	■	14			
15			16					■	17			
■	■	■	18			■	19	20				
21	22	23			■	24				■	■	■
25				■	26					27	28	■
29			■	30					■	31		32
■	33		34					■	35			
■	■	■	36				■	37				
38	39	40				■	41			■	■	■
42				■	43	44				45	46	47
48				■	49				■	50		
51				■	■	52			■	53		

39. Nickel or dime
40. Make over
41. Tubular pasta
44. Align the crosshairs
45. Diaper holder
46. "What was ___ think?"
47. No, slangily

Solution on Page 340

ACROSS

1. U-turn from SSE
4. Official with a whistle
7. Like Lindbergh's flight
11. Swelling reducer
12. Tanguay and Gabor
14. "Fargo" director Joel
15. Pro slugger's workplace
17. "This can't be!"
18. Place with swinging doors
19. "___ don't say!"
21. Naval letters
22. Cowboy's rope
26. Bert's buddy
29. Brit. flyboys
30. Common Father's Day gift
31. "Let's Get It On" singer
32. Indent key
33. Beach bird
34. Coin-___ (candy machines, e.g.)
35. Neb. neighbor
36. Multiplied by
37. Director Spielberg
39. MSN rival
40. Mich. neighbor
41. Golf shoe features
45. Actions on heartstrings and pant legs
48. Heavenly
50. Dick and Jane's dog
51. Frame of mind
52. TV maker
53. Falafel bread
54. Call to a calf
55. Electrical unit

DOWN

1. Pen points
2. Final Four org.
3. Place to make a wish
4. Tranquillity
5. Roy's wife Dale
6. Distant
7. Search high and low
8. Fireworks reaction
9. Football Hall-of-Famer Dawson
10. Lennon's lady
13. Bygone space station
16. Nephew of Donald Duck
20. Clodhopper
23. Big-ticket ___
24. Suffix with billion
25. Change for a twenty
26. They give people big heads
27. Engrossed
28. Nasdaq rival
29. Operated
32. Bicycle for two
33. Bathroom floor installer
35. Barbie's beau

Puzzle 107

1	2	3	■	4	5	6	■	■	7	8	9	10
11			■	12			13	■	14			
15			16					■	17			
18						■	19	20		■	■	■
■	■	■	21			■	22			23	24	25
26	27	28			■	29			■	30		
31				■	32			■	33			
34			■	35			■	36				
37			38			■	39			■	■	■
■	■	■	40			■	41			42	43	44
45	46	47		■	48	49						
50				■	51				■	52		
53				■	■	54			■	55		

36. "Holy" Ohio town
38. "Hasta la ___, baby!"
39. Sound heard before "Gesundheit!"
42. Prefix with nautical
43. R.p.m. indicator
44. Grand ___
45. Cooking meas.
46. Reuters competitor
47. "___ Milk?"
49. ___ Sawyer

Solution on Page 340

ACROSS

1. Basinger of "Batman"
4. Very center
8. Prefix with god
12. ___ cream
13. Tied
14. "X" or "Y," on a graph
15. Flop
16. China's ___ Xiaoping
17. Actress Garr
18. Ex-Mrs. Trump
20. Assail
21. Lend ___ (listen)
23. Wharton degs.
25. ___ Strauss & Co.
26. Israel's Golda
27. ___ Lilly and Company
30. Crude shelter
32. Alternative to digital
34. Mo. metropolis
35. Steals from
37. Medal recipient
38. Queue
39. Soapbox derby entrant
40. Lady's title
43. Seize (from)
45. Get one's ducks in ___
46. Hawaii's "Valley Isle"
47. Floor covering
50. "The Magic Mountain" author
51. Cheshire cat feature
52. The Monkees' "___ Believer"
53. Beame and Burrows
54. The "M" in YMCA
55. Part of a baseball uniform

DOWN

1. "The Karate ___" (1984)
2. Hosp. area for emergency cases
3. Like feudal times
4. Closet wood
5. Kiln
6. Change the title of
7. Where London is: abbr.
8. Goes out with
9. Former spouses
10. Swampy ground
11. "___ something I said?"
19. "You're So ___" (Carly Simon hit)
20. Hayloft's location
21. "___ Well That Ends Well"
22. Hair removal brand
24. Slant
26. '60s NASA target
27. Running off current
28. Oral history
29. Dr. Frankenstein's assistant
31. Quick haircut
33. Discoverers' cries
36. "___ the Ides of March"

Puzzle 108

1	2	3	■	4	5	6	7	■	8	9	10	11
12			■	13				■	14			
15			■	16				■	17			
■	■	18	19				■	20				
21	22				■	23	24			■	■	■
25				■	26				■	27	28	29
30				31		■	32		33			
34			■	35		36		■	37			
■	■	■	38				■	39				
40	41	42			■	43	44				■	■
45				■	46				■	47	48	49
50				■	51				■	52		
53				■	54				■	55		

38. Suburban expanses
39. Jockey's handful
40. Nursery cry
41. Riyadh resident
42. Finished
44. Damage beyond repair
46. "The Wizard of Oz" studio
48. Thurman of "Pulp Fiction"
49. Generation ___

Solution on Page 340

ACROSS

1. iPhone download
4. Box lightly
8. "I ___, I saw, I conquered"
12. ___ chi
13. Brazilian soccer great
14. Burn soother
15. Explosive letters
16. Kind of sax
17. Laze about
18. State with conviction
20. Apportions, with "out"
21. Tenant
24. Swift
27. Auction grouping
28. "Norma ___"
31. "___ My Party"
32. Homo sapiens
33. Novelist Clancy
34. Welcome ___
35. Long. crosser
36. Refine, as metal
38. Nap in Oaxaca
40. Dieter's lunch
44. Goodies
48. Vigoda and Lincoln
49. Make yawn
51. Go one better
52. Some male dolls
53. "Beware the ___ of March"
54. La-la intro
55. ___ Lee of Marvel Comics
56. Cough syrup amts.
57. Dissenting vote

DOWN

1. "___ boy!"
2. Partner of pots
3. Peach centers
4. Dealt leniently with
5. Animal hides
6. Ctrl-___-Delete
7. Bygone car
8. Auto racer Yarborough
9. Plenty
10. Beauty mark
11. Snaky swimmers
19. Quarterback Manning
20. Encountered
22. List of candidates
23. Long, long time
24. Canyon edge
25. One step ___ time
26. Attention getter
28. Letter carrier's assignment: abbr.
29. Popular ISP
30. CPR pro
32. ___ tai (cocktail)
35. It was dropped in the '60s
36. Emphasize

Puzzle 109

37. Ginnie ___ (mortgage agency)
39. Throat ailment
40. ___ Fifth Avenue
41. Aid and ___
42. Horne or Olin
43. Professional grp.
45. Abbr. on an envelope
46. ___ Bora (Afghan region)
47. Fix, as a cat
49. Bridle part
50. Takes too much, for short

Solution on Page 341

ACROSS

1. XXX x X
4. "___ fair in love and war"
8. Write on metal
12. Bit of sunshine
13. High-protein beans
14. Richard of "Chicago"
15. Unrestrained
17. Coral formation
18. Midpoints
19. Shea team
20. Suffix with ethyl
21. Notice
23. Think-tank products
26. Auction offer
27. Classic auto
28. Go under
29. Capp and Capone
30. Clark of the "Daily Planet"
31. A-Team muscleman
32. Macadamia, for one
33. "If I ___ do it all over again . . ."
34. Brawny
36. Small bit, as of cream
37. Peel
38. Roll-on alternative
42. Cornmeal bread
43. Geometric curve
44. Designer Chanel
45. The Beatles' "___ a Woman"
46. Jar part
47. ___ chic
48. Sounds of disapproval
49. Come-___ (inducements)

DOWN

1. Gator's cousin
2. Chaplin prop
3. Shade of blue
4. Quaking trees
5. Peter of "Casablanca"
6. Soapmaking substances
7. U-turn from NNW
8. Wading bird
9. Balanced on the brink
10. Moon shape
11. Playboy founder, familiarly
16. Porterhouse, e.g.
19. Pre___ student
21. Bad-mouth
22. "The Wizard of Oz" dog
23. Distinctive doctrines
24. Poverty-stricken
25. The way in
26. PBJ alternative
29. Mo. before Labor Day
30. Shish ___
32. SSW's opposite
33. Give a hard time
35. Black-and-white cookies

Puzzle 110

1	2	3	■	4	5	6	7	■	8	9	10	11
12			■	13				■	14			
15			16					■	17			
18							■	19				■
■	■	■	20			■	21					22
23	24	25			■	26			■	27		
28				■	29			■	30			
31			■	32			■	33				
34			35			■	36			■	■	■
■	37				■	38				39	40	41
42				■	43							
44				■	45				■	46		
47				■	48				■	49		

36. Bo of "10"
38. Sounds of relief
39. Fly alone
40. Actress Lena
41. Young fellows
42. Meas. of interest
43. "Hey you!"

Solution on Page 341

ACROSS

1. "The Joy Luck Club" writer Tan
4. "Return of the Jedi" creature
8. Smooth-talking
12. Butt
13. Princess who battles the Death Star
14. Kennedy matriarch
15. Broadcast regulatory org.
16. Depression
17. PDA entry
18. Disgrace
20. Lock openers
22. Use a crowbar
24. Milky gems
28. Winnie-the-___
31. Reply to "Are you hurt?"
34. Fan setting
35. Bar code
36. Part of a bicycle wheel
37. Airport overseer: abbr.
38. ___ Shop Boys
39. Sampras of tennis
40. Have a yen for
41. Listerine alternative
43. Play-___ (kids' clay)
45. Possesses
48. Church doctrine
52. Six-sided solid
55. Brand for Fido
57. "Chocolate" dog
58. Sheepish sounds
59. Twosome
60. Olive ___ (Popeye's sweetie)
61. Move to and fro
62. Spy Aldrich
63. San Francisco/Oakland separator

DOWN

1. Barks
2. Sound-speed number
3. 1978 Village People hit
4. Church officer
5. Tiny
6. Sty sound
7. "Kiss Me, ___"
8. Understand
9. Chop off
10. AOL, for one
11. "Wanna ___?"
19. Dashboard abbr.
21. Oxen's harness
23. "Egad!"
25. ___ Romeo (Italian car)
26. Bank transaction
27. Whack
28. Litter members
29. Oil cartel acronym
30. Twice tetra-
32. Bon ___ (clever remark)
33. Gave a thumbs-up
36. Eject, as lava

Puzzle 111

1	2	3	■	4	5	6	7	■	8	9	10	11
12			■	13				■	14			
15			■	16				■	17			
18			19	■	20		21		■	■	■	■
■	■	■	22		23	■	■	24		25	26	27
28	29	30		■	31	32	33		■	34		
35			■	36					■	37		
38			■	39				■	40			
41			42		■	■	43	44		■	■	■
■	■	■	45		46	47	■	48		49	50	51
52	53	54		■	55		56		■	57		
58				■	59				■	60		
61				■	62				■	63		

40. "___ goes there?"
42. Flowery verse
44. Aromas
46. California wine valley
47. Close with a bang
49. Dollop
50. Author Angelou
51. With skill
52. Rather's network
53. Motor City gp.
54. Sheep's sound
56. ___ in the sky

Solution on Page 341

ACROSS

1. Family docs
4. "Take This ___ and Shove It"
7. Music with jazz-like riffs
10. Hoof sound
11. "Have you ___ wool?"
12. Palo ___, Calif.
14. Unadulterated
15. "The Simpsons" bartender
16. Nautilus captain
17. Input data again
19. Precipitous
20. Show showers
21. Where the buoys are
22. Comic book punch sound
25. "Turn, soldier!"
30. "It's a Sin to Tell ___"
32. www.aspca.___
33. Historic times
34. Pay attention
37. Network with an eye logo
38. Do sums
39. Scarlet
41. Human trunk
44. Confronts boldly
48. Persia, today
49. Educ. group
50. "Here comes trouble!"
51. Reebok rival
52. One for the Germans
53. It's a long story
54. Neighbor of Aus.
55. Verizon forerunner
56. A conceited person has a big one

DOWN

1. Sticky stuff
2. Skin opening
3. Paid out
4. Ian Fleming creation
5. ___ about (roughly)
6. "Later!"
7. Capital of New Mexico
8. Swiss artist Paul
9. "Look ___ (I'm in Love)"
10. EMT's skill
13. Alley-___ (basketball maneuver)
18. New Deal org.
19. "Quiet on the ___!"
21. Big crop in Hawaii
22. Buddy
23. Bullring shout
24. ". . . ___ one for the Gipper"
26. Metal to be refined
27. ___ de Triomphe
28. Taxi
29. Letter before tee
31. Lou Grant portrayer
35. Brouhaha
36. VCR button

Puzzle 112

■	1	2	3	■	4	5	6	■	7	8	9	■
10				■	11			■	12			13
14				■	15			■	16			
17				18			■	19				
■	■	■	20			■	21			■	■	■
22	23	24	■	25		26				27	28	29
30			31	■	32			■	33			
34				35				36	■	37		
■	■	■	38			■	39		40	■	■	■
41	42	43			■	44				45	46	47
48				■	49			■	50			
51				■	52			■	53			
■	54			■	55			■	56			■

40. Extinguish
41. ___ Pan Alley
42. Not a dup.
43. Gather leaves
44. Going ___ (bickering)
45. Uneven hairdo
46. Like takeout orders
47. Al Green's "___-La-La"
49. Wooden pin

Solution on Page 341

ACROSS

1. "I ___ You Babe"
4. Drink with sushi
8. Date with a Dr.
12. "King Kong" studio
13. Online auction house
14. Word with hay or live
15. Estrange
17. Scored 100% on
18. The blahs
19. 401(k) alternatives
20. Low digit?
21. Followed orders
23. Eyelid cosmetic
26. Jamaican liquor
27. Numero ___
28. Like ___ of bricks
29. King in a Steve Martin song
30. Not pro
31. Taxpayer's ID
32. Big wine holder
33. Top of a wave
34. Talked back to
36. Links peg
37. Mosquito repellent ingredient
38. Blankety-blank type
42. State south of Ky.
43. Stretchables
44. Lip
45. Model
46. "I don't think so"
47. Swiss painter Paul
48. Rental units: abbr.
49. "Are you a man ___ mouse?"

DOWN

1. Metric weight
2. Neighbor of Ark.
3. Slave away
4. 12th grader
5. Humiliate
6. Shakespearean shrew
7. Needle hole
8. Cognizant
9. Petty
10. Gifts
11. Rocker Nugent
16. Consumed
19. Apple alternative
21. Gone for the day
22. ___-yourself kit
23. Young woman
24. Words with a handshake
25. Hogwash
26. Wagon track
29. Tiny bit
30. "___ You Glad You're You?"
32. Dog doc
33. Puts an end to
35. Have a feeling

Puzzle 113

1	2	3	■	4	5	6	7	■	8	9	10	11
12			■	13				■	14			
15			16					■	17			
18							■	19				■
■	■	■	20			■	21					22
23	24	25			■	26			■	27		
28				■	29			■	30			
31			■	32			■	33				
34			35			■	36			■	■	■
■	37				■	38				39	40	41
42				■	43							
44				■	45				■	46		
47				■	48				■	49		

36. Raise a glass to
38. Sow chow
39. Flintstones pet
40. Surgery souvenir
41. Worker protection org.
42. "Naughty, naughty!"
43. Clean air org.

Solution on Page 342

ACROSS

1. Major prank
5. Word with pitch or mo
8. "Things aren't as bad as they ___"
12. Actress Bancroft
13. Murphy's ___
14. Wheel shaft
15. View from a beach house
17. ___-edged (highest quality)
18. "To Each ___ Own"
19. Aircraft-carrier letters
20. Fee schedule
21. Globes
23. Bushy 'do
26. "___ we now our gay apparel"
27. Solemn promise
30. Fit for farming
33. Present to Goodwill, e.g.
35. Short flight
36. Approves
38. "___ upon a time . . ."
39. In-flight attendant
42. Sail supports
45. ___-friendly (green)
46. Pen name
49. Home to Honolulu
50. Follow
52. Much-kicked body part
53. Go out with
54. Lots
55. Recipe measures: abbr.
56. Ques. response
57. Athletic supporters?

DOWN

1. Corned beef concoction
2. "That's ___ haven't heard"
3. Santa ___ (hot winds)
4. Deletes, with "out"
5. Cut, as prices
6. Was not renewed
7. Have debts
8. Long stories
9. Way out
10. Model Macpherson
11. New York nine
16. Drinking vessel
20. Nevada city
21. Weep loudly
22. Reel's partner
23. Ooh and ___
24. Not to
25. Grammy category
27. Delivery vehicle
28. AMEX alternative
29. Minuscule
31. Plenty
32. ___ out (supplement)
34. Silent acknowledgment
37. Bjorn Borg's homeland

Puzzle 114

39. Astonishes
40. Partner of pains
41. ___ v. Wade
42. Lion's share
43. Satisfied sounds
44. Use FedEx, say
46. ___ carotene
47. Have ___ good authority
48. Hoodwinks
50. Drunk ___ skunk
51. U.K. military fliers

Solution on Page 342

ACROSS

1. Compassionate letters
4. Fire residue
7. Bali ___
10. Stadium cheer
11. Swimmer's woe
13. Some IHOP drinks
14. Turkey part
16. 5th month in France
17. Broke some ground
18. Open-eyed
20. Wyoming range
23. Apparel for a young diner
24. Twisted
25. Long-eared hound
28. Corp. bigwig
29. Piece of dinnerware
31. Tycoon Onassis
33. Gawks
35. Chicago paper, briefly
36. Blend
37. Downhill ski race
39. Deputized group
42. Disfigure
43. "Evil Woman" rock grp.
44. Loser at the dice table
49. Tiger Woods' org.
50. Pooped out
51. Wapiti
52. A barber has to work around it
53. Compaq products
54. Tire-pressure letters

DOWN

1. La-la leader
2. ___ Cruces, NM
3. Ho ___ Minh City
4. Zodiacal Ram
5. Hourglass fill
6. Medical care grp.
7. Catcher's base
8. Not quite closed
9. "What time ___?"
11. "Let's get crackin'!"
12. Kudos
15. Cry to a matey
19. Scale amts.
20. Tic-___-toe
21. She sheep
22. Fox or turkey follower
23. Cave dweller
25. ___-relief sculpture
26. ___ of Sandwich
27. Duet plus one
29. Catholic clergyman
30. "Superman" arch-villain Luthor
32. "Think" sloganeer
34. Pro-___ (some tourneys)
35. Housebroken
37. "Land ___!"

Puzzle 115

1	2	3	■	■	4	5	6	■	■	7	8	9
10			■	11				12	■	13		
14			15						■	16		
■	■	■	17				■	18	19			
20	21	22				■	23			■	■	■
24				■	■	25				26	27	■
28			■	29	30				■	31		32
■	33		34				■	■	35			
■	■	■	36			■	37	38				
39	40	41			■	42				■	■	■
43			■	44	45					46	47	48
49			■	50					■	51		
52			■	■	53			■	■	54		

38. Told a whopper
39. Cartoon skunk Le Pew
40. Korbut of the 1972 Olympics
41. Fly into the wild blue yonder
42. Cleopatra's love ___ Antony
45. ___ and tuck
46. Slangy affirmative
47. Raised railways
48. Go downhill fast?

Solution on Page 342

ACROSS

1. Nicholas I or II
5. Split ___ soup
8. Quarrel
12. Ready for picking
13. Surgery spots, for short
14. Well-___ (prosperous)
15. Partner of crafts
16. ___ Tafari (Haile Selassie)
17. Oodles
18. "Hey, you!"
19. Opposite of WNW
20. Flag-maker Betsy
21. Agrees
24. Philosopher who wrote the "Republic"
27. Depot: abbr.
28. Cry of discovery
31. Copier need
32. Indiana basketballer
34. Mattress problem
35. Wriggly fish
38. Cosmetician Lauder
39. Unpaid debt
41. "September ___" (Neil Diamond hit)
44. Civil War soldier
45. "___ boy!"
49. Parched
50. Heavenly body
51. Fly high
52. Western writer Grey
53. Actress ___ Dawn Chong
54. Roman wrap
55. Lodge members
56. Hog haven
57. Thick slice

DOWN

1. Snare
2. Knights' titles
3. Places for rent: abbr.
4. Say another way
5. Skin openings
6. Cleans the blackboard
7. Concurrence
8. Constellation components
9. Sport on horseback
10. Bustles
11. Little tykes
22. More tender
23. Become narrower
24. TDs are worth six
25. Mauna ___ (Hawaiian volcano)
26. "The Ice Storm" director ___ Lee
28. Do something
29. Part of a giggle
30. "You ___ here"
33. Lends a hand
36. Goofs

Puzzle 116

1	2	3	4	■	5	6	7	■	8	9	10	11
12				■	13			■	14			
15				■	16			■	17			
18				■	19			■	20			
■	■	■	21	22				23		■	■	■
24	25	26			■	27			■	28	29	30
31					■	■	■	32	33			
34			■	35	36	37	■	38				
■	■	■	39				40			■	■	■
41	42	43		■	44			■	45	46	47	48
49				■	50			■	51			
52				■	53			■	54			
55				■	56			■	57			

37. Regard with lust
39. Peruvian peaks
40. Westminster ___
41. Lab rat's challenge
42. Not written
43. Ice hockey venue
46. Hammer or saw
47. Epic tale
48. United ___ Emirates

Solution on Page 342

ACROSS

1. Lo-___: lite
4. Golfing standard
7. Actress Jessica
12. "___ the only one?"
13. Mail Boxes ___
14. Perfect
15. Swab
16. Never-ending
18. "I've got it!"
20. Letter after chi
21. Baseball's Hershiser
22. 6, on a phone dial
24. Roseanne, once
28. Alias, for short
30. Sun or moon
32. Alehouse
33. Prime-rate setter, with "the"
35. The Little Mermaid
37. Shar-___ (wrinkly dog)
38. Chopper
39. Old what's-___-name
40. Burnt ___ crisp
42. Roman tyrant
44. Rep.'s opponent
46. Stew
49. Wednesday's child is full of it
51. Canada's capital
53. "Y"-shaped weapon
57. Nervous twitch
58. Tough question
59. "Telephone Line" rock grp.
60. Single: prefix
61. Distress signal
62. Forty winks
63. Cpl.'s superior

DOWN

1. Small part played by a big name
2. Stevie Wonder's "My Cherie ___"
3. One who can see what you're saying
4. Legendary actor Gregory
5. Mr. T's group
6. "His Master's Voice" co.
7. Falsehoods
8. Improvise
9. Maiden name preceder
10. Stove option
11. Ernie on the links
17. Germ cell
19. BPOE member
23. Cacophony
25. Equipment
26. ___ the day
27. Slugger's stat
29. "How nice!"
31. Diner sandwich
33. Devotee
34. Devon river

Puzzle 117

1	2	3	■	4	5	6	■	7	8	9	10	11
12			■	13			■	14				
15			■	16			17					
18			19			■	20			■	■	■
21				■	22	23		■	24	25	26	27
■	■	28		29	■	30		31	■	32		
33	34		■	35	36				■	37		
38			■	39			■	40	41		■	■
42			43	■	44		45	■	46		47	48
■	■	■	49	50		■	51	52				
53	54	55				56			■	57		
58					■	59			■	60		
61					■	62			■	63		

36. Disney World attractions
41. Frequently
43. Title holder
45. Dinero
47. "Dallas" family name
48. Unspoken
50. Shrek, for one

52. 'Vette roof option
53. Tanning lotion abbr.
54. Cyber-guffaw
55. "Love ___ Battlefield"
56. Barnyard clucker

Solution on Page 343

ACROSS

1. Lampblack
5. OR personnel
8. ___ good example
12. Vases
13. Suffix with cloth or cash
14. Baldwin of "30 Rock"
15. Watergate's ___ Throat
16. Bell and Barker
17. Aspiring atty.'s exam
18. Tippler
19. Wall St. watchdog
20. What roots connect to
21. "It must be him, ___ shall die . . ." (Vikki Carr line)
23. Hamilton bills
25. Not silently
27. "A Boy Named ___"
28. Decline
31. 14-line poem
33. Moses parted it
35. Clamor
36. "Alias" org.
38. Label anew
39. Wheelchair access
40. Inventor Whitney
41. Cavalry sword
44. Cushion
46. "And here's to you, ___ Robinson . . ."
49. Old flames
50. Teacher's favorite
51. Word repeated before "Don't tell me!"
52. Roger Bannister's distance
53. Tabby
54. Jazz singer James
55. ___ of Capri
56. "You'll never know unless you ___"
57. Keg contents

DOWN

1. Lather
2. Creme-filled cookie
3. Life-size replica's ratio
4. Cough medicine amt.
5. Thin coin
6. Responds
7. AARP members
8. Smelling ___
9. Otherwise
10. Sports squad
11. Book after John
19. Motorcycle attachment
20. Smiled scornfully
22. Seek office
24. Where Switz. is
25. Volcanic fallout
26. Singer Rawls or Reed
28. Pre-repair job figure
29. "Who Wants to ___ Millionaire?"
30. Sack
32. QB Tebow

Puzzle 118

1	2	3	4	■	5	6	7	■	8	9	10	11
12				■	13			■	14			
15				■	16			■	17			
18			■	19			■	20				
■	■	21	22		■	23	24			■	■	■
25	26				■	27			■	28	29	30
31					32	■	33		34			
35			■	36		37	■	38				
■	■	■	39				■	40			■	■
41	42	43			■	44	45		■	46	47	48
49				■	50			■	51			
52				■	53			■	54			
55				■	56			■	57			

34. Dover's state: abbr.
37. Come into view
39. View again
41. Half: prefix
42. Line of rotation
43. Ringer
45. Bar member: abbr.
47. Baptism, for one
48. Symbol on the Hollywood Walk of Fame
50. Mtge. point, for example
51. Spider's creation

Solution on Page 343

ACROSS

1. Singer Guthrie
5. "Thar ___ blows!"
8. Energetic
12. Clubs or hearts
13. Coal delivery unit
14. Poke
15. "This ___ laughing matter!"
16. Blushing
17. Minimum points
18. Felt hat
20. Midterms and finals
22. Chaney of horror films
23. The ___ Moines Register
24. Makes it to class
28. Bookcase part
32. "___ do you do?"
33. Uncle ___
35. One of the Three Stooges
36. Bunch of bees
39. Eating alcove
42. Tally (up)
44. Piece of turf
45. Grace under pressure
47. Fit for consumption
51. Containers
52. ___ for the course
54. Head's opposite
55. ___ as a button
56. ___ and vinegar
57. Kind of sch.
58. Blockhead
59. Give it a whirl
60. Cub Scout groups

DOWN

1. "Like, no way!"
2. Trick
3. Swedish soprano Jenny
4. "Lawrence of Arabia" star
5. Locks of hair
6. Gardener's tool
7. Finished
8. Swimming pool sound
9. High-school dance
10. Spreadsheet lines
11. Units of three feet: abbr.
19. Wood of the Rolling Stones
21. ___ out (deletes)
24. Sighs of contentment
25. Wrecker's job
26. Former Pan Am rival
27. Unhappy
29. Ambulance worker, for short
30. Real estate unit
31. Doctor's charge
34. Scrooge-like
37. Reared
38. Physicians, for short
40. "Yes" gesture

Puzzle 119

1	2	3	4	■	5	6	7	■	8	9	10	11
12				■	13			■	14			
15				■	16			■	17			
18				19		■	20	21				■
■	■	■	22			■	23			■	■	■
24	25	26				27	■	28		29	30	31
32			■	■	33		34	■	■	35		
36			37	38	■	39		40	41			
■	■	■	42		43	■	44			■	■	■
■	45	46				■	47			48	49	50
51				■	52	53		■	54			
55				■	56			■	57			
58				■	59			■	60			

41. Checked copy
43. Train stop
45. Legendary Bunyan
46. Aware of
48. Cotton unit
49. Claim on property
50. Stately trees
51. New Deal agcy.
53. Televise

Solution on Page 343

ACROSS

1. Playtex products
5. Yes, in Yokohama
8. Goatee site
12. Eyelid attachment
13. Surgery sites, for short
14. Arizona Indian
15. Diva's song
16. Five-sided figure
18. Flashlight's projection
19. Oct. follower
20. Reverse, as an action
23. Beaded calculators
28. Not quite oneself
31. Wheel tracks
33. "___ hardly wait!"
34. Former PLO leader
36. On-the-job learner
38. Winslet of "Titanic"
39. Knitter's ball
41. Thoroughfares: abbr.
42. One-pot dinners
44. Stitched
46. "Gonna ___ with a little help from my friends"
48. Kindergarten learning
52. Everything considered
57. 50% off event
58. Campus military org.
59. Stage signal
60. Comet competitor
61. Money on hand
62. CPR giver
63. ___ Gaga

DOWN

1. Tell all
2. Scarce
3. Where the Himalayas are
4. SeaWorld whale
5. Go like a bunny
6. "We ___ amused"
7. "Money ___ object!"
8. "___-ching!" (cash register noise)
9. Animal in a sty
10. Wall St. debut
11. Palindromic diarist
17. Flood control proj.
21. Firearms org.
22. Assigned task
24. Drill insert
25. One-spot cards
26. Golfing vehicle
27. Lodges
28. Sturdy trees
29. People rush to get in here
30. Destiny
32. Father
35. Not many
37. SSE's opposite

Puzzle 120

1	2	3	4	■	5	6	7	■	8	9	10	11
12				■	13			■	14			
15				■	16			17				
18				■	■	19			■	■	■	■
■	■	■	20	21	22		■	23	24	25	26	27
28	29	30	■	31			32	■	33			
34			35			■	36	37				
38				■	39	40			■	41		
42				43	■	44			45	■	■	■
■	■	■	■	46	47		■	■	48	49	50	51
52	53	54	55				56	■	57			
58				■	59			■	60			
61				■	62			■	63			

40. Sanctuary
43. RR depot
45. ___ decongestant
47. Indy 500, e.g.
49. Mexican peninsula
50. Attired
51. Like Playboy models
52. Lob's path
53. Hawaii's Mauna ___
54. Columbo and others: abbr.
55. German "I"
56. Allow

Solution on Page 343

ACROSS

1. Hitcher's hope
5. Theater admonition
8. World's fair
12. Elec., e.g.
13. Half a bray
14. Ship's front
15. Tale of woe
17. Hamster's home
18. "48 ___" (Nick Nolte film)
19. Trouble
20. Toys on strings
21. Popular nightclub
23. Birthday dessert
26. Palindromic cheer
27. Lifeguard's skill, for short
30. Is wild about
33. Hairpiece
35. Slumber party garb
36. Florist's vehicle
38. "Song ___ Blue" (Neil Diamond hit)
39. Last Beatles album
42. Go bad
45. "Give it the old college ___"
46. "Gross!"
49. Ear part
50. Flowering vine
52. Similar
53. Family
54. Not much
55. "As Good as It ___" (1997)
56. Since 1/1: abbr.
57. When tripled, a WWII movie

DOWN

1. ___-hour traffic
2. "Believe ___ Not!"
3. Have ___ on (claim)
4. Golfer Ernie
5. "Darn it!"
6. Rejection of church dogma
7. "You there!"
8. Disney World attraction
9. Like Superman's vision
10. Cartoon possum
11. Is in arrears
16. "Terrible" age
20. Toy on a string
21. "On ___ Majesty's Secret Service"
22. Sajak or Boone
23. Beanie
24. Pt. of speech
25. Ring victories
27. PC core
28. Paper Mate product
29. ___ U.S. Pat. Off.
31. Daredevil Knievel
32. Used a stool
34. "___ it or lose it"

Puzzle 121

1	2	3	4	■	5	6	7	■	8	9	10	11
12				■	13			■	14			
15				16				■	17			
18			■	19			■	20				
■	■	■	21				22			■	■	■
23	24	25		■	■	26			■	27	28	29
30				31	32	■	33		34			
35			■	36		37	■	■	38			
■	■	■	39				40	41		■	■	■
42	43	44			■	45			■	46	47	48
49				■	50				51			
52				■	53			■	54			
55				■	56			■	57			

37. Lamebrain
39. Property claims
40. The way things are going
41. First-round pass
42. Smelting waste
43. ___ fun at (ridicule)
44. Newspaper notice
46. "What've you been ___?"
47. Camping stuff
48. "If I ___ hammer . . ."
50. Shade of blue
51. Rat-a-___ (drum sound)

Solution on Page 344

ACROSS

1. Applaud
5. Some NCOs
9. "Where ___ sign?"
12. Missing
13. Furniture wood
14. Baby docs
15. Sills solo
16. Prefix meaning "both"
17. Zero
18. Boot camp affirmative
20. Tranquilize
22. B&O and Reading
24. Lab maze runner
25. Departure's opposite: abbr.
28. Tennis unit
29. Frees (of)
32. Big name in movie theaters
34. "___ Rheingold"
36. Horn sound
37. "___ to leap tall buildings . . ."
38. The ___ Four (The Beatles)
40. One of the Bobbsey twins
41. College website suffix
43. Winter woe
44. Necklace fasteners
47. Stern and Newton
52. The "L" of L.A.
53. Identical
55. Arterial blockage
56. Grow older
57. Writer Hunter
58. In ___ land (spacy)
59. "The ___ Squad" of '60s–'70s TV
60. Student's book
61. ___-friendly (easy to operate)

DOWN

1. Potter's medium
2. Folk wisdom
3. Sale tag words
4. School orgs.
5. Played the lead
6. Ruby, for one
7. Day planner features
8. Mogul negotiator
9. Charitable gift
10. Final notice
11. ___ of Man
19. April 15 org.
21. Bull's-eye hitter
23. Workers on duty
25. Fla. neighbor
26. Stick up
27. Set free
30. ___ good job (perform well): 2 wds.
31. Train stop: abbr.
33. Marries
35. Prominent, as a feature
39. Public vehicle

Puzzle 122

42. Unexpected sports outcome
44. Chowder morsel
45. NBC's peacock, e.g.
46. Put away for a rainy day
48. Rights org.
49. "Woe is me!"
50. Nat King ___
51. Constellation component
54. To the ___ (fully)

Solution on Page 344

ACROSS

1. Delivery room doctors, for short
4. "Do not open 'til ___"
8. Nuke
11. "Peanuts" expletive
13. "___ of Eden"
14. Roth ___
15. Rice Krispies sound
16. Space org.
17. "Right in the kisser!" preceder
18. Tennessee footballer
20. ___ fat
22. Part of an act
24. Live in fear of
26. "The Man Who Knew ___ Much"
27. Brand for Bowser
29. Rope fiber
32. North Pole toymaker
33. Clues, to a detective
35. Floppy rabbit feature
36. Countrywide: abbr.
38. Big furniture retailer
39. Ike's monogram
40. Clydesdale, e.g.
42. Medicinal plants
44. Dictation taker
46. Forbidden
48. ___ & Perrins (sauce brand)
49. Chooses
51. Chances
54. Mess up
55. 1/500 of the Indianapolis 500
56. Breathe rapidly
57. Cleverness
58. On ___ (without a contract)
59. Farm bale

DOWN

1. Hosp. areas
2. Prohibit
3. Technologically advanced
4. TV's warrior princess
5. Rustic film couple
6. Dolt
7. Governor's domain
8. "Song of the South" song
9. Elvis ___ Presley
10. Cat's feet
12. Rotate
19. Greenish blue
21. Cheer
22. British gun
23. Pepsi, e.g.
25. Took a taxi
28. Aloha gifts
30. Created
31. Oval Office occupant, briefly
34. Swedish car
37. Actor Chaney
41. Hotel offerings

Puzzle 123

1	2	3	■	■	4	5	6	7	■	8	9	10
11			12	■	13				■	14		
15				■	16				■	17		
■	■	18		19			■	20	21			
22	23				■	24	25				■	■
26			■	27	28			■	29		30	31
32			■	33				34	■	35		
36			37	■	38				■	39		
■	■	40		41			■	42	43			
44	45				■	46	47				■	■
48			■	49	50			■	51		52	53
54			■	55				■	56			
57			■	58				■	■	59		

43. Aerobatic maneuver
44. Whole bunch
45. Actress Hatcher
47. "Wait just ___!"
50. "Great Expectations" boy
52. Crime lab evidence
53. Piggery

Solution on Page 344

ACROSS

1. Cries of aversion
5. Hosts, briefly
8. Model in a bottle
12. Potatoes' partner
13. Mil. mail drop
14. ___-Cola
15. Ballerina's knee bend
16. What a cow chews
17. Cain's victim
18. Victory sign
20. Valuable vein
21. Colorado resort
24. Partner of born
27. Strong cleaner
28. Religion of the Koran
30. Where cranberries grow
33. Old cable inits.
34. Harsh reflection
35. "Top Hat" studio
36. Nov. preceder
37. Scrooge
38. Lend a hand
39. Kismet
40. Bill of Microsoft
42. Michelle Wie's org.
45. Author Kesey
46. Not theirs
47. Ripen
49. Guys' partners
53. Fail to mention
54. U-turn from SSW
55. ___ and polish
56. Spigots
57. "Annie Get Your ___"
58. Deuce topper, in cards

DOWN

1. Strike caller
2. Hair stiffener
3. "Bali ___" ("South Pacific" song)
4. Martin or McQueen
5. Riot spray
6. Computer's core, briefly
7. Instant lawn
8. Burn with hot liquid
9. Traveling tramp
10. Frosted
11. Ashen
19. Mystery
21. Voice below soprano
22. Lip-___ (not really sing)
23. Confined, with "up"
24. Nonchalant
25. Seldom seen
26. Come out
29. Narrow opening
30. Enfant terrible
31. Dust Bowl migrant
32. Deities

Puzzle 124

1	2	3	4	■	5	6	7	■	8	9	10	11
12				■	13			■	14			
15				■	16			■	17			
■	■	■	18	19		■	■	■	20			
21	22	23			■	24	25	26		■	■	■
27			■	28	29				■	30	31	32
33			■	34					■	35		
36			■	37					■	38		
■	■	■	39				■	40	41			
42	43	44		■	■	■	45			■	■	■
46				■	47	48		■	49	50	51	52
53				■	54			■	55			
56				■	57			■	58			

39. Abstains from eating
41. Feeling of anxiety
42. Plunder
43. Mountain lion
44. Tight hold
45. Like an eagle's vision
47. "Hulk" director Lee
48. African antelope
50. Mar. follower
51. Untruth
52. Pigpen

Solution on Page 344

ACROSS

1. Baseball officials, for short
5. The Almighty
8. Old wound mark
12. ___ the bill (pay)
13. Gun enthusiast's org.
14. Partner of Crosby and Stills
15. Not fooled by
16. Ornamental vase
17. ___ cost (free)
18. Takes too much, briefly
20. Came to terms
22. No longer fresh
25. ___ firma
26. Boy king of ancient Egypt
27. Blazing
31. Long, long ___
32. "If ___ say so myself"
33. Billy the ___
36. Nuisances
38. "Just ___ suspected!"
39. Neck and neck
43. Smidgens
45. Extends a subscription
47. J. Edgar Hoover's org.
48. Not odd
49. Guerrilla Guevara
51. Easter bloom
55. Hoover Dam's lake
56. "Washboard" muscles
57. "Yikes!"
58. Morays
59. Bon ___ (witticism)
60. Canines

DOWN

1. ET's craft
2. "___ Dieu!"
3. Flower holder
4. Pub perch
5. Wildebeests
6. Bobby of the NHL
7. "The X-Files" agent Scully
8. Trap
9. Supply food for a fee
10. Ed of "Lou Grant"
11. "The Mary Tyler Moore Show" spinoff
19. U.S. antitrafficking grp.
21. Former Telecom giant
22. Railroad stop: abbr.
23. Yank
24. From "___ Z" (totally)
28. "For shame!"
29. Doorkeepers' demands, briefly
30. Decompose
33. Krazy ___ of the comics
34. "This ___ stickup!"
35. Insult, in slang
36. Church bench

Puzzle 125

37. Close relative, for short
39. ___ de menthe
40. Flood embankment
41. Ryan or Tatum
42. Dispatches
44. Like smooth-running machines
46. Con game
47. Suffix with Oktober
50. SHO alternative
52. "Can ___ now?"
53. Get a little behind
54. Gridiron gains: abbr.

Solution on Page 345

ACROSS

1. Elec. company, e.g.
5. Oohs and ___
8. Spanish Surrealist Joan
12. Mediocre
13. Recipe amount
14. NYSE rival
15. Give off
16. "We ___ People . . ."
17. Ill-mannered
18. Robert of "Raging Bull"
20. Phonograph inventor
22. Your and my
23. Put on, as clothes
24. Perfumes
27. Gives in
31. One, in Bonn
32. Army bed
33. Alehouse
37. Dodged
40. Zodiac lion
41. To a ___ (without exception)
42. Passionate
45. Imbeciles
49. TV's Griffin
50. Actor Affleck
52. Peter, Paul, and Mary, e.g.
53. Curse
54. Tree feller
55. Start of a counting-out rhyme
56. "___ your side!"
57. Rep. foe
58. Boozers

DOWN

1. Secondhand
2. "Sock it ___!"
3. "Beauty ___ the eye . . ."
4. Skin soother
5. Cast members
6. "What'd you say?"
7. Rapid
8. Gomer Pyle was one
9. Don of talk radio
10. Overhaul
11. Beasts of burden
19. Groove
21. "___ look like a mind reader?"
24. "Game, ___, match!"
25. Cloak-and-dagger org.
26. Ltr. holder
28. Type of PC screen
29. Fawn's mother
30. Regular: abbr.
34. 7-___
35. Stimpy's TV pal
36. "Pretty good!"
37. "8 Mile" rapper
38. Young boy
39. Brings together

Puzzle 126

1	2	3	4	■	5	6	7	■	8	9	10	11
12				■	13			■	14			
15				■	16			■	17			
18				19		■	20	21				
■	■	■	22			■	23			■	■	■
24	25	26				■	27			28	29	30
31			■	■	■	■	■	■	■	32		
33			34	35	36	■	37	38	39			
■	■	■	40			■	41			■	■	■
42	43	44				■	45			46	47	48
49				■	50	51		■	52			
53				■	54			■	55			
56				■	57			■	58			

42. Both: prefix
43. Paper purchase
44. First 007 film
46. Black-and-white cookie
47. Salon job
48. Beans used for tofu
51. Program file extension

Solution on Page 345

ACROSS

1. Ames and Asner
4. Ask for alms
7. Charged atoms
11. "___ Woman" (Reddy song)
12. Door-to-door cosmetics company
14. Supreme Court justice ___ Bader Ginsburg
15. Opposite SSW
16. Psychic communication
18. Battleship blast
20. Custard dessert
21. Data-sharing syst.
22. Suppress
26. Tilts
28. Coffee, in slang
29. Afr. neighbor
30. Jane who loved Mr. Rochester
31. ___ Luis Obispo
32. ___ Millions (multistate lottery)
33. Educator's org.
34. Tool with teeth
35. Student's jottings
36. Wily
38. Keebler cookie maker
39. Spirited horse
41. Like Pisa's tower
44. Pie filling
48. Singer Orbison
49. Kind of beer
50. Worldwide: abbr.
51. Labor Day mo.
52. Harbor vessels
53. It breaks in the morning
54. Duet number

DOWN

1. ___, zwei, drei
2. Comic Carvey
3. Suspect dishonesty
4. Conductors' sticks
5. Eden woman
6. Tiger's game
7. Tehran native
8. Away from home
9. Advanced degree
10. Reserved
13. South Africa's Mandela
17. ___ de foie gras
19. Windmill blade
23. One way to jump in
24. Winter Olympics sled
25. Chapters in history
26. Singer Horne
27. Watcher
28. Uppercut's target
31. Deli meat
32. Shed, as skin
34. Positive
35. In an uncluttered way

Puzzle 127

1	2	3	■	4	5	6	■	■	7	8	9	10
11			■	12			13	■	14			
15			■	16				17				
18			19		■	20				■	■	■
■	■	21			■	■	22			23	24	25
26	27				■	28			■	29		
30				■	31			■	32			
33			■	34			■	35				
36			37			■	■	38			■	■
■	■	■	39			40	■	41			42	43
44	45	46					47		■	48		
49				■	50				■	51		
52				■	■	53			■	54		

37. Almanac tidbits
40. Flex
42. Theater chain founder Marcus
43. Proofreader's find
44. "The A-Team" star
45. Debt acknowledgment
46. Yuletide beverage
47. One ___ time

Solution on Page 345

ACROSS

1. Mount Olympus dwellers
5. Proofs of age, for short
8. Self-satisfied
12. Spicy Asian cuisine
13. "___ a problem"
14. Sit for a portrait
15. Seep
16. "For Whom ___ Bell Tolls"
17. "___ sesame"
18. Mount Everest guide
20. Author Hemingway
22. ___ center
23. Fix illegally
24. Despot
27. Derisive looks
31. Halen or Morrison
32. Online chuckle
33. Horse sense
37. Pencil end
40. Noah's craft
41. Like Abner
42. Display on a pedestal
45. Takes into one's family
49. Stuck in ___
50. Preschooler
52. Owl sound
53. Rock's partner
54. Pool stick
55. Pond organism
56. Helper
57. Aaron's 755: abbr.
58. Neatnik's opposite

DOWN

1. Old Pontiac muscle cars
2. Cry of anticipation
3. Stupefy
4. ___ Leone
5. All there
6. Cry from Homer Simpson
7. Takes the helm
8. Kind of cake
9. Sulk
10. Takes advantage of
11. Lady's man
19. Farm enclosure
21. ___ Tin Tin
24. Boob tubes
25. Candied veggie
26. Genetic material
28. Chicago trains
29. Caviar
30. Camera choice, in brief
34. Baby's noisemaker
35. Capote, for short
36. Artist's rendering
37. Makes very happy
38. Free (of)
39. Hawaiian greetings

Puzzle 128

1	2	3	4	■	5	6	7	■	8	9	10	11
12				■	13			■	14			
15				■	16			■	17			
18				19		■	20	21				
■	■	■	22			■	23			■	■	■
24	25	26				■	27			28	29	30
31			■	■	■	■	■	■	■	32		
33			34	35	36	■	37	38	39			
■	■	■	40			■	41			■	■	■
42	43	44				■	45			46	47	48
49				■	50	51		■	52			
53				■	54			■	55			
56				■	57			■	58			

42. "___ Smile" (1976 Hall & Oates hit)
43. Captain Picard's counselor
44. "Should ___ acquaintance . . ."
46. Survey
47. Fast-food option
48. Knife wound
51. "Days of ___ Lives"

Solution on Page 345

ACROSS

1. Singer Davis
4. Rx watchdog org.
7. Draw an outline of
12. "This ___ test . . ."
13. More than -er
14. Pass along
15. Wed. follower
16. Three-letter sandwich
17. Lessen
18. New Age composer John
20. "Today ___ man" (Bar Mitzvah declaration)
22. Golf legend Sam
24. Map lines: abbr.
25. Peat source
28. ___ down (softened)
30. Prefix meaning "one"
31. "Time to leave"
34. Happenings
37. Brian of Roxy Music
38. Newswoman Shriver
40. Wrigley Field flora
41. "___ me with a spoon!"
42. "Me and Bobby ___"
46. Morse ___
47. ___ of Fame
48. Ice house
51. Stanley Cup org.
54. Cambridge sch.
55. Stadium levels
56. Actress Susan
57. Chinese chairman
58. Battery terminal
59. Firefighter's tool
60. The Beach Boys' "Barbara ___"

DOWN

1. Catchers' gloves
2. Pale-faced
3. Make happen
4. Leap day's mo.
5. Cable alternative
6. Garb
7. Aerial railway cars
8. Country's McEntire
9. ___ carte
10. Manx or Siamese
11. CBS logo
19. Derbies and fedoras
21. Viper
23. Three ___ Night
25. Hot dog holder
26. Mich. neighbor
27. USO audience
29. Desert wanderer
31. Luau souvenir
32. Ltr. carrier
33. Yo-yo or Slinky
35. Energy

Puzzle 129

36. "To ___ his own"
39. Meeting plan
41. Mother ___
43. Beta's follower
44. Cuban boat boy González
45. Rock's ___ John
46. Firewood measure
48. Give ___ shot
49. Cotton ___
50. Author Buscaglia
52. Evil spell
53. Caustic chemical

Solution on Page 346

ACROSS

1. Christmas drink
4. Brain wave readout, for short
7. Yo-Yo Ma's instrument
12. Sheep's bleat
13. "___ Baba and the 40 Thieves"
14. Loud, as a crowd
15. Map collections
17. Inclined
18. Slow-witted
19. Gathers leaves
20. Sierra Nevada lake
23. "You da ___!"
24. "Son ___ Preacher Man"
25. It wasn't built in a day
28. Barbie or Ken
32. It's perpendicular to long.
33. Phone book listings: abbr.
34. Sturgeon eggs
35. Slave Scott
37. Rolling stones lack it
39. Director's cry
40. Skating surface
42. "Holy smokes!"
44. "The Simpsons" dad
47. Sales agent, for short
48. Tickle pink
49. Tommy gun noise
53. Ran in neutral
54. Fed. biomedical research agency
55. Med. plan
56. Fashionably outdated
57. Pub order
58. ___ out (withdraw)

DOWN

1. Hoopsters' org.
2. Cereal grain
3. Lass
4. Less difficult
5. Type of school: abbr.
6. Amer. soldiers
7. "It's a Wonderful Life" director
8. Gofer's job
9. "___, ma! No hands!"
10. Narrow street
11. Raw metals
16. Fuss
20. Tattled
21. At a distance
22. Detest
23. Army chow
26. "This one's ___"
27. Dairy farm sound
29. "Jaws" boat
30. Earsplitting
31. Answer to "Shall we?"
36. Calorie counter
38. Boil
41. Words to live by

Puzzle 130

1	2	3	■	4	5	6	■	7	8	9	10	11
12			■	13			■	14				
15			16				■	17				
■	■	■	18			■	■	19				
20	21	22			■	■	23			■	■	■
24			■	25	26	27		■	28	29	30	31
32			■	■	33			■	■	34		
35			36	■	37			38	■	39		
■	■	■	40	41		■	■	42	43			
44	45	46			■	■	47			■	■	■
48					■	49				50	51	52
53					■	54			■	55		
56					■	57			■	58		

43. Valedictorian's pride, for short
44. ___ to the throne
45. Ye ___ Shoppe
46. Beer ingredient
47. Train track
49. Genetic letters
50. However, briefly
51. Sound booster
52. Tyke

Solution on Page 346

ACROSS

1. Delta deposit
5. Bout enders, for short
9. Outdo
12. On the road
13. Pile
14. Prefix for center
15. Huckleberry ___
16. Jane of literature
17. Cal. Tech. rival
18. Make beloved
20. ___ Monkey Trial
22. ___ green
24. Instigate litigation
25. "Pipe down!"
28. Domino dot
29. Sea creature that moves sideways
32. "___ on truckin'"
34. "Uh-uh"
36. Angel's headgear
37. Assuming that's true
38. Person with a beat
40. Family member
41. Ill temper
43. Immigrant's course: abbr.
44. To the rear, on a ship
47. Coin flips
52. Auditor, for short
53. Uncontrolled anger
55. Curbside call
56. "Star Wars" pilot Solo
57. Musical work
58. "Shake ___!"
59. CPR expert
60. "___ Make a Deal"
61. Part of MIT: abbr.

DOWN

1. Ump's call
2. "Heads ___, tails you lose"
3. Terra firma
4. Actress Daly
5. "___ lies a tale"
6. Lock opener
7. Paddles
8. Eyeglasses, for short
9. Poster paints
10. Sheriff Taylor's kid
11. The ___ (awful)
19. PC program
21. "That hurts!"
23. Quickly
25. Compete in a slalom
26. Playboy Mansion guy
27. Wavering
30. Rope-a-dope boxer
31. Duck for apples
33. Look (over)
35. It's her party

Puzzle 131

1	2	3	4	■	5	6	7	8	■	9	10	11
12				■	13				■	14		
15				■	16				■	17		
18				19		■	20		21			
■	■	■	■	22		23	■	24			■	■
25	26	27	■	28			■	■	29		30	31
32			33	■	34		35	■	36			
37				■	■	38		39	■	40		
■	■	41		42	■	43			■	■	■	■
44	45				46	■	47		48	49	50	51
52			■	53		54		■	55			
56			■	57				■	58			
59			■	60				■	61			

39. Mideast grp.
42. Swashbuckling Flynn
44. Feel sore
45. Junk e-mail
46. Neck part
48. RBI or ERA
49. Store event
50. Business VIP
51. Sorrowful sound
54. ___ reaction

Solution on Page 346

ACROSS

1. Father
4. Actor Neeson
8. Cry like a baby
12. Take advantage of
13. Pale
14. Peek___
15. Green-lights
16. Comparison word
17. Ripped
18. Business mag
20. Stir up
22. "___, Martin, and John"
26. The "I" in ICBM
27. "Stay" singer Lisa
28. Belgrade native
30. Vinyl records
31. Court
32. Yank's foe
35. Front-page stuff
36. U.S. disaster relief org.
37. Wedding site
41. "Chilean" fish
43. Poland's capital
45. Capp's ___ Abner
46. Run ___ (go wild)
47. LP player
50. "This ___ shall pass"
53. Great review
54. Community gym site
55. Not at work
56. ___ Scott Decision, 1857
57. Pouches
58. Squeal (on)

DOWN

1. Twosome
2. "___ not what your country . . ."
3. Longs for
4. Door fastener
5. Kind of: suffix
6. "So that's it!"
7. Talking bird
8. Conductor's stick
9. "It's not ___ the money"
10. Not as good
11. Recluse
19. Catch red-handed
21. Chest bone
22. ___ or nothing
23. Hit on the head
24. "___ forgive our debtors"
25. Cat calls
29. Pink wine
32. Home shower
33. Printer's measures
34. English majors' degs.
35. Gun lobby, briefly
36. "The X-Files" org.
37. Prize

Puzzle 132

1	2	3	■	4	5	6	7	■	8	9	10	11
12			■	13				■	14			
15			■	16				■	17			
■	■	18	19		■	■	20	21				
22	23				24	25	■	26				
27				■	28		29		■	■	■	■
30			■	■	31			■	■	32	33	34
■	■	■	■	35				■	36			
37	38	39	40		■	41		42				
43					44	■	■	45			■	■
46				■	47	48	49		■	50	51	52
53				■	54				■	55		
56				■	57				■	58		

38. Tennessee senator Alexander
39. Treasure ___
40. Inquired
42. Assumed name
44. Explanations
48. John Denver's "Thank God ___ Country Boy"
49. Govt. media watchdog
51. "Scent ___ Woman"
52. Frequently, in verse

Solution on Page 346

ACROSS

1. Blacken
5. Govt. health watchdog
8. Foldable beds
12. Tortoise's race opponent
13. Response to an online joke
14. Puts on TV
15. Writing fluids
16. Barn bird
17. Large number
18. Classify
20. Not quite right
22. ___Moines
23. Coop dweller
24. "With it"
27. Gym pad
29. "What's the ___ that can happen?"
33. A Gabor sister
34. Unruly crowd
36. Mooer
37. ___-Goldwyn-Mayer
40. West Bank grp.
42. Santa ___ winds
43. Boise's state: abbr.
45. Hurricane's center
47. More rational
49. Viewpoints
53. Cops enforce them
54. Refusals
56. Lopsided victory
57. Make eyes at
58. "___ we having fun yet?"
59. "The ___ Ranger"
60. "Porgy and ___"
61. A's opposite, in England
62. Depict unfairly

DOWN

1. ___ Pet (cultivatable gift)
2. ___ Christian Andersen
3. Clumsy boats
4. Patch the lawn
5. Jetsam's partner
6. ___ Jones industrials
7. To whom a Muslim prays
8. Vegas attraction
9. Lubricates
10. Number between dos and cuatro
11. Away from NNE
19. Sleep acronym
21. Cat call
24. Skirt's edge
25. "___ Got a Secret"
26. Frisk, with "down"
28. Blouse or shirt
30. Big TV maker
31. Prince, to a king
32. Former rival of Pan Am
35. Holy
38. Gets the soap off

Puzzle 133

1	2	3	4	■	5	6	7	■	8	9	10	11
12				■	13			■	14			
15				■	16			■	17			
18				19		■	20	21				■
■	■	■	22			■	23			■	■	■
24	25	26	■	27		28	■	29		30	31	32
33			■	■	34		35	■	■	36		
37			38	39	■	40		41	■	42		
■	■	■	43		44	■	45		46	■	■	■
■	47	48				■	49			50	51	52
53				■	54	55		■	56			
57				■	58			■	59			
60				■	61			■	62			

39. "___ to Joy"
41. Popeye's Olive ___
44. Desi of "I Love Lucy"
46. Some noblemen
47. Stuffing seasoning
48. Shoemaker's tools
50. Cozy corner
51. Jukebox choice
52. One-dish meal
53. High tennis shot
55. Miner's load

Solution on Page 347

ACROSS

1. NBA tiebreakers
4. Loan org.
7. Makes, as a salary
12. Stove top item
13. ___ Angeles Dodgers
14. Southwestern home material
15. Greek "H"
16. Spellbound
18. Have a connection
20. Sixth sense, for short
21. "You said it!"
22. Bark sharply
24. Use a stopwatch
28. Vegas's ___ Grand
30. Apollo component
32. December dairy case offering
33. "___ Yankee Doodle dandy"
35. Capri and Wight
37. What it takes to tango
38. Like a fiddle
39. Sticky stuff
40. Doberman's warning
42. Notion
44. Old Ford model
46. Three feet
49. Easy as ___
51. First game of the season
53. Next to
57. Amtrak stop: abbr.
58. Cowboy contest
59. "___ Pepper's Lonely Hearts Club Band"
60. Caesar's three
61. "M*A*S*H" clerk
62. "For ___ a jolly good fellow"
63. Perfect gymnastics score

DOWN

1. Met offering
2. ___ pole
3. Inconclusive conclusion
4. Fly like a butterfly
5. Hive product
6. Fit ___ fiddle
7. Big rabbit features
8. Get used (to)
9. L. ___ Hubbard
10. "Friends" network
11. View
17. Sioux shelter
19. "Brokeback Mountain" director Lee
23. Parcel out
25. On the way
26. Cut the grass
27. Id's counterpart
29. Russian-built fighter aircraft
31. "No ___" (Chinese menu phrase)
33. "___ were you . . ."
34. Prefix with life or wife

Puzzle 134

36. Shoe bottoms
41. Deli bread
43. Sleep problem
45. Jump out of the way
47. Knot again
48. Sink outlet
50. Composer Stravinsky
52. Dogs and cats
53. Timetable abbr.
54. Mauna ___ volcano
55. Peculiar
56. It's like "-like"

Solution on Page 347

ACROSS

1. Hydrant attachment
5. Classifieds, e.g.
8. Air safety org.
11. SASE, e.g.
12. Disease research org.
13. ___ serif
14. "___ my lips!"
15. High card
16. Bowlers' targets
17. Prepare for unpleasantness
20. Be sorry
21. "Today I ___ man" (bar mitzvah phrase)
22. Stretchy, as a waistband
26. March 17 honoree, for short
30. Mover's vehicle
31. Clean the floor
33. Prefix with center
34. Vice President Spiro
37. Afternoon show
40. Tic ___: mint
42. Yang's complement
43. Nuclear explosion aftermath
50. Pretentious
51. Pub drink
52. Simplicity
53. Go yachting
54. Envy or gluttony
55. Not now
56. Popular camera type, for short
57. Explosive inits.
58. Soapy froth

DOWN

1. Parsley, sage, rosemary, or thyme
2. R.E.M.'s "The ___ Love"
3. Improvisational singing style
4. Church officials
5. Disneyland's locale
6. Casino cubes
7. Biblical land with a queen
8. Flunk
9. Green Gables girl
10. Mgr.'s aide
13. Water balloon sound
18. Boy king of Egypt
19. Stammerer's syllables
22. Zsa Zsa's sister
23. Not keep up
24. Raggedy doll
25. Dot-___ (Internet company)
27. Ballpoint, e.g.
28. King Kong, e.g.
29. Ascot
32. Creditor's demand
35. Gas additive
36. Armed conflict
38. ___-tac-toe
39. Small bays

Puzzle 135

1	2	3	4	■	5	6	7	■	■	8	9	10
11				■	12			■	13			
14				■	15			■	16			
17				18				19				
■	■	■	20			■	21			■	■	■
22	23	24				25	■	26		27	28	29
30			■	■	31		32	■	■	33		
34			35	36	■	37		38	39			
■	■	■	40		41	■	42			■	■	■
43	44	45				46				47	48	49
50				■	51			■	52			
53				■	54			■	55			
56			■	■	57			■	58			

41. Seashore
43. Church service
44. Russia's ___ Mountains
45. Use a swizzle stick
46. Lena or Ken of film
47. Diamond Head locale
48. Not new
49. Family rooms

Solution on Page 347

ACROSS

1. Snow vehicle
5. Scannable mdse. bars
8. Woes
12. Broadway "Auntie"
13. Architect I. M.
14. Brother of Abel
15. "Semper fi" org.
16. Death Valley is below it
18. "___ she blows!"
19. Leopold's co-defendant
20. Part of SASE
23. Day of "Pillow Talk"
27. Carryall
31. Warrior princess of TV
32. Jimmy and Rosalynn's daughter
33. Standoffish
36. "Paper or plastic?" item
37. Labor Day mo.
39. Something new in LA?
41. Bull's sound
43. Sot's spot
44. Zealous
47. Unmannerly
51. Reverend
55. Captain of the Pequod
56. Read quickly
57. CBS forensic series
58. ___ bene
59. Workout centers
60. ___ flask (liquor container)
61. "If ___ only knew!"

DOWN

1. Censor's target
2. Mascara target
3. Poet Lazarus
4. Edict
5. ___ and downs
6. Orange throwaway
7. "See you later!"
8. Fridge, old-style
9. Loo
10. Perjure oneself
11. Eddie Murphy's old show, for short
17. ___ Zeppelin (rock group)
21. LeBron James's org.
22. Actor Kilmer
24. Singer McEntire
25. "Back ___ hour" (shop sign)
26. Droops
27. Old Soviet news agency
28. Prophetic sign
29. Printing goof
30. Hot tar, e.g.
34. Globe
35. Ala. neighbor
38. Choo-choos
40. Straying
42. Tubes

Puzzle 136

45. Something to scratch
46. He loved Lucy
48. "We're in trouble"
49. Palm fruit
50. Online auction site
51. Flavor enhancer
52. "If looks could kill" type of stare
53. '60s war zone, briefly
54. Tear

Solution on Page 347

ACROSS

1. Golfer's shout
5. Sighing words
9. Campbell's container
12. Amazes
13. Wordsworth work
14. Losing tic-tac-toe row
15. Cubicle fixture
16. Univ. military program
17. Bullring "Bravo!"
18. Fainthearted
20. 1950s Ford flop
22. Tooth covering
24. Gave grub to
25. Idiot
26. Studio stands
29. Have no ___ for
30. Letters between "K" and "O"
31. Co. that merged with Time Warner
33. Bothers greatly
36. Foil maker
38. Put a spell on
39. UFO crew
40. Follow
43. Thespian
44. Cut off, as branches
45. ___-of-the-moment
47. Neet rival
50. Calf's cry
51. Answering-machine sound
52. Blues singer James
53. Not outgoing
54. Makes a choice
55. Metal that Superman can't see through

DOWN

1. Craze
2. Part of IOU
3. Interstate relaxation station
4. ___ Pie (ice cream treat)
5. Showery month
6. Engine cover
7. Ran into
8. Roasts' hosts
9. Whispers sweet nothings
10. Auto shaft
11. Christmas song
19. Stag party attendees
21. Ike's initials
22. Big bird
23. "Schnozzola"
24. Groupie
26. CPR specialist
27. Tear jaggedly
28. Before long
30. Calif. airport
32. ___ Palmas, Spain
34. Day of the wk.
35. Takes care of

Puzzle 137

1	2	3	4	■	5	6	7	8	■	9	10	11
12				■	13				■	14		
15				■	16				■	17		
■	■	18		19			■	20	21			
22	23					■	24			■	■	■
25					■	26				27	28	■
29			■	■	30			■	■	31		32
■	33		34	35			■	36	37			
■	■	■	38			■	39					
40	41	42			■	43					■	■
44			■	45	46			■	47		48	49
50			■	51				■	52			
53			■	54				■	55			

36. PC key
37. Big name in toy trains
39. Land measures
40. "Desire Under the ___"
41. Ark builder
42. Neuter
43. Em, to Dorothy
46. "___ Goes the Weasel"
48. "Let's call ___ day"
49. "Far out"

Solution on Page 348

ACROSS

1. Cries out loud
5. Head-shakers' syllables
9. Links org.
12. One-named New Age singer
13. 2002 Winter Olympics locale
14. "___ Are My Sunshine"
15. Mississippi's Trent
16. Actress Spelling
17. Creepy Chaney
18. Sassy
20. Not strict
22. Unlocked
24. "Yuck!"
27. "How the West Was ___" (1962)
28. "___ can you see . . ."
32. Scanty
34. Not outdoors
36. Auction off
37. "___ Had a Hammer"
38. Jammies
39. Maximum extent
42. Led down the aisle
45. Holey cheese
50. "Peggy ___ Got Married"
51. "Take ___ from me!"
53. "___ a man with seven wives"
54. ___ capita
55. Da Vinci's "___ Lisa"
56. Senate errand runner
57. Basic version: abbr.
58. Limerick, e.g.
59. Midterm, e.g.

DOWN

1. "To thine own ___ be true"
2. ___ about (approximately)
3. Eight bits
4. College entrance exams
5. Egypt's King ___
6. Like some kisses and bases
7. Singing Carpenter
8. "Rise and ___!"
9. "Gomer ___, USMC"
10. Hired thug
11. Uncle's partner
19. Inventor Elias
21. They're exchanged at the altar
23. "Un momento, ___ favor"
24. Speakers' pause fillers
25. "Fancy that!"
26. Actor Holbrook
29. Taste the soup
30. Modifying wd.
31. Affirmative response
33. Rubber cement, e.g.
34. Suppositions
35. Things to pick
37. Antiseptic element
40. "Lady and the ___"

Puzzle 138

1	2	3	4	■	5	6	7	8	■	9	10	11
12				■	13				■	14		
15				■	16				■	17		
18				19	■	20			21			
■	■	■	■	22	23					■	■	■
24	25	26	■	27			■	■	28	29	30	31
32			33			■	34	35				
36				■	■	37			■	38		
■	■	■	39	40	41				■	■	■	■
42	43	44					■	45	46	47	48	49
50			■	51			52	■	53			
54			■	55				■	56			
57			■	58				■	59			

41. "Ditto"
42. Delivery org.
43. Fatty treat for birds
44. Group of buffalo
46. Towel (off)
47. Giant-screen theater
48. Nintendo competitor
49. Flower stalk
52. Shriver of tennis

Solution on Page 348

ACROSS

1. Corn on the ___
4. Mafia bigwigs
8. Famous cookie man
12. Family card game
13. TV's "How ___ Your Mother"
14. Toy block brand
15. Printer's widths
16. Ferris wheel or bumper cars
17. Lounge
18. Confidential matter
20. Miniature
22. Form 1040 org.
23. Heavens
24. Barbecue entrée
27. Average guy
28. Comment made while slapping the forehead
31. Trivial
35. Vicious of the Sex Pistols
36. Chatter
37. Mil. fliers
38. Blubber
39. "___ voyage!"
41. Pinball palace
44. Turns away
48. Command to a dog
49. ___ and shine
51. Hunky-dory
52. Snakelike fish
53. Related
54. "Med" or "law" lead-in
55. Store goods: abbr.
56. Telescope part
57. Logging tool

DOWN

1. Billiard sticks
2. "This round's ___"
3. Popular pear
4. More grim
5. Leaves out
6. A Beatty
7. Child by marriage
8. Back street
9. Cat call
10. Leer at
11. Fillet of ___
19. Put on the line
21. Managed, with "out"
24. ER workers
25. Jr.'s son
26. "A" followers
27. Poke
28. Put down, slangily
29. Thurman of "The Avengers"
30. Playboy Hugh, familiarly
32. "Holy moly!"
33. Side-to-side
34. ___ buggy

Puzzle 139

1	2	3	■	4	5	6	7	■	8	9	10	11
12			■	13				■	14			
15			■	16				■	17			
18			19			■	20	21				
■	■	■	22			■	23			■	■	■
24	25	26		■	■	27			■	28	29	30
31				32	33				34			
35			■	36			■	■	37			
■	■	■	38			■	39	40		■	■	■
41	42	43				■	44			45	46	47
48				■	49	50			■	51		
52				■	53				■	54		
55				■	56				■	57		

38. Not true
39. Place to wash up
40. Pizzeria fixtures
41. Throat-clearing sound
42. Marsh plant
43. Cartoon frames
45. Knocks lightly
46. Synagogue scroll
47. Distort
50. "I Like ___"

Solution on Page 348

ACROSS

1. Fireplace fuel
5. ___-American relations
9. Dylan or Dole
12. Fourth-down play
13. "___ I care!"
14. Mr. Onassis
15. Play the lead
16. Fabric fuzz
17. Psychedelic drug
18. Stockholm natives
20. Co. honchos
21. Shirt part
22. "Obviously!"
24. Japanese cartoon style
27. Apartment dwellers
31. Wrestling win
32. Cut off
34. Three: prefix
35. Passes, as time
37. Patriot Allen
39. "See ya"
40. "___, humbug!"
41. Golfers' goals
44. Beauty parlors
47. Feel sorry about
48. Currier and ___
50. "Just the facts, ___"
52. It's west of Que.
53. Sugar source
54. Bullets, e.g.
55. Norm: abbr.
56. Simple
57. Leak slowly

DOWN

1. CD precursors
2. Inning-enders
3. Chew (on)
4. Creek
5. Oregon's capital
6. Wife of Osiris
7. Writer Anaïs
8. Many a time
9. Hay bundle
10. Roughly
11. Auction actions
19. Fancy, as clothes
20. When repeated, a ballroom dance
22. "Look at Me, I'm Sandra ___"
23. Imaginary
24. Animal that beats its chest
25. Nothing
26. Put ___ good word for
27. Sets in dens
28. Utmost
29. ___ la la (singing syllables)
30. ___ City (Las Vegas)
33. Wide shoe designation
36. Big Bird's network

Puzzle 140

1	2	3	4	■	5	6	7	8	■	9	10	11
12				■	13				■	14		
15				■	16				■	17		
■	18			19			■	■	20			
■	■	■	21			■	22	23		■	■	■
24	25	26			■	27				28	29	30
31			■	32	33				■	34		
35			36				■	37	38			
■	■	■	39			■	40			■	■	■
41	42	43		■	■	44				45	46	■
47			■	48	49			■	50			51
52			■	53				■	54			
55			■	56				■	57			

38. Clarence of the Supreme Court
40. Moisten the turkey
41. Major-leaguers
42. Jemima, e.g.
43. On a pension: abbr.
44. Fortuneteller
45. Partner of rank and serial number
46. "___ Time, Next Year"
48. PC maker
49. Neckline shape
51. Unruly head of hair

Solution on Page 348

ACROSS

1. Auditor's org.
4. ___ Deco
7. Rotten
10. "That oughta ___!"
12. ___ boom bah
13. New Haven campus
14. Divide
16. ___ even keel
17. "Citizen ___"
18. Twenty questions attempt
19. Pointed a pistol
22. Switchboard worker: abbr.
24. Future atty.'s exam
25. China, Japan, etc.
29. Ichthyologist's study
30. Photo ___ (White House events)
31. Shoe bottom
32. Pre-cable need
34. Burden of proof
35. Mama ___ of the Mamas and the Papas
36. Out in the open
37. Prince of Darkness
40. Scotch and ___
42. Out of control
43. Rate a horse
47. Ration (out)
48. "Act your ___!"
49. Auto parts giant
50. Night school subj.
51. Craven or Unseld
52. Howard of "Happy Days"

DOWN

1. Co. photo badges, e.g.
2. Salmon eggs
3. Drink slowly
4. Straight ___ arrow
5. It's part of growing up
6. When doubled, an African fly
7. The ___ of one's existence
8. "Oh, woe!"
9. Lairs
11. Be extraordinary
13. 1972 Carly Simon hit
15. Half a diam.
18. Eur. country
19. ___ Romeo (sports car)
20. "The doctor ___"
21. Sail support
23. Faux ___ (blunder)
26. Super-duper
27. Disparaging remark
28. Midterm or final
30. Light switch positions
33. Palindromic Bobbsey twin
36. Eccentric
37. "The Sweetest Taboo" singer
38. Singer Tori

Puzzle 141

39. Turnpike charge
41. Singles
43. Hem and ___
44. Garage contents
45. Mil. address
46. Pot's partner

Solution on Page 349

ACROSS

1. Website ID
4. Like a rock
9. Blubber
12. Actress Zadora
13. Swap
14. Civil War general
15. Slick
16. Monastery head
17. Young ___
18. Polite refusal
20. Flow back
22. Letters after a proof
24. Wave tops
27. Triumphant cries
30. Wide shoe width
32. Sticky stuff
33. Bert Bobbsey's twin
34. "K–O" connection
35. Colorant
36. Make a sweater
38. Shack
39. Not fem.
40. St. Francis of ___
42. ___ Tomé
44. PC key
45. Chubby Checker's dance
49. Toward the stern
51. "Remember the ___!"
55. "This instant!"
56. Pecan or cashew
57. Batman's sidekick
58. CBS drama
59. College sr.'s test
60. "All That Jazz" director Bob
61. Derby, for one

DOWN

1. Go ___ smoke
2. Puerto ___
3. Big name in chips
4. Gawk (at)
5. Crystal ball, e.g.
6. Experiment site
7. Words before "You may kiss the bride"
8. Dissuade
9. Scotch mixer
10. Stimpy's sidekick
11. Word of assent
19. Brainpower stats
21. Implore
23. New ___, India
24. Pennies
25. Aerosmith album "___ in the Attic"
26. Blueprint detail
27. Paul who sang "Diana"
28. Skater Brinker
29. Licorice-flavored liqueur
31. Down Under bird

Puzzle 142

1	2	3	■	4	5	6	7	8	■	9	10	11
12			■	13					■	14		
15			■	16					■	17		
18			19		■	■	■	20	21		■	■
■	■	■	22		23	■	24				25	26
27	28	29		■	30	31		■	32			
33			■	■	34			■	■	35		
36			37	■	38			■	39			
40				41		■	42	43		■	■	■
■	■	44			■	■	■	45		46	47	48
49	50		■	51	52	53	54		■	55		
56			■	57					■	58		
59			■	60					■	61		

37. "___ the wind and nothing more"
39. Cut the lawn
41. Winter neckwear
43. Make amends
46. 1/12 of a foot
47. Cubs slugger Sammy
48. Nincompoop
49. Director Lee
50. Mink or sable
52. British bathroom
53. Belly muscles
54. Prefix for giving or taking

Solution on Page 349

ACROSS

1. Gulf War missile
5. Writer Bombeck
9. Mauna ___
12. Stun
13. Ball-___ hammer
14. Feel poorly
15. Showy flower
16. Lazily
17. Dutch airline
18. Letter openers?
20. Follows the leader
22. "Who shot J. R.?" show
25. "___ luck?"
26. Laziness
27. Least restrained
30. Chicken drumstick
31. Thanksgiving side dish
32. Escape, as from jail
34. Made airtight
37. Hackneyed
39. Back talk
40. Wore away
41. Wee
44. Singer Redding
45. Comparative suffix
46. Eyebrow shape
48. Eve's man
52. Mai ___ (tropical drink)
53. Quote
54. Start for Rooter or tiller
55. Terminus
56. Practice boxing
57. Thanksgiving side dish

DOWN

1. Reagan's "Star Wars" prog.
2. Saturn, for one
3. Commando weapon
4. Treat, as seawater
5. Grand stories
6. Funnyman Foxx
7. Funnyman Brooks
8. "Tennis, ___?"
9. Erie or Huron
10. Greasy
11. Handouts
19. "___! Humbug!"
21. "See ya!"
22. Broadband inits.
23. Pub drinks
24. Theater box
25. Limb
27. It's all the rage
28. Moved on ice
29. "Little Man ___" (Jodie Foster film)
31. "Uh-huh!"
33. ___ school
35. Sum total
36. Purple flowers

Puzzle 143

1	2	3	4	■	5	6	7	8	■	9	10	11
12				■	13				■	14		
15				■	16				■	17		
■	■	■	18	19			■	20	21			
22	23	24				■	25			■	■	■
26					■	27				28	29	■
30			■	■	31			■	■	32		33
■	34		35	36			■	37	38			
■	■	■	39			■	40					
41	42	43			■	44				■	■	■
45			■	46	47			■	48	49	50	51
52			■	53				■	54			
55			■	56				■	57			

37. Prefix with cycle or angle
38. Prayer beads
40. Bygone anesthetic
41. Locale
42. Nasty
43. Saharan
44. Eight: comb. form
47. ___ Van Winkle
49. ER pronouncement
50. Green machine?
51. Cal. pages

Solution on Page 349

ACROSS

1. Heidi's home
5. Eco-friendly org.
8. Bed support
12. Scarlett's home
13. Acted as a guide
14. "___ Gynt"
15. Upper canine
17. Price of a ride
18. Psychic power
19. Greets the day
21. "The Raven" poet
22. "___ a real nowhere man . . ."
23. Optimistic
25. Mexican dish
28. Hold in high regard
31. "I smell ___"
32. Sunrise direction
33. School break
36. Warns
38. Like arson evidence
39. Central
40. "Cheers" setting
42. ___ Martin (James Bond car)
44. It's "big" in London
47. Stratford-upon-___
49. Mexican food staple
51. Sharpen, as a knife
52. Pitcher's stat
53. Throw in the towel
54. Loretta of "M*A*S*H"
55. Gibson of "Braveheart"
56. Flippered mammal

DOWN

1. To ___ (exactly)
2. Puts down
3. Kind of school
4. Plopped down
5. Plaza Hotel girl of fiction
6. Four-footed friends
7. Stick (to)
8. Beach lotion letters
9. Calendar phenomenon
10. Prefix with space
11. Shade giver
16. Hershiser on the mound
20. Letters of distress
22. Despises
24. War horse
25. ___ and feather
26. "___ you sure?"
27. What Yankee Doodle called the feather
29. Superlative suffix
30. Everest and Rainier: abbr.
34. ___ Na Na
35. The "S" in CBS
36. Unconcerned with right and wrong
37. It's trapped on laundry day

Puzzle 144

1	2	3	4	■	5	6	7	■	8	9	10	11
12				■	13			■	14			
15				16				■	17			
18			■	19				20	■	21		
■	■	■	22			■	23		24		■	■
25	26	27				■	28				29	30
31				■	■	■	■	■	32			
33				34	35	■	36	37				
■	■	38				■	39			■	■	■
40	41		■	42		43			■	44	45	46
47			48	■	49				50			
51				■	52			■	53			
54				■	55			■	56			

40. Cries of contempt
41. Confess
43. Ripped
44. Sky-colored
45. Film director Kazan
46. Part of NFL: abbr.
48. Tennis court divider
50. Mensa members have high ones

Solution on Page 349

ACROSS

1. Sales agents, briefly
5. Learning inst.
8. Drink from a flask
12. Home furnishings chain
13. Calf call
14. Fey of "30 Rock"
15. Game show legend Griffin
16. Climbing plant
17. Like printers' fingers
18. Horse house
20. Sniffer
21. Sr.'s test
22. Food-additive letters
24. Juliet's beloved
27. Mental quickness
28. Total (up)
31. Wayne film "___ Bravo"
32. Humpback, e.g.
34. ___ sauce
35. ___-mo replay
36. Half a dozen
37. "___ not, want not"
39. Freshly painted
40. Gun a motor
41. Unexciting
44. Neater
47. Fury
48. Toddler
49. Mimicked
51. Eggs ___ easy
52. Color
53. Fork prong
54. Boggs of baseball
55. 12-mo. periods
56. Greenspan's subj.

DOWN

1. What an air ball doesn't touch
2. ___ out a living (barely scrapes by)
3. Sassy
4. Barbaric
5. "Say cheese!"
6. Bat's home
7. Cow chow
8. Bee injury
9. Overindulger of the grape
10. Squid squirts
11. Singer Marvin
19. Shop without buying
22. Thickness measure
23. Prepared, as tomatoes
24. Train lines: abbr.
25. Lubricant
26. Cattle call
27. Floor application
28. Sure-footed work animal
29. Period
30. Hair coloring
33. Big success

Puzzle 145

1	2	3	4	■	5	6	7	■	8	9	10	11
12				■	13			■	14			
15				■	16			■	17			
■	18			19			■	■	20			
■	■	■	21			■	22	23		■	■	■
24	25	26			■	27			■	28	29	30
31			■	32	33				■	34		
35			■	36			■	37	38			
■	■	■	39			■	40			■	■	■
41	42	43		■	■	44				45	46	■
47				■	48			■	49			50
51				■	52			■	53			
54				■	55			■	56			

38. Fly a plane
39. "Now ___ was I?"
40. Religious ceremonies
41. Furrowed part of the head
42. Molten rock
43. Got gray
44. ___ de force
45. Heroic tale
46. City near Lake Tahoe
48. "___ will be done"
50. Lair

Solution on Page 350

ACROSS

1. Abbr. at the end of a company's name
4. Environmental prefix
7. Bygone Russian space station
10. Milne character
12. Drink like a dog
13. Sugar source
14. Christmas tree decoration
16. URL starter
17. Exploding star
18. Google competitor
19. Maxim
22. Eins + zwei
24. "Star Trek: TNG" counselor Deanna
25. Hurrying
29. "Death in Venice" author
30. Air traffic control agcy.
31. The hunted
32. Cowboy hat
34. "Holy cow!"
35. Parsley or sage
36. "___ Jacques" (children's song)
37. Threaded fastener
40. Piercing tools
42. Dragon's ___ (early video game)
43. Large sailing vessel
47. "___ bitten, twice shy"
48. Anonymous John
49. Eliot of "The Untouchables"
50. Co. that merged into Verizon
51. Traveler's stopover
52. Sandwich initials

DOWN

1. Stock debut, for short
2. ". . . ___ a lender be"
3. Bamboozle
4. Hgt.
5. Pizza topping
6. Take your pick
7. SAT section
8. Get ___ shape
9. "___ Man" (Estevez film)
11. Stay the course
13. Committee head
15. A Stooge
18. Pro vote
19. After-hours money sources, for short
20. "Dang!"
21. Top-notch
23. Genetic trait carrier
26. Egg on
27. Burn
28. Jekyll's counterpart
30. "___ Your Eyes Only"
33. Use needle and thread
36. Mel's Diner waitress

Puzzle 146

37. Plod through the mud
38. Quitter's word
39. Paddy product
41. "___ Harry Met Sally . . ."
43. '80s defense prog.
44. Kan. neighbor
45. Subj. for immigrants
46. Letters after "Q"

Solution on Page 350

ACROSS

1. Ref.'s relative
4. They're kissable
8. "No ___ luck!"
12. "Once Upon a Mattress" legume
13. "Take ___ from me . . ."
14. Poet Pound
15. PC monitor
16. Femur or fibula
17. MGM symbol
18. Presidential rejection
20. Poorly lit
22. Prepare presents
25. Desert spring
29. Actress Moore
32. Daybreak
34. MSN, for one
35. Paranormal showman Geller
36. Copenhageners, e.g.
37. 4.0 is a great one: abbr.
38. Grand ___ (sporty Pontiacs)
39. Kuwaiti leader
40. ___ and wherefores
41. Machine tool
43. Surrender
45. Reaction to the cold
47. Poison ivy symptom
50. Long car, for short
53. Long ago
56. Wide shoe specification
58. Hat's edge
59. In ___ (stuck)
60. Young man
61. Belgrade resident
62. Writing points
63. Football scores, for short

DOWN

1. ___ symbol (bar code)
2. "___ Griffin's Crosswords"
3. Chopped liver spread
4. Toil
5. "Am ___ blame?"
6. Bowling target
7. Raced
8. 1965 Alabama march site
9. Israeli submachine gun
10. ___-Magnon man
11. ___ Solo of "Star Wars"
19. Prefix with light
21. Charged particles
23. Sandler of "Big Daddy"
24. Lose one's cool
26. Audible breath
27. '60s TV show with Bill Cosby and Robert Culp
28. Health resorts
29. Twofold
30. Columnist Bombeck
31. "Gorillas in the ___"
33. "___ #1!"
36. Bucks and does

Puzzle 147

40. "Slippery when ___"
42. Cold War threat
44. Lose-weight schemes
46. Meg of "Sleepless in Seattle"
48. Boston hoopster, for short
49. Lettuce unit
50. Scale units: abbr.
51. Dander
52. Former Russian space station
54. ". . . ___ quit!" (ultimatum ending)
55. ___ down (massage)
57. Sullivan and Harris

Solution on Page 350

ACROSS

1. Mil. rank
4. Dem.'s opponent
7. Engagement gift
11. Maidenform product
12. Sen. Bayh of Indiana
14. Prepare for publication
15. Superman's symbol
16. 1990 Macaulay Culkin film
18. Way past ripe
20. "Long ___ and far away . . ."
21. College official
22. Flirts
26. Narcotic
28. Tough time
29. Take the odds
30. Actress ___ Marie Saint
31. Academy Awards
35. Playwright Sean
38. Kind of food or group
39. Swindles
40. Pontiac muscle car
41. Skin art
44. "A ___ Named Desire"
48. NYPD alert
49. Naughty child's Christmas gift
50. Catches some rays
51. "The Facts of Life" actress Charlotte
52. Hawkeye State
53. Quilting party
54. Foxlike

DOWN

1. Trucker with a handle
2. ". . . ___ I'm told"
3. Desperate, as an effort
4. Prepare leftovers
5. Tennis champ Goolagong
6. Actress Dawber
7. Insert fresh cartridges
8. Bachelor's last words
9. Diarist Anaïs
10. Former AT&T rival
13. "Cool!"
17. Ripening agent
19. Steeped beverage
23. Experiences dizziness
24. Roof edge
25. Knock off
26. Double-reed instrument
27. Termite, e.g.
32. Actress Lansbury
33. ___ of passage
34. F. ___ Fitzgerald
35. Gas rating
36. Not fine-grained
37. Picnic pest

Puzzle 148

1	2	3	■	4	5	6	■	■	7	8	9	10
11			■	12			13	■	14			
15			■	16				17				
18			19			■	20			■	■	■
■	■	21				■	22			23	24	25
26	27					■	28					
29			■	■	■	■	■	■	■	30		
31			32	33	34	■	35	36	37			
38						■	39				■	■
■	■	■	40			■	41				42	43
44	45	46				47			■	48		
49				■	50				■	51		
52				■	■	53			■	54		

42. October birthstone
43. Follow orders
44. Poli-____
45. "A Bridge ____ Far"
46. Like sushi
47. It's hailed in cities

Solution on Page 350

ACROSS

1. Atlas contents
5. Camera type, for short
8. First mo.
11. "Do I dare to ___ peach?"
12. Weed digger
13. Actress Turner
14. "___ does it!"
15. "Lost" network
16. "The King ___"
17. Lend a hand
19. Sex ___
21. "Q–U" link
22. HP products
23. Heaven's gatekeeper
27. "___ of Endearment"
31. Youngster
32. Actor Stephen of "The Crying Game"
34. Motorists' org.
35. Minimum
38. Home of Disney World
41. "Eureka!"
43. One side in checkers
44. Musical ladders
47. Can be found
51. Suffix with million
52. B&B beverages
54. Give out cards
55. D.C. baseball team
56. Turner who led a revolt
57. "___ Have to Do Is Dream"
58. Shipwreck signal
59. Letters on an ambulance
60. Downhill racer

DOWN

1. "I ___ man with seven wives . . ."
2. Sounds of satisfaction
3. Sch. orgs.
4. Lampoon
5. Break into bits
6. Arcing shot
7. Summary
8. Author Austen
9. Wing ___ prayer
10. Hammer's target
13. Run out, as a subscription
18. Fast jet, for short
20. Agts. usually get 10
23. Letters on a Cardinal's cap
24. Oft-stubbed digit
25. School fund-raising grp.
26. ___ Speed Wagon
28. Skedaddled
29. Off one's rocker
30. ___ Tomé and Príncipe
33. Hauls down to the station
36. Corporate department
37. "That'll be ___ day!"

Puzzle 149

1	2	3	4	■	5	6	7	■	■	8	9	10
11				■	12			■	13			
14				■	15			■	16			
17				18		■	19	20				
■	■	■	21			■	22			■	■	■
23	24	25				26	■	27		28	29	30
31			■	■	32		33	■	■	34		
35			36	37	■	38		39	40			
■	■	■	41		42	■	43			■	■	■
44	45	46				■	47			48	49	50
51				■	52	53		■	54			
55				■	56			■	57			
58			■	■	59			■	60			

39. Superman's nemesis Luthor
40. Nike rival
42. In unison
44. Without
45. "See you," in Sorrento
46. Sciences' partner
48. Peddle
49. "A ___ of Two Cities"
50. Glided
53. Toast topper

Solution on Page 351

ACROSS

1. Outback birds
5. Prefix with "understanding"
8. Fizzling sound
12. Entertainer Minnelli
13. Hole-punching tool
14. Friend in war
15. Go bankrupt
16. Take care of a bill
17. Pager's sound
18. "Alice" diner
20. "No Ordinary Love" singer
21. Nook
24. Play the ponies
26. Frontiersman Daniel
27. "Our ___ Will Come"
28. Used a shovel
31. Prickly seedcase
32. Nary a soul
34. Grp. putting on shows for troops
35. Since 1/1, to a CPA
36. And so on: abbr.
37. Sheets, pillowcases, etc.
39. ADA member
40. Ebb
41. High spirits
44. Rigatoni relative
45. Enthusiastic review
46. Goo in a 'do
47. Declines
51. Like summer tea
52. ___-Columbian era
53. "Don't go!"
54. Marine's meal
55. Lawn makeup
56. Go left or right

DOWN

1. Santa's helper
2. Soccer star Hamm
3. Israeli gun
4. Upstream swimmer
5. Syrup source
6. "As ___ saying . . ."
7. Stallone's nickname
8. Blue Ribbon brewer
9. Parasitic insect
10. Ran away from
11. Hunt and peck
19. Smoothed (out)
21. "Dear" advice-giver
22. Oaf
23. Parachute part
24. Forbid
25. Shoelace hole
27. "What's up, ___?"
28. Sand hill
29. Preowned
30. Used up
33. Fifth qtrs.

Puzzle 150

1	2	3	4	■	5	6	7	■	8	9	10	11
12				■	13			■	14			
15				■	16			■	17			
■	■	■	18	19			■	■	20			
21	22	23				■	24	25		■	■	■
26					■	27			■	28	29	30
31			■	32	33				■	34		
35			■	36			■	37	38			
■	■	■	39			■	40					
41	42	43		■	■	44				■	■	■
45				■	46			■	47	48	49	50
51				■	52			■	53			
54				■	55			■	56			

38. Most chilling
39. Ownership papers
40. Irritated
41. ___ Reaper
42. Doily material
43. Nights before holidays
44. Goose egg
46. Modern navigation syst.
48. A/C meas.
49. Saloon
50. Thesaurus wd.

Solution on Page 351

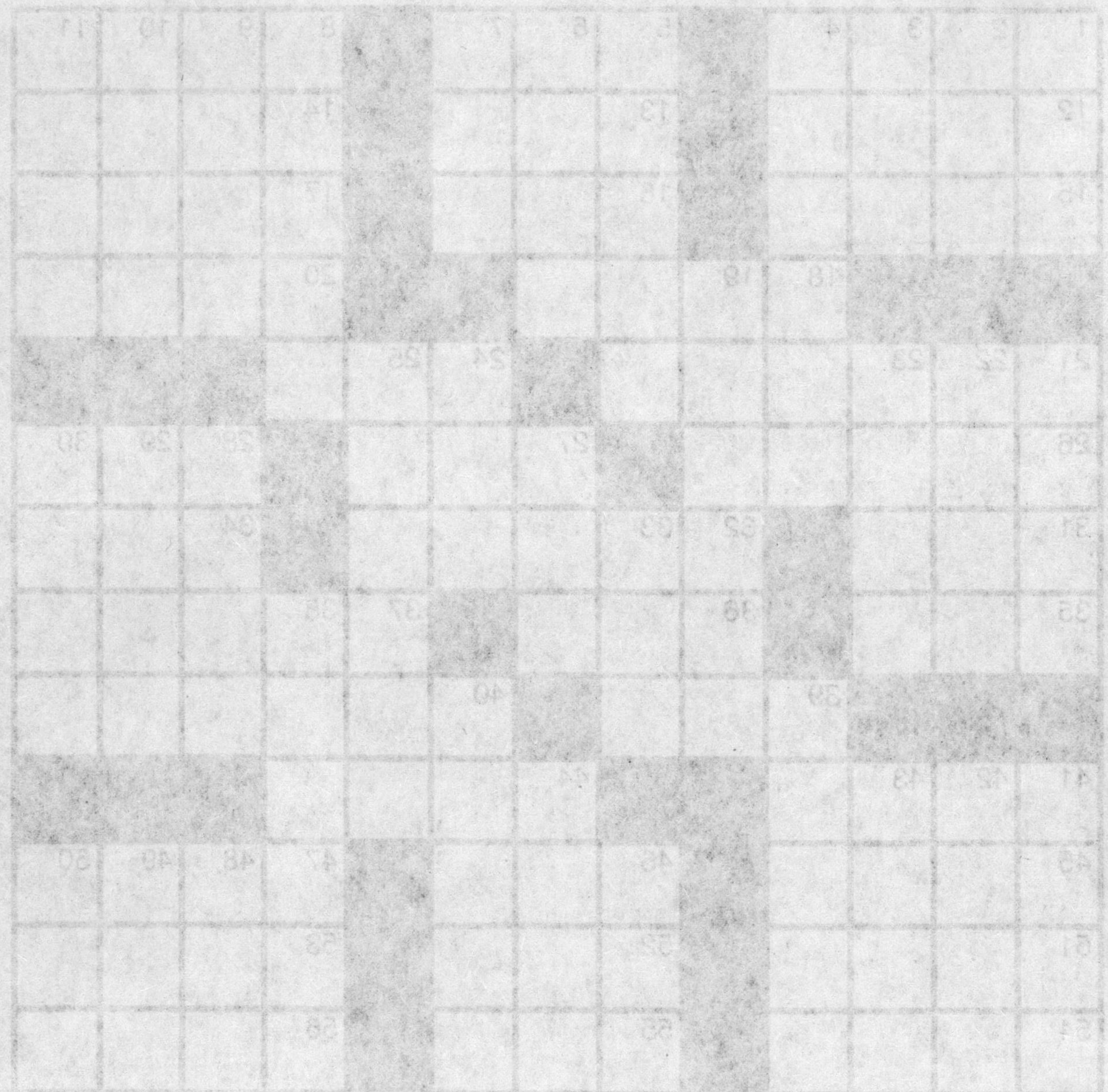

Answers

L	E	E	■	R	A	P	T	■	L	I	D	S
Y	I	N	■	E	L	I	A	■	S	A	R	A
E	N	D	A	N	G	E	R	■	A	T	O	P
■	■	■	D	E	A	R	■	S	T	E	P	S
M	A	R	I	E	■	C	A	P	S	■	■	■
E	L	I	E	■	S	E	G	A	■	O	R	A
E	P	L	U	R	I	B	U	S	U	N	U	M
T	S	E	■	O	G	R	E	■	N	I	L	E
■	■	■	S	I	N	O	■	L	I	T	E	R
B	A	S	I	L	■	S	P	O	T	■	■	■
A	C	E	R	■	I	N	A	S	E	N	S	E
M	I	N	E	■	M	A	R	E	■	S	O	N
A	D	D	S	■	A	N	T	S	■	A	X	E

Puzzle 1

G	A	L	E	■	M	D	S	E	■	R	A	M
A	S	I	S	■	T	O	L	L	■	E	R	A
T	I	P	S	■	V	I	A	L	■	S	E	T
E	A	S	E	■	■	N	Y	E	■	T	A	S
■	■	■	S	A	N	G	■	N	E	E	■	■
M	A	P	■	S	O	S	A	■	D	A	M	S
C	R	E	A	S	E	■	C	E	S	S	N	A
S	C	A	N	■	S	O	R	T	■	Y	O	N
■	■	R	N	A	■	P	E	A	S	■	■	■
R	O	T	■	M	A	E	■	■	L	E	S	S
O	A	R	■	A	U	R	A	■	A	L	E	G
O	R	E	■	S	T	A	G	■	T	I	N	T
T	S	E	■	S	O	S	O	■	S	A	T	S

Puzzle 2

C	L	A	D	■	C	O	N	■	S	T	I	R
P	E	T	E	■	B	R	A	■	T	I	N	Y
A	I	M	S	■	S	E	N	T	E	N	C	E
S	A	S	E	■	■	S	U	R	E	■	■	■
■	■	■	R	A	G	■	■	U	L	T	R	A
S	A	L	T	I	N	E	■	■	S	O	O	N
I	K	E	■	L	U	N	G	E	■	O	A	K
D	I	A	L	■	■	V	E	R	A	N	D	A
E	N	R	O	N	■	■	M	S	G	■	■	■
■	■	■	N	I	N	O	■	■	A	S	W	E
S	E	R	E	N	A	D	E	■	S	L	A	W
I	C	E	R	■	S	I	R	■	S	A	G	E
D	O	N	S	■	T	E	N	■	I	V	E	S

Puzzle 3

H	Y	D	E	■	C	P	U	■	C	R	O	P
B	O	R	N	■	A	L	T	■	H	O	U	R
O	K	E	D	■	T	E	A	R	I	N	T	O
■	E	W	O	K	■	A	H	S	■	■	■	■
■	■	■	W	I	T	S	■	T	R	A	S	H
L	I	D	■	S	H	E	D	■	A	L	O	E
E	L	A	P	S	E	■	A	S	H	O	R	E
A	I	D	E	■	M	A	T	E	■	T	E	L
P	E	S	T	O	■	D	E	E	M	■	■	■
■	■	■	■	W	O	O	■	P	A	L	S	■
S	A	Y	O	N	A	R	A	■	M	O	A	T
A	T	O	P	■	H	E	M	■	A	N	I	N
P	L	U	S	■	U	R	I	■	S	I	L	T

Puzzle 4

Puzzle 5

A	S	A	P		L	E	A		S	H	I	P
P	A	L	E		I	N	S		N	E	A	R
P	L	I	E		L	O	T		A	R	M	Y
S	T	E	L	L	A		R	E	G			
				A	C	R	I	D		M	A	P
E	A	S	E	D		E	D	U	C	A	T	E
A	G	E	D		S	U	E		P	I	N	E
R	E	A	S	O	N	S		T	A	L	O	N
P	S	T		D	E	E	R	E				
			S	E	A		A	L	T	A	R	S
C	A	S	E		K	A	T		O	P	A	L
N	Y	S	E		E	N	E		M	O	L	E
N	E	E	D		R	I	D		S	P	E	D

Puzzle 6

Puzzle 7

Puzzle 8

T	W	I	G		I	D	O	S		L	E	T
O	H	N	O		D	E	L	L		I	C	H
S	I	F	T		A	N	D	I		F	H	A
S	M	O	O	T	H		E	D	I	T	O	R
				L	O	A	N	E	R			
T	S	K		C	A	B			A	H	S	O
W	A	I	F		N	U	N		Q	U	A	D
A	L	M	A			S	A	W		G	P	S
			C	A	M	E	R	A				
S	C	H	E	M	E		R	H	O	N	D	A
N	A	Y		I	N	C	A		W	E	A	N
I	S	M		S	L	O	T		L	I	N	D
P	A	N		H	O	M	E		S	L	A	Y

Puzzle 9

S	C	A	B		S	P	A	S		N	P	R
C	A	S	A		T	A	U	T		Y	E	A
U	S	S	R		A	S	T	O		S	A	Y
M	E	T	E	O	R		O	R	D	E	R	S
				P	L	A	S	M	A			
S	I	P		S	I	X			M	A	S	C
K	I	E	V		T	I	E		P	U	L	P
Y	I	P	E			O	N	S		G	R	R
			N	O	R	M	A	L				
I	S	A	I	A	H		M	O	S	A	I	C
R	P	M		R	I	F	E		L	U	S	H
K	I	M		E	N	C	L		A	T	N	O
S	N	O		D	O	C	S		B	O	O	P

Puzzle 10

L	M	N		A	P	E	D		S	L	I	P
O	O	O		L	O	S	E		T	A	D	A
B	O	N		B	E	L	A		R	O	L	L
S	T	O	N	E			N	O	I	S	E	S
			I	R	K		S	O	P			
S	M	I	T	T	E	N		P	E	N	C	E
O	A	F			N	A	Y			O	U	R
N	O	I	S	Y		G	E	T	E	V	E	N
			T	A	D		N	E	D			
I	N	T	A	K	E			N	U	R	S	E
T	O	O	T		A	B	C	S		Y	T	D
S	U	L	U		L	U	R	E		E	E	G
A	N	D	S		T	R	O	D		S	P	Y

Puzzle 11

M	P	H		P	E	E	P		A	W	L	S
D	E	Y		A	L	L	A		L	O	C	H
S	A	P		R	I	M	S		I	N	D	Y
	K	E	G	S			T	U	G			
			R	E	A	M		S	N	O	U	T
F	L	U	E		H	A	R	M		U	F	O
R	E	G	G	I	E	J	A	C	K	S	O	N
E	E	L		S	M	O	G		I	T	S	Y
T	R	Y	S	T		R	U	S	T			
			W	O	K			L	E	F	T	
D	I	N	E		I	L	I	E		L	O	G
I	T	B	E		D	O	S	E		A	O	L
T	A	C	T		S	P	A	T		T	K	O

Puzzle 12

O	U	C	H		S	O	F	T		I	R	A
K	N	E	E		T	R	U	E		R	U	B
S	O	L	I	T	A	I	R	E		E	B	B
			D	U	G			N	I	N	E	R
S	P	L	I	T		S	T	Y	L	E		
T	O	E			A	P	U		E	C	O	N
E	L	M	S		R	A	T		T	A	P	E
P	O	O	H		T	R	U			R	E	X
		N	O	O	S	E		S	T	A	R	T
M	E	L	O	N			C	H	E			
A	V	A		T	O	P	B	A	N	A	N	A
S	E	W		O	D	I	E		D	D	A	Y
H	R	S		P	E	E	R		S	O	M	E

Puzzle 13

G	S	A		T	H	U			B	L	A	B
R	O	W		H	I	P	S		L	I	M	A
E	S	O	T	E	R	I	C		A	P	P	T
G	A	L	O	R	E		R	P	M			
			T	E	D		E	L	E	C	T	
L	I	M	E			H	E	Y		L	O	O
B	R	E	D		H	U	N		L	A	R	D
S	A	N		M	O	B			O	W	E	D
	S	U	S	A	N		S	I	R			
			L	Y	E		T	O	N	S	I	L
P	Y	R	E		S	T	O	N	E	A	G	E
B	E	E	P		T	I	K	I		Y	E	N
S	A	L	T			P	E	A		S	T	D

Puzzle 14

B	R	A		U	G	H	S		I	N	D	Y
B	I	C		N	E	E	T		D	A	D	A
C	O	L		D	R	N	O		A	T	T	Y
	T	U	B	E			P	A	H			
			O	R	G	Y		C	O	U	P	E
B	L	E	W		L	O	F	T		S	A	G
L	O	G		S	O	D	A	S		D	I	G
T	U	G		O	W	E	D		Z	A	N	Y
S	T	O	O	D		L	E	G	O			
			M	A	C			R	O	A	D	
P	Y	L	E		O	L	G	A		M	A	J
L	O	I	N		P	E	E	P		F	R	O
O	N	U	S		A	X	L	E		M	E	G

Puzzle 15

D	O	M			S	T	D		A	D	O	S
E	D	I	T		T	U	E		P	A	R	A
C	O	R	E		A	B	S		A	N	I	N
A	R	E	N	A	S		S	A	L			
			E	C	H	O	E	D		A	V	A
T	A	S	T	E		R	R	S		C	I	D
A	L	E	S		R	A	T		S	E	N	D
T	A	X		G	E	T		B	A	S	E	S
A	N	Y		R	H	E	S	U	S			
			D	E	E		A	S	S	E	S	S
S	A	S	E		A	P	R		E	L	L	E
I	L	I	E		T	E	A		S	L	A	T
N	I	T	S		S	T	N			A	M	A

Puzzle 16

Puzzle 17

MDSE CRO CARA
RIPS HEN APAL
ERIC AVA RUNS
DENALI NEB
PARADE HUG
MONEY LOG OFA
OPED EON SHOT
LEO CNN CHOSE
TNN IAGREE
SAC HEARST
OBIE TWI TUNE
NUKE ERN HEIR
TREK DYE ESPN

Puzzle 18

Puzzle 19

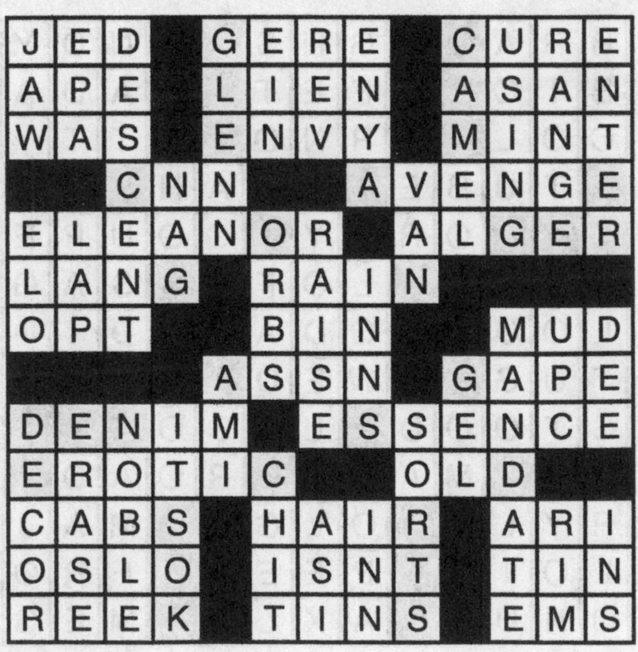

Puzzle 20

Puzzle 21

D	A	M	E	S		W	O	N		A	M	A
A	G	I	L	E		A	Y	E		R	A	D
D	O	G	P	A	D	D	L	E		I	N	D
			A	N	D			R	O	S	I	E
L	U	I	S		S	A	G		A	T	A	D
A	R	D	O	R		L	O	T	T	O		
D	I	E		E	V	I	T	A		T	I	P
		N	O	L	I	E		T	A	L	I	A
P	A	T	H		M	N	O		N	E	I	N
S	L	I	M	E			R	I	G			
A	B	C		A	R	E	A	C	O	D	E	S
L	E	A		R	U	N		B	R	A	V	O
M	E	L		P	E	G		M	A	N	E	S

Puzzle 22

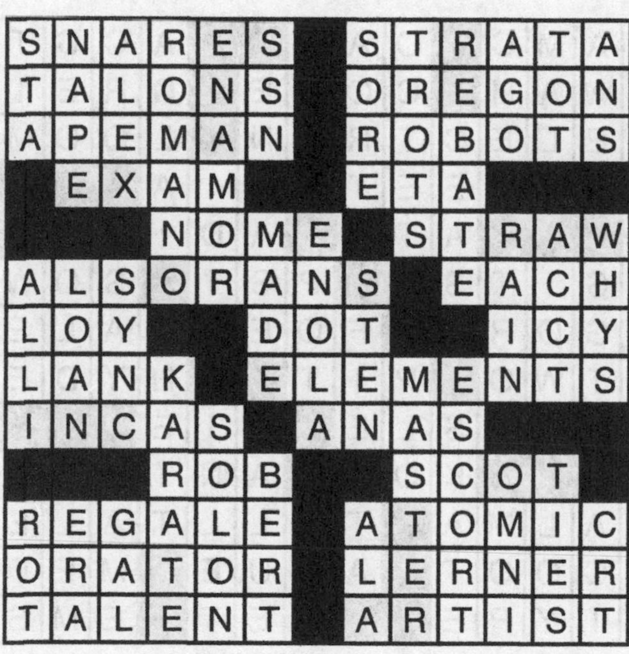

Puzzle 23

Puzzle 24

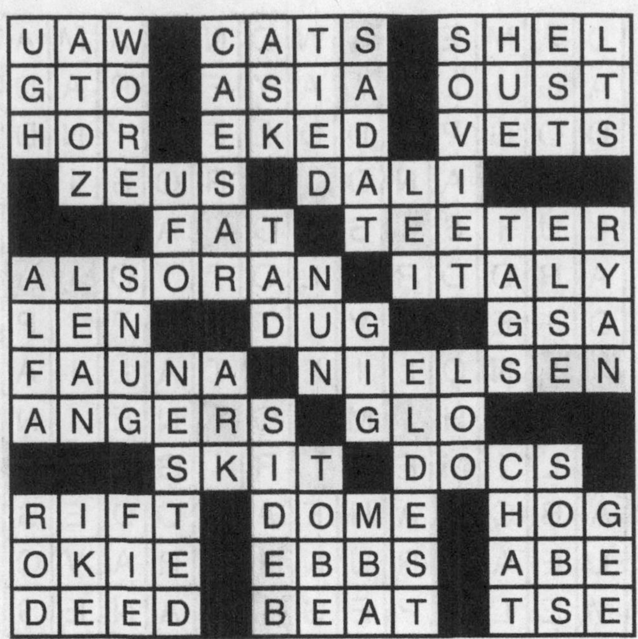

Puzzle 25

O	K	L	A	■	G	L	O	P	■	I	D	A
B	I	O	S	■	L	I	T	E	■	N	E	B
S	A	Y	C	H	E	E	S	E	■	A	M	C
■	■	■	I	O	N	■	■	V	A	L	I	D
A	D	M	I	T	■	H	Y	E	N	A	■	■
T	E	A	■	■	D	E	A	■	E	T	C	H
T	E	R	A	■	U	M	P	■	W	H	O	A
A	R	K	S	■	D	A	S	■	■	E	R	R
■	■	T	W	E	E	N	■	C	A	R	E	T
S	A	W	E	D	■	■	C	E	L	■	■	■
U	M	A	■	I	N	T	H	E	L	O	O	P
R	B	I	■	C	A	V	E	■	I	N	D	O
F	I	N	■	T	H	A	W	■	N	O	D	E

Puzzle 26

Puzzle 27

Puzzle 28

Puzzle 29

U	K	E		A	M	E	N		S	L	A	V
F	I	N		M	A	N	Y		T	O	N	E
O	N	A		B	Y	T	E		R	O	T	E
		M	O	L	A	R		E	A	T	E	R
O	C	O	M	E		A	B	L	Y			
D	A	R	N		A	P	A	L		C	O	G
O	N	E	I	L	L		L	E	T	H	A	L
R	E	D		O	V	I	D		H	A	T	E
			B	R	A	S		A	R	I	S	E
S	C	O	L	D		R	E	R	U	N		
C	O	V	E		D	A	M	S		S	I	S
A	M	E	S		N	E	M	O		A	S	K
T	A	N	S		A	L	A	N		W	H	Y

Puzzle 30

Puzzle 31

Puzzle 32

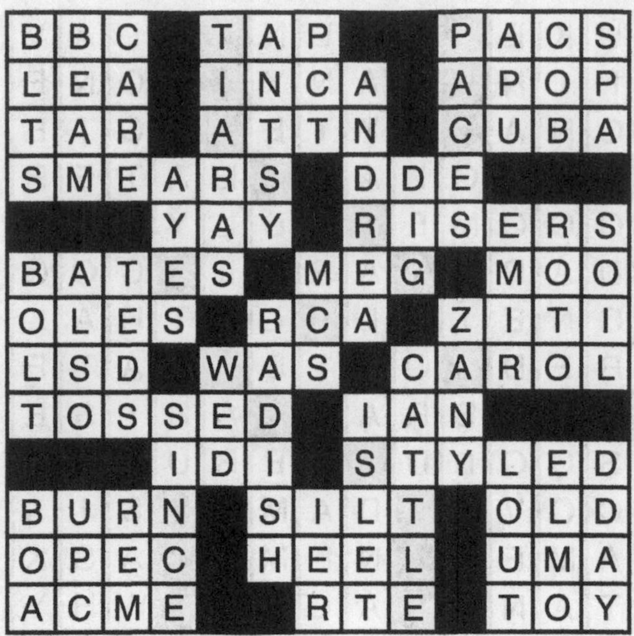

Puzzle 33

BRIT SAP MINI
ROOK CSI ISIT
ANNOTATE SELL
RBI STEEL
RINSE TAIL
UNITY CADETS
GATE FHA TRUE
NEPALI POEMS
ARON AESOP
SPASM TIC
LONI LINESMAN
AGED OMS EINE
TOTE GET CRAW

Puzzle 34

Puzzle 35

Puzzle 36

Puzzle 37

SAGS RAP ASPS
SITE ATM SHAG
EDEN MIS PEST
SWAT LISTS
AGREE SIR
LEASE OTTERS
LET RDS AMS
SEANCE TAROT
SHA OMEGA
SNAIL ACNE
LAVA ALE NCAA
ADIN AVE DEPP
PADS HAS SOUP

Puzzle 38

Puzzle 39

BEE ATO SANE
AMY SONS TINA
TIE LATECOMER
STORES LOO
POET ENGINE
SLEEPS SEESAW
ION ONA
NIECES SEASON
ENRICO ERIC
NON CARESS
ALIENATES LEO
LOAM RIDE ERN
ANNA NED SAY

Puzzle 40

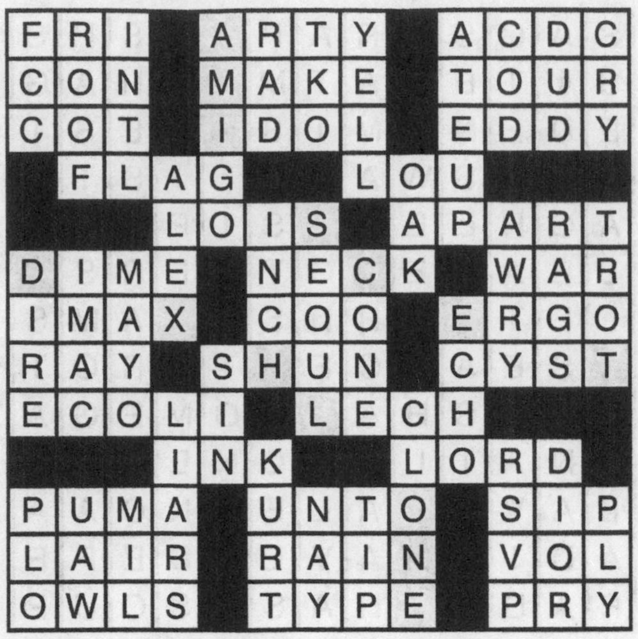

F	R	I		A	R	T	Y		A	C	D	C
C	O	N		M	A	K	E		T	O	U	R
C	O	T		I	D	O	L		E	D	D	Y
	F	L	A	G			L	O	U			
			L	O	I	S		A	P	A	R	T
D	I	M	E		N	E	C	K		W	A	R
I	M	A	X		C	O	O		E	R	G	O
R	A	Y		S	H	U	N		C	Y	S	T
E	C	O	L	I		L	E	C	H			
			I	N	K			L	O	R	D	
P	U	M	A		U	N	T	O		S	I	P
L	A	I	R		R	A	I	N		V	O	L
O	W	L	S		T	Y	P	E		P	R	Y

Puzzle 41

B	A	R	S		O	F	F	S		C	A	W
C	A	A	N		B	A	L	E		O	W	E
D	A	M	E		I	T	E	R	A	T	E	D
			A	B	E		D	I	T			
S	M	O	K	E				A	L	E	C	S
T	O	N		E	A	S	E	L		A	R	I
O	T	C			T	O	Y			T	A	G
I	O	U		P	E	T	E	R		A	N	N
C	R	E	P	E				O	A	T	E	S
			H	A	M		L	B	S			
R	O	A	D	R	A	C	E		C	A	S	T
A	O	K		L	R	O	N		A	V	O	W
G	P	A		S	C	O	T		P	E	S	O

Puzzle 42

S	A	S	E		G	E	E		A	H	A	S
O	R	G	Y		O	N	S		S	A	S	H
B	I	T	E		O	D	S		S	L	A	Y
S	A	S	S	E	S		E	A	T			
			O	C	E	A	N	S		S	Y	N
A	S	T	R	O		S	C	H		A	A	A
L	O	R	E		F	O	E		L	I	L	T
O	R	E		M	A	N		S	A	L	E	S
T	E	E		A	R	E	N	O	T			
			S	E	E		O	P	E	R	A	S
S	A	D	E		A	W	E		R	O	L	L
A	I	R	E		S	A	L		A	T	T	A
P	R	E	S		T	D	S		L	O	O	T

Puzzle 43

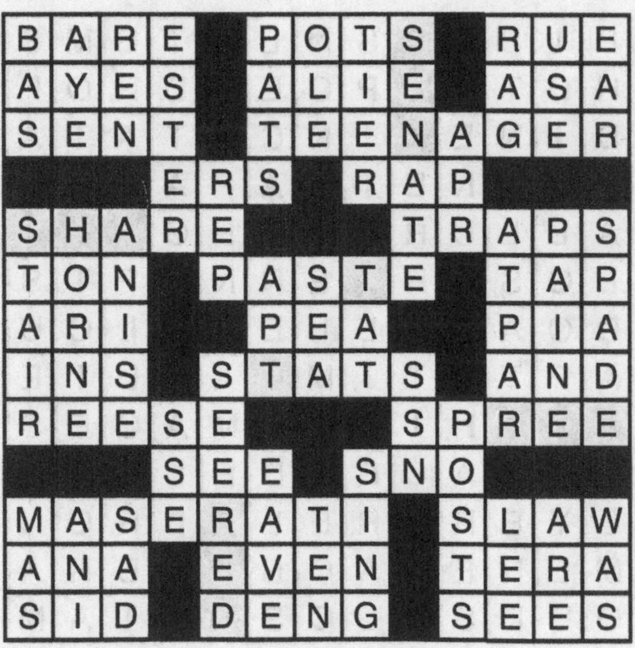

B	A	R	E		P	O	T	S		R	U	E
A	Y	E	S		A	L	I	E		A	S	A
S	E	N	T		T	E	E	N	A	G	E	R
			E	R	S		R	A	P			
S	H	A	R	E				T	R	A	P	S
T	O	N		P	A	S	T	E		T	A	P
A	R	I			P	E	A			P	I	A
I	N	S		S	T	A	T	S		A	N	D
R	E	E	S	E				S	P	R	E	E
			S	E	E		S	N	O			
M	A	S	E	R	A	T	I		S	L	A	W
A	N	A		E	V	E	N		T	E	R	A
S	I	D		D	E	N	G		S	E	E	S

Puzzle 44

N	F	L			D	D	E		B	O	I	L
O	L	E	S		A	U	G		A	N	N	A
R	U	N	T		N	O	G		R	A	N	G
M	E	T	R	I	C		E	B	B			
			O	R	E	I	D	A		S	T	L
T	E	L	L	S		N	O	D		O	R	I
A	W	O	L		M	A	N		R	U	E	D
R	A	S		U	A	W		B	O	R	E	S
A	N	S		P	E	E	R	E	D			
			U	S	S		I	D	E	A	L	S
H	E	R	R		T	A	N		O	V	A	L
E	V	E	L		R	I	D		S	I	N	E
W	E	B	S		O	M	S			D	E	W

Puzzle 45

I	T	T	O		A	M	A			C	P	A
C	H	O	P		M	O	D		S	H	U	N
B	A	R	E		A	N	D		A	I	N	T
M	I	N	N	E	S	O	T	A	F	A	T	S
			S	O	S		O	N	A			
B	T	U		N	E	D		I	R	I	S	H
L	U	R	E		D	O	S		I	N	C	A
T	E	N	T	H		C	I	D		K	I	D
			H	I	P		N	U	T			
M	U	S	I	C	A	L	C	H	A	I	R	S
O	T	I	C		N	E	E		M	O	A	T
S	A	G	S		A	I	R		P	U	M	A
S	H	H			M	A	E		A	S	S	N

Puzzle 46

P	U	B			C	H	A	T		H	A	D
G	R	A	B		P	O	P	E		I	C	Y
A	L	G	A		A	B	B	R		V	I	E
			I	F	S	O		S	H	E	D	S
C	A	C	T	I			Z	E	E			
O	H	M		B	O	N	O		H	U	L	A
G	O	O		S	A	I	N	T		N	O	R
S	Y	N	C		F	L	E	W		D	O	M
			P	C	S			I	C	O	N	S
O	C	T	A	L		B	E	N	Z			
H	U	B		A	J	A	X		A	R	F	S
M	R	S		S	A	K	E		R	E	B	A
Y	E	P		P	R	E	S			B	I	D

Puzzle 47

J	A	N		A	W	L			D	U	E	L
E	G	O		M	O	E			E	R	M	A
S	A	L		P	E	N	S		S	L	U	G
T	I	T	H	E		S	A	C	K			
S	N	E	E	R			H	A	S	S	L	E
			R	E	N	T	A	L		T	E	X
L	O	I	S		E	U	R		H	U	G	E
I	R	S		C	A	B	A	L	A			
T	E	A	S	E	R			A	L	T	O	S
			P	E	E	R		S	T	R	U	T
B	I	T	E		R	O	T	S		A	T	E
A	C	N	E			D	O	I		I	D	A
T	E	N	D			S	E	E		L	O	L

Puzzle 48

Puzzle 49

	F	I	R		O	N	A		P	A	R	
M	A	M	E		P	E	N		A	H	O	Y
A	W	O	L		T	W	A		S	A	V	E
O	N	K	E	Y		T	S	E	T	S	E	S
			A	D	D		T	E	A			
C	L	A	S	S	I	C	A	L		D	Y	E
H	O	N	E		M	O	S		S	O	R	E
A	L	T		D	E	M	I	T	A	S	S	E
			S	S	N		A	I	D			
C	A	M	E	L	O	T		S	N	A	R	L
E	L	E	V		V	O	L		E	L	E	C
L	U	R	E		E	T	A		S	E	N	D
	M	E	N		L	O	W		S	G	T	

Puzzle 50

Puzzle 51

Puzzle 52

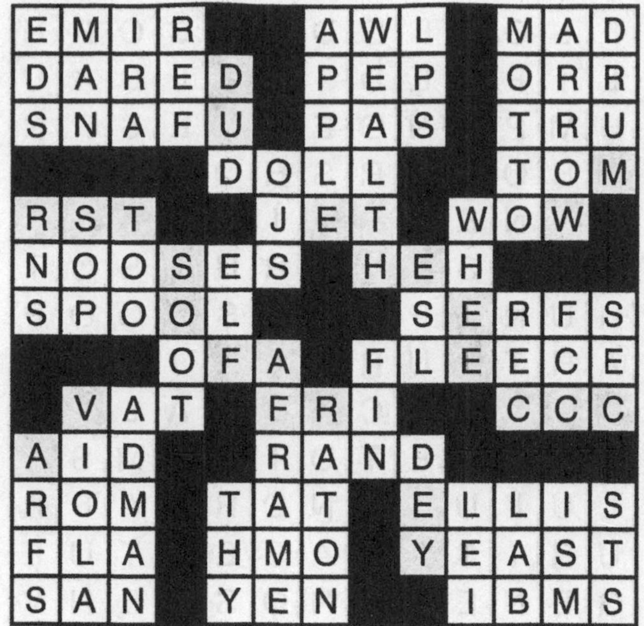

Puzzle 53

R	A	M	A		S	K	A			S	P	A
E	L	I	E		T	E	N		S	L	O	G
P	S	S	T		E	N	G		L	I	N	E
S	O	O	N	E	R	O	R	L	A	T	E	R
			A	L	E		Y	E	T			
M	D	S		M	O	M		M	E	S	A	S
I	O	U	S		S	A	C		S	O	P	H
S	A	N	T	A		P	A	C		P	O	E
			O	F	T		B	O	A			
I	D	E	N	T	I	C	A	L	T	W	I	N
B	R	I	E		N	O	R		B	A	S	E
I	N	N	S		T	O	E		A	R	O	W
D	O	S			S	S	T		T	E	N	T

Puzzle 54

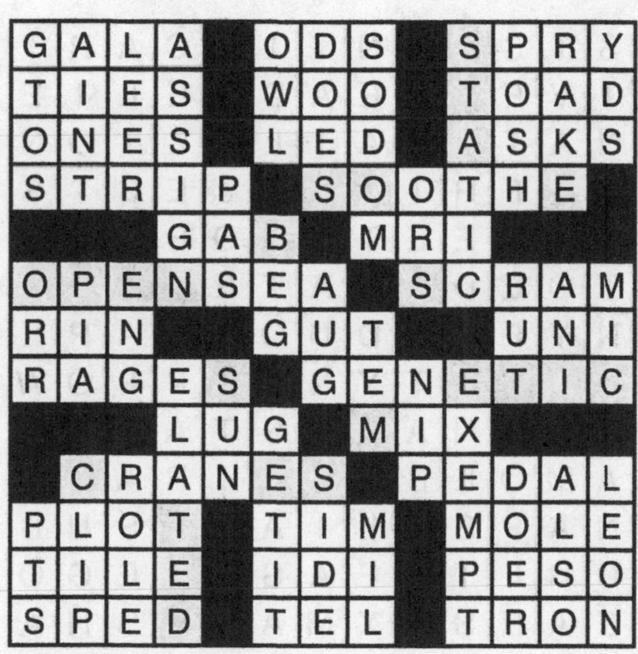

Puzzle 55

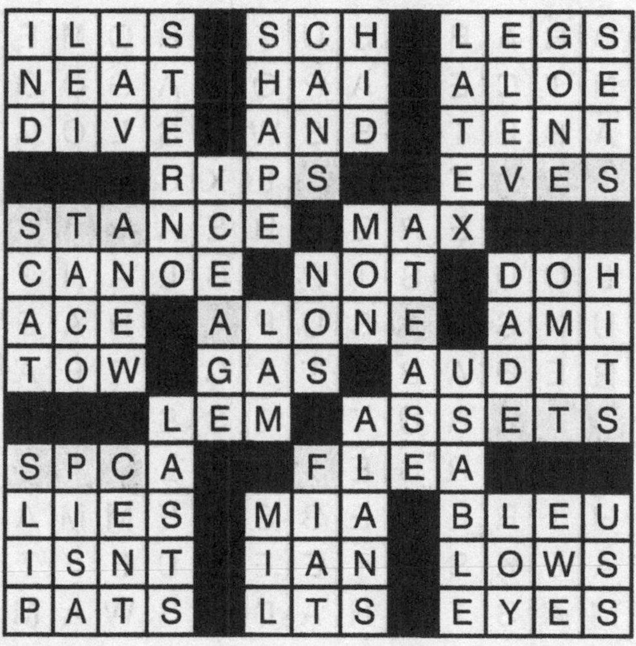

Puzzle 56

A	T	E	E		R	E	C		D	O	W	N
P	A	V	E		E	A	R		E	R	I	E
P	R	E	Y		S	T	U		M	E	S	S
S	T	R	O	D	E		S	N	O	O	P	S
			R	E	N		O	F	T			
L	A	M	E	N	T		E	L	E	C	T	S
I	V	E								A	R	K
V	E	N	E	E	R		A	R	A	B	I	A
			N	Y	E		G	I	L			
O	R	A	T	E	S		E	N	L	I	S	T
H	O	P	E		T	A	N		I	N	T	O
I	T	O	R		E	S	T		E	D	E	N
O	O	P	S		D	I	S		S	O	W	S

Puzzle 57

F	L	O		R	O	D			C	O	R	N
L	I	P		E	D	I	T		L	U	A	U
U	M	P		N	O	E	S		E	S	P	N
	B	O	X	E	R	S	H	O	R	T	S	
		N	E	W			I	N	K			
F	O	E	S			T	R	U		S	C	I
H	U	N		P	A	N	T	S		O	O	P
A	R	T		U	R	N			J	U	D	O
			A	R	C			P	A	L		
	C	O	M	E	T	O	T	E	R	M	S	
L	U	L	U		I	N	O	R		A	P	R
U	R	I	S		C	A	G	E		T	U	E
G	E	N	E			N	O	S		E	N	V

Puzzle 58

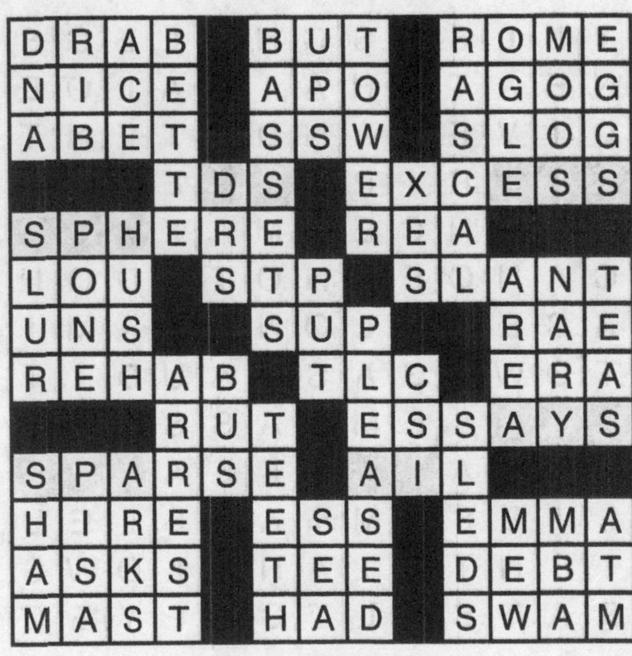

D	R	A	B		B	U	T		R	O	M	E
N	I	C	E		A	P	O		A	G	O	G
A	B	E	T		S	S	W		S	L	O	G
			T	D	S		E	X	C	E	S	S
S	P	H	E	R	E		R	E	A			
L	O	U		S	T	P		S	L	A	N	T
U	N	S			S	U	P			R	A	E
R	E	H	A	B		T	L	C		E	R	A
			R	U	T		E	S	S	A	Y	S
S	P	A	R	S	E		A	I	L			
H	I	R	E		E	S	S		E	M	M	A
A	S	K	S		T	E	E		D	E	B	T
M	A	S	T		H	A	D		S	W	A	M

Puzzle 59

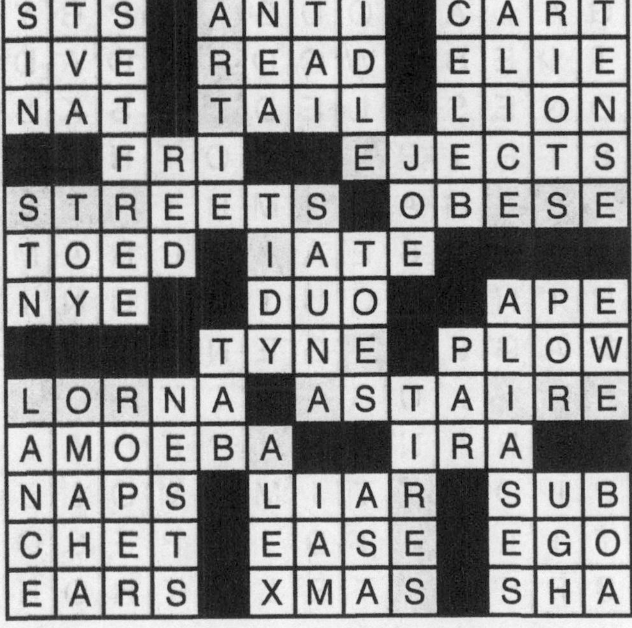

S	T	S		A	N	T	I		C	A	R	T
I	V	E		R	E	A	D		E	L	I	E
N	A	T		T	A	I	L		L	I	O	N
		F	R	I			E	J	E	C	T	S
S	T	R	E	E	T	S		O	B	E	S	E
T	O	E	D		I	A	T	E				
N	Y	E			D	U	O			A	P	E
				T	Y	N	E		P	L	O	W
L	O	R	N	A		A	S	T	A	I	R	E
A	M	O	E	B	A			I	R	A		
N	A	P	S		L	I	A	R		S	U	B
C	H	E	T		E	A	S	E		E	G	O
E	A	R	S		X	M	A	S		S	H	A

Puzzle 60

Puzzle 61

ALS ARR LASSO
SAT HEE ASKEW
IDO SAC SPIEL
ALL SUIT
NEET ORG DON
INN ONSALE
LOADS PANDA
INSEAM SRS
EEK RAT HOSS
TILE ROT
ASTRO ORD ANA
TENTS FEE LIL
MATES TOM SAL

Puzzle 62

Puzzle 63

Puzzle 64

Puzzle 65

P	B	S		A	B	U	T		U	N	I	T
F	I	T		S	A	S	H		S	O	D	A
F	L	U		T	R	O	Y		S	N	O	B
T	E	N	U	R	E			D	R	E	S	S
			M	O	R	O	S	E				
T	A	R	P	S		N	U	N		I	C	Y
H	I	P	S		Z	A	P		I	P	O	D
E	L	M		P	E	I		I	D	O	L	S
				E	N	R	A	G	E			
L	A	L	A	W			I	N	A	S	E	C
I	M	A	X		F	I	D	O		O	X	O
M	E	T	E		I	C	E	R		U	P	S
O	R	E	L		R	U	S	E		L	O	T

Puzzle 66

Puzzle 67

Puzzle 68

Puzzle 69

A	S	P	S		L	A	C	E		H	A	T
O	P	I	E		A	N	O	N		A	M	I
N	A	N	A		C	A	P	E		Z	E	E
E	N	E	M	I	E	S			H	E	N	S
			A	N	S		B	R	R			
B	A	R	N	S		S	E	E	S	R	E	D
E	S	S		A	L	I	N	E		E	V	A
T	I	T	A	N	I	C		S	A	F	E	S
			G	E	E		P	E	R			
C	A	S	E			E	A	S	I	E	S	T
A	P	E		S	A	Y	S		S	A	W	S
S	E	W		A	X	E	S		T	R	I	P
A	D	S		W	E	R	E		A	L	M	S

Puzzle 70

Puzzle 71

Puzzle 72

Puzzle 73

NBC SECS SLAB
BOO CTRL EAVE
AOK OCTO EYED
BEST THY
USPS AARON
TIDE OOHS EMU
WHITEELEPHANT
OOO ATOM IRIS
SPRAT SILK
BAD AERO
TRAY IMON OKS
EATS VANE ORG
DYES ADOS MAT

Puzzle 74

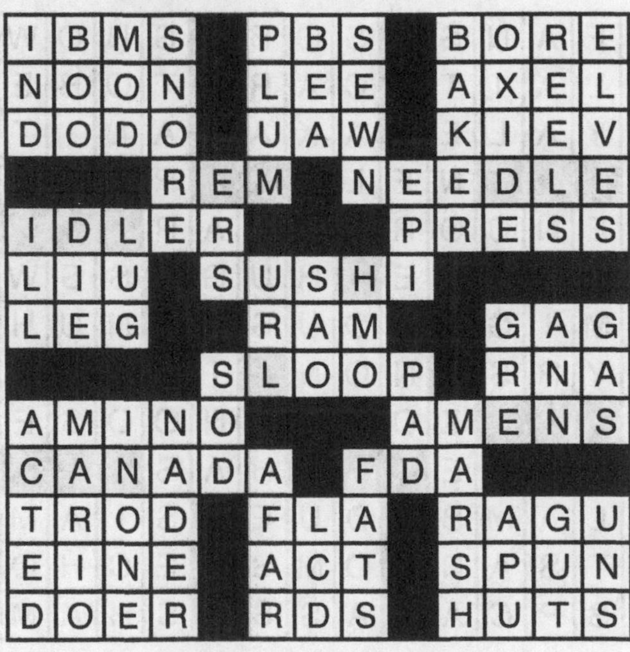

Puzzle 75

Puzzle 76

Puzzle 77

D	R	A	T		U	S	C		C	O	P	A
D	I	N	E		N	O	D		A	V	O	N
T	O	Y	S		T	A	S		P	E	R	K
			T	T	O	P		K	O	R	E	A
S	H	E	E	R			P	I	T			
T	E	T	R	A		D	E	T	E	S	T	
P	A	T			W	A	G			M	I	C
	L	E	E	W	A	Y		L	A	U	R	A
			R	O	D			A	N	T	E	D
S	A	L	O	N		B	A	B	E			
P	L	O	D		P	A	C		M	A	M	E
I	T	B	E		R	A	D		I	R	O	N
T	A	S	S		E	S	C		A	C	E	D

Puzzle 78

Puzzle 79

Puzzle 80

Puzzle 81

L	A	N		A	B	L	E		S	I	P	S
T	I	E		Z	E	A	L		H	E	A	R
D	D	S		T	A	S	K		A	R	M	S
	S	T	Y	E			S	O	D			
			A	C	T	S		T	E	S	L	A
T	A	R	P		E	K	E	S		L	A	P
O	T	I	S		D	E	A		L	O	N	E
P	M	S		U	S	E	R		O	W	E	S
S	E	E	D	S		T	S	K	S			
			Y	A	P			N	E	S	S	
M	O	R	E		A	N	T	E		T	I	S
A	F	A	R		P	A	L	E		A	L	L
C	A	W	S		A	B	C	S		T	O	Y

Puzzle 82

Puzzle 83

Puzzle 84

Puzzle 85

S	P	I	C	E		C	R	Y		S	P	A
T	E	N	O	R		H	U	E		O	R	B
U	N	S	E	R		R	N	S		B	O	O
			D	E	M	O			M	E	N	D
C	P	U		D	E	M		B	A	R	G	E
H	I	S			R	E	L	I	C			
I	T	A	L	I	C		I	N	S	T	E	P
			A	V	I	A	N			H	E	M
S	A	R	G	E		C	D	S		O	K	S
H	M	O	S			C	A	L	F			
O	B	S		C	O	O		O	R	B	I	T
V	E	E		A	P	R		P	E	A	C	E
E	R	S		L	S	D		E	T	H	E	L

Puzzle 86

Puzzle 87

Puzzle 88

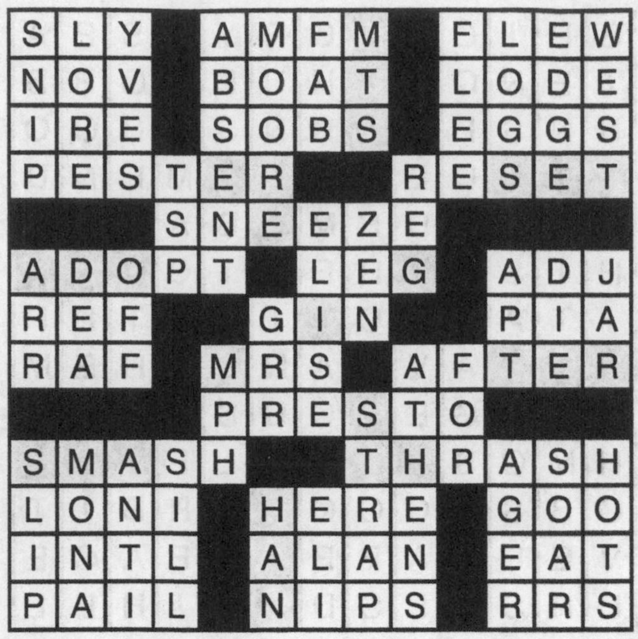

S	L	Y		A	M	F	M		F	L	E	W
N	O	V		B	O	A	T		L	O	D	E
I	R	E		S	O	B	S		E	G	G	S
P	E	S	T	E	R			R	E	S	E	T
			S	N	E	E	Z	E				
A	D	O	P	T		L	E	G		A	D	J
R	E	F			G	I	N			P	I	A
R	A	F		M	R	S		A	F	T	E	R
				P	R	E	S	T	O			
S	M	A	S	H			T	H	R	A	S	H
L	O	N	I		H	E	R	E		G	O	O
I	N	T	L		A	L	A	N		E	A	T
P	A	I	L		N	I	P	S		R	R	S

Puzzle 89

E	A	R	S		L	B	S		S	T	E	M
S	T	Y	E		O	L	E		T	A	R	A
S	E	E	R		O	U	T		A	T	I	T
			E	I	N	E		T	R	E	E	S
P	L	A	N	E		I	T	O	R			
O	I	L	E	R		N	O	T		A	C	T
E	S	L			R	T	E			C	A	R
M	A	I		A	A	H		D	A	N	T	E
			T	Y	N	E		D	R	E	S	S
L	A	T	H	E		F	A	T	E			
A	L	O	E		F	A	T		N	A	S	A
L	E	I	S		A	C	E		A	L	A	N
A	X	L	E		N	E	E		S	E	N	D

Puzzle 90

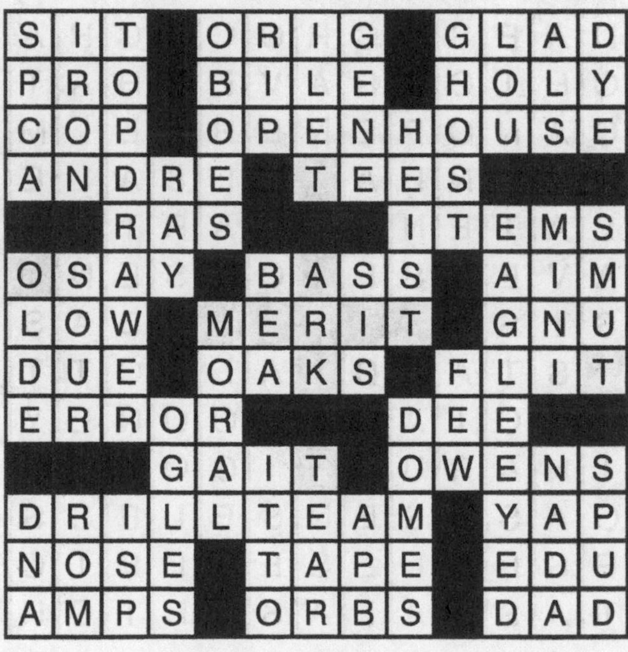

S	I	T		O	R	I	G		G	L	A	D
P	R	O		B	I	L	E		H	O	L	Y
C	O	P		O	P	E	N	H	O	U	S	E
A	N	D	R	E		T	E	E	S			
		R	A	S				I	T	E	M	S
O	S	A	Y		B	A	S	S		A	I	M
L	O	W		M	E	R	I	T		G	N	U
D	U	E		O	A	K	S		F	L	I	T
E	R	R	O	R				D	E	E		
			G	A	I	T		O	W	E	N	S
D	R	I	L	L	T	E	A	M		Y	A	P
N	O	S	E		T	A	P	E		E	D	U
A	M	P	S		O	R	B	S		D	A	D

Puzzle 91

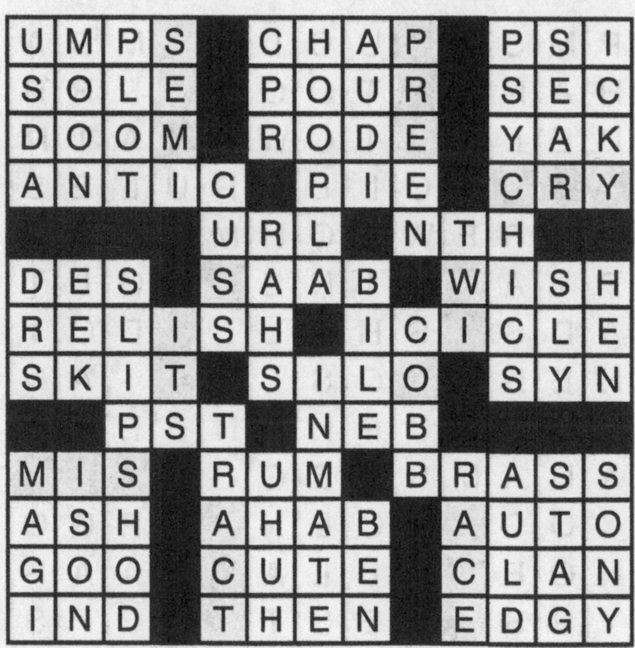

U	M	P	S		C	H	A	P		P	S	I
S	O	L	E		P	O	U	R		S	E	C
D	O	O	M		R	O	D	E		Y	A	K
A	N	T	I	C		P	I	E		C	R	Y
				U	R	L		N	T	H		
D	E	S		S	A	A	B		W	I	S	H
R	E	L	I	S	H		I	C	I	C	L	E
S	K	I	T		S	I	L	O		S	Y	N
		P	S	T		N	E	B				
M	I	S		R	U	M		B	R	A	S	S
A	S	H		A	H	A	B		A	U	T	O
G	O	O		C	U	T	E		C	L	A	N
I	N	D		T	H	E	N		E	D	G	Y

Puzzle 92

S	L	I	D		O	F	F	S		B	R	R
P	E	S	O		F	O	A	M		Y	O	U
U	N	I	T		F	E	T	E		T	A	D
N	O	S	E	S				L	E	E	R	Y
				O	R	A	C	L	E			
G	M	T		B	E	L	A		N	O	I	R
R	E	A	P		S	I	B		Y	A	L	E
R	A	G	E		I	B	I	D		K	L	M
			E	L	N	I	N	O				
S	T	A	K	E				G	L	O	S	S
P	U	B		E	B	B	S		O	C	T	A
E	B	B		R	O	T	E		B	T	U	S
W	A	R		S	O	U	P		S	O	N	S

Puzzle 93

G	R	E		R	E	F			S	P	R	Y
M	O	N		O	W	E	S		P	L	E	A
T	U	G		G	A	Z	A		R	A	N	K
	T	A	K	E	N		C	H	A	N	T	
		G	E	T		P	R	A	Y			
B	R	I	G			H	E	M		P	J	S
Y	I	N		T	O	A	D	S		R	A	H
E	G	G		R	N	S			D	E	N	Y
			W	E	R	E		C	A	T		
	H	A	I	K	U		L	A	Y	E	R	
B	O	R	N		S	P	U	R		N	O	T
C	H	I	C		H	A	L	T		S	I	S
D	O	Z	E			C	U	E		E	L	K

Puzzle 94

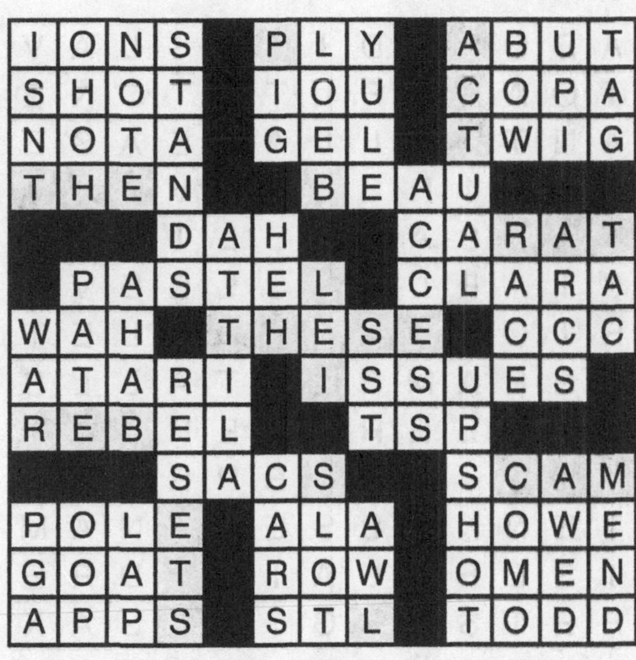

I	O	N	S		P	L	Y		A	B	U	T
S	H	O	T		I	O	U		C	O	P	A
N	O	T	A		G	E	L		T	W	I	G
T	H	E	N			B	E	A	U			
			D	A	H			C	A	R	A	T
	P	A	S	T	E	L		C	L	A	R	A
W	A	H		T	H	E	S	E		C	C	C
A	T	A	R	I		I	S	S	U	E	S	
R	E	B	E	L			T	S	P			
			S	A	C	S			S	C	A	M
P	O	L	E		A	L	A		H	O	W	E
G	O	A	T		R	O	W		O	M	E	N
A	P	P	S		S	T	L		T	O	D	D

Puzzle 95

F	B	I		C	I	D			T	O	M	E
L	A	N		O	R	A	L		I	V	A	N
O	J	S		C	O	M	E		D	I	N	G
P	A	T	R	O	N		T	R	A	D	E	R
			Y	A	Y		T	E	L			
P	Y	L	E			H	E	X		N	F	L
L	E	I	S		G	E	R		D	I	E	T
Y	T	D		M	R	S			O	P	E	D
			T	U	E		M	I	D			
T	I	R	A	D	E		A	N	O	I	N	T
O	R	E	M		T	H	I	N		N	E	W
F	A	D	E		S	I	N	E		C	H	I
U	S	S	R			P	E	R		H	I	T

Puzzle 96

Puzzle 97

TINY MACE CHA
OHIO PLOP LAS
SONG HALO ARK
SPEAK SEC PTS
ELK HAT
CHE ROAM TRAM
POPART ARMADA
URIS SINO PJS
SKI NNW
HBO MED SANDS
OLD PRIM REAL
WOE EGGO CARA
LTS LOOM HTTP

Puzzle 98

Puzzle 99

Puzzle 100

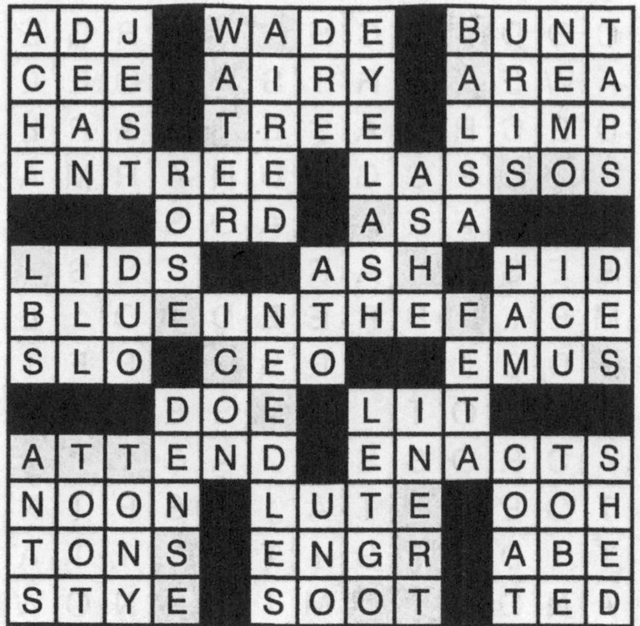

Puzzle 101

BIRD MOBS TAP
AGUE GNAT AYE
DOTS MESA PEP
ETHIC GEESE
ARISEN
MON PINT CRAM
RUBE DUO LUBE
STAY ESPN BEG
RAREST
LASER HOSTS
ABC ACDC WHOA
BOO BOAR LADD
SOT SONY SHOE

Puzzle 102

Puzzle 103

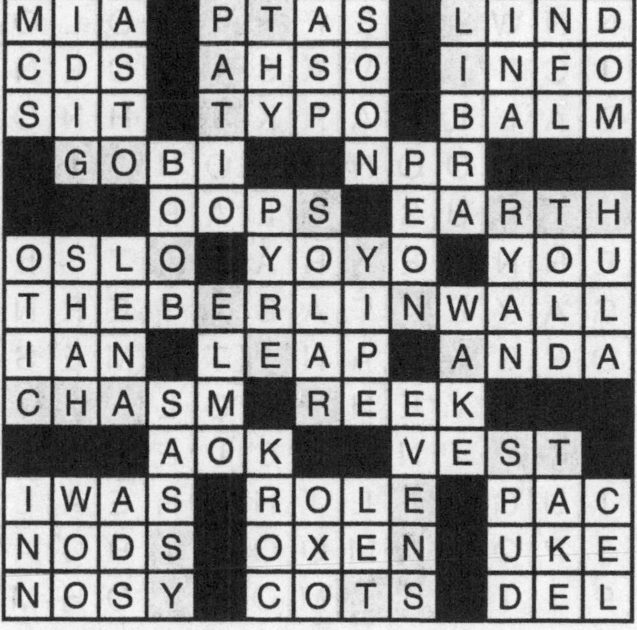

Puzzle 104

K	O	S		I	N	T	O		Y	O	D	A
E	K	E		N	E	O	N		A	B	E	T
D	I	P		S	A	W	S		N	O	L	O
S	E	T	T	E	R			S	K	E	I	N
			A	T	S	T	A	K	E			
M	E	E	T	S		O	R	I	E	N	T	S
C	A	W			A	N	T			B	A	Y
S	T	E	E	P	L	E		T	R	A	I	N
			A	T	I	S	S	U	E			
S	P	A	R	S			A	R	O	M	A	S
P	E	N	N		M	I	T	T		A	P	T
E	T	T	E		E	V	I	L		R	E	A
W	E	E	D		T	Y	N	E		S	S	N

Puzzle 105

C	O	D		S	C	H			U	R	G	E
A	W	E		I	R	I	S		N	O	E	L
D	E	C	R	E	A	S	E		E	A	R	L
			E	G	G		D	H	A	R	M	A
K	N	I	F	E		T	A	O	S			
L	E	S	S		A	R	T	L	E	S	S	
M	E	L		B	R	E	E	D		O	I	L
	D	E	L	E	T	E	S		P	F	F	T
			O	T	I	S		S	E	A	T	S
A	C	R	O	S	S		Z	A	G			
T	O	E	S		T	A	I	L	S	P	I	N
T	I	D	E		S	I	T	S		I	T	A
A	N	O	N			M	I	A		N	O	W

Puzzle 106

N	N	W		R	E	F			S	O	L	O
I	C	E		E	V	A	S		C	O	E	N
B	A	L	L	P	A	R	K		O	H	N	O
S	A	L	O	O	N		Y	O	U			
			U	S	S		L	A	R	I	A	T
E	R	N	I	E		R	A	F		T	I	E
G	A	Y	E		T	A	B		T	E	R	N
O	P	S		K	A	N		T	I	M	E	S
S	T	E	V	E	N		A	O	L			
			I	N	D		C	L	E	A	T	S
T	U	G	S		E	T	H	E	R	E	A	L
S	P	O	T		M	O	O	D		R	C	A
P	I	T	A			M	O	O		O	H	M

Puzzle 107

K	I	M		C	O	R	E		D	E	M	I
I	C	E		E	V	E	N		A	X	I	S
D	U	D		D	E	N	G		T	E	R	I
		I	V	A	N	A		B	E	S	E	T
A	N	E	A	R		M	B	A	S			
L	E	V	I		M	E	I	R		E	L	I
L	E	A	N	T	O		A	N	A	L	O	G
S	T	L		R	O	B	S		H	E	R	O
			L	I	N	E		R	A	C	E	R
M	A	D	A	M		W	R	E	S	T		
A	R	O	W		M	A	U	I		R	U	G
M	A	N	N		G	R	I	N		I	M	A
A	B	E	S		M	E	N	S		C	A	P

Puzzle 108

A	P	P		S	P	A	R		C	A	M	E
T	A	I		P	E	L	E		A	L	O	E
T	N	T		A	L	T	O		L	O	L	L
A	S	S	E	R	T			M	E	T	E	S
			L	E	S	S	E	E				
R	A	P	I	D		L	O	T		R	A	E
I	T	S			M	A	N			T	O	M
M	A	T		L	A	T		S	M	E	L	T
				S	I	E	S	T	A			
S	A	L	A	D			T	R	E	A	T	S
A	B	E	S		B	O	R	E		T	O	P
K	E	N	S		I	D	E	S		T	R	A
S	T	A	N		T	S	P	S		N	A	Y

Puzzle 109

C	C	C		A	L	L	S		E	T	C	H
R	A	Y		S	O	Y	S		G	E	R	E
O	N	A	S	P	R	E	E		R	E	E	F
C	E	N	T	E	R	S		M	E	T	S	
			E	N	E		D	E	T	E	C	T
I	D	E	A	S		B	I	D		R	E	O
S	I	N	K		A	L	S		K	E	N	T
M	R	T		N	U	T		H	A	D	T	O
S	T	R	O	N	G		D	A	B			
	P	A	R	E		A	E	R	O	S	O	L
P	O	N	E		P	A	R	A	B	O	L	A
C	O	C	O		S	H	E	S		L	I	D
T	R	E	S		T	S	K	S		O	N	S

Puzzle 110

A	M	Y		E	W	O	K		G	L	I	B
R	A	M		L	E	I	A		R	O	S	E
F	C	C		D	E	N	T		A	P	P	T
S	H	A	M	E		K	E	Y	S			
			P	R	Y			O	P	A	L	S
P	O	O	H		I	M	O	K		L	O	W
U	P	C		S	P	O	K	E		F	A	A
P	E	T		P	E	T	E		W	A	N	T
S	C	O	P	E			D	O	H			
			O	W	N	S		D	O	G	M	A
C	U	B	E		A	L	P	O		L	A	B
B	A	A	S		P	A	I	R		O	Y	L
S	W	A	Y		A	M	E	S		B	A	Y

Puzzle 111

	G	P	S		J	O	B		S	K	A	
C	L	O	P		A	N	Y		A	L	T	O
P	U	R	E		M	O	E		N	E	M	O
R	E	E	N	T	E	R		S	T	E	E	P
			T	V	S		S	E	A			
P	O	W		A	B	O	U	T	F	A	C	E
A	L	I	E		O	R	G		E	R	A	S
L	E	N	D	A	N	E	A	R		C	B	S
			A	D	D		R	E	D			
T	O	R	S	O		A	C	C	O	S	T	S
I	R	A	N		P	T	A		U	H	O	H
N	I	K	E		E	I	N		S	A	G	A
	G	E	R		G	T	E		E	G	O	

Puzzle 112

G	O	T		S	A	K	E		A	P	P	T
R	K	O		E	B	A	Y		W	I	R	E
A	L	I	E	N	A	T	E		A	C	E	D
M	A	L	A	I	S	E		I	R	A	S	
			T	O	E		O	B	E	Y	E	D
L	I	N	E	R		R	U	M		U	N	O
A	T	O	N		T	U	T		A	N	T	I
S	S	N		V	A	T		C	R	E	S	T
S	A	S	S	E	D		T	E	E			
	D	E	E	T		S	O	A	N	D	S	O
T	E	N	N		E	L	A	S	T	I	C	S
S	A	S	S		P	O	S	E		N	A	H
K	L	E	E		A	P	T	S		O	R	A

Puzzle 113

H	O	A	X		S	L	O		S	E	E	M
A	N	N	E		L	A	W		A	X	L	E
S	E	A	S	C	A	P	E		G	I	L	T
H	I	S		U	S	S		R	A	T	E	S
			S	P	H	E	R	E	S			
A	F	R	O			D	O	N		V	O	W
A	R	A	B	L	E		D	O	N	A	T	E
H	O	P		O	K	S			O	N	C	E
			S	T	E	W	A	R	D			
M	A	S	T	S		E	C	O		B	I	C
O	A	H	U		A	D	H	E	R	E	T	O
S	H	I	N		S	E	E		A	T	O	N
T	S	P	S		A	N	S		F	A	N	S

Puzzle 114

T	L	C			A	S	H			H	A	I
R	A	H		C	R	A	M	P		O	J	S
A	S	I	A	M	I	N	O	R		M	A	I
			H	O	E	D		A	L	E	R	T
T	E	T	O	N	S		B	I	B			
A	W	R	Y			B	A	S	S	E	T	
C	E	O		P	L	A	T	E		A	R	I
	S	T	A	R	E	S			T	R	I	B
			M	I	X		S	L	A	L	O	M
P	O	S	S	E		M	A	I	M			
E	L	O		S	N	A	K	E	E	Y	E	S
P	G	A		T	I	R	E	D		E	L	K
E	A	R			P	C	S			P	S	I

Puzzle 115

T	S	A	R		P	E	A		S	P	A	T
R	I	P	E		O	R	S		T	O	D	O
A	R	T	S		R	A	S		A	L	O	T
P	S	S	T		E	S	E		R	O	S	S
			A	S	S	E	N	T	S			
P	L	A	T	O		S	T	A		A	H	A
T	O	N	E	R				P	A	C	E	R
S	A	G		E	E	L		E	S	T	E	E
			A	R	R	E	A	R	S			
M	O	R	N		R	E	B		I	T	S	A
A	R	I	D		O	R	B		S	O	A	R
Z	A	N	E		R	A	E		T	O	G	A
E	L	K	S		S	T	Y		S	L	A	B

Puzzle 116

Puzzle 117

SOOT DRS SETA
URNS IER ALEC
DEEP MAS LSAT
SOT SEC STEMS
ORI TENS
ALOUD SUE EBB
SONNET REDSEA
HUE CIA RETAG
RAMP ELI
SABER PAD MRS
EXES PET WAIT
MILE CAT ETTA
ISLE TRY BEER

Puzzle 118

Puzzle 119

Puzzle 120

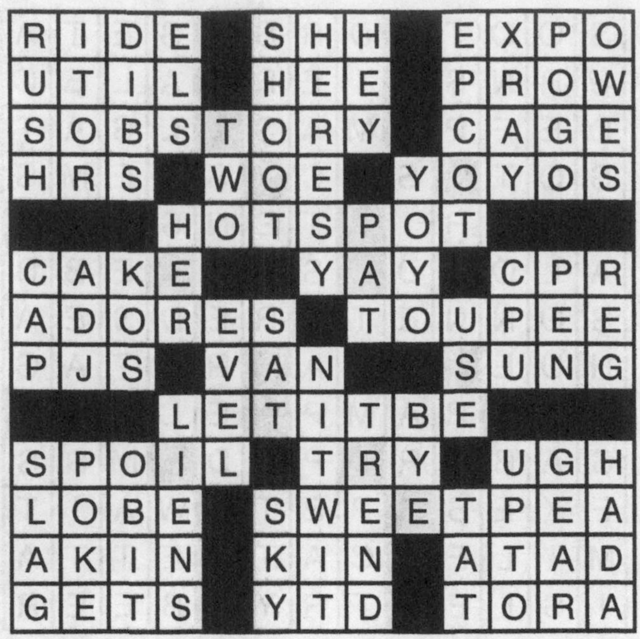

Puzzle 121

CLAP SGTS DOI
LOST TEAK OBS
ARIA AMBI NIL
YESSIR SEDATE
RRS RAT
ARR SET RIDS
LOEW DAS TOOT
ABLE FAB NAN
EDU FLU
CLASPS ISAACS
LOS SAME CLOT
AGE EVAN LALA
MOD TEXT USER

Puzzle 122

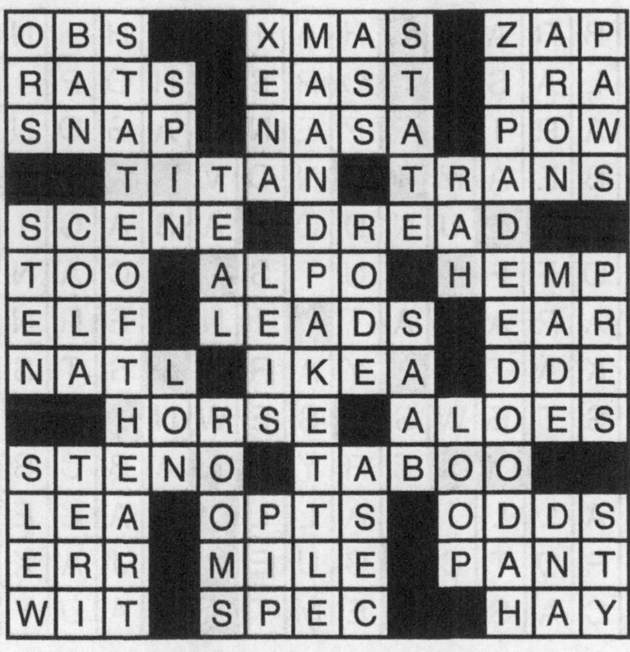

Puzzle 123

Puzzle 124

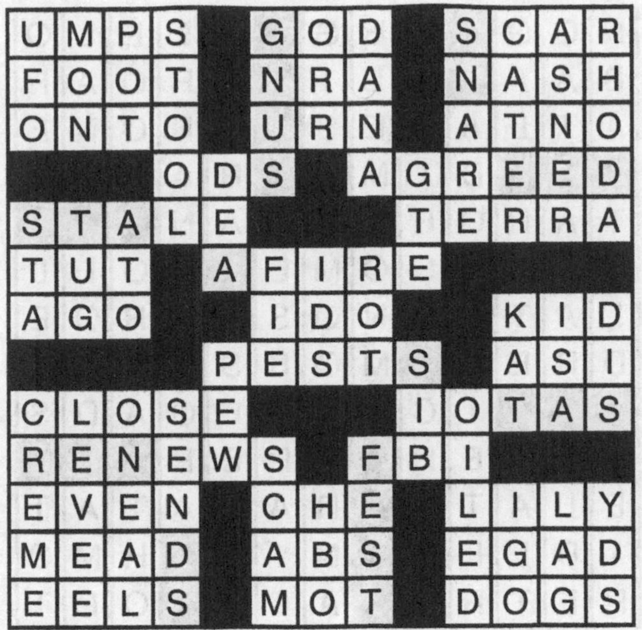

Puzzle 125

UTIL AHS MIRO
SOSO CUP AMEX
EMIT THE RUDE
DENIRO EDISON
OUR DON
SCENTS YIELDS
EIN COT
TAVERN ELUDED
LEO MAN
ARDENT IDIOTS
MERV BEN TRIO
BANE AXE EENY
IMON DEM SOTS

Puzzle 126

Puzzle 127

Puzzle 128

M	A	C		F	D	A		T	R	A	C	E
I	S	A		E	S	T		R	E	L	A	Y
T	H	U		B	L	T		A	B	A	T	E
T	E	S	H			I	A	M	A			
S	N	E	A	D		R	D	S		B	O	G
			T	O	N	E	D			U	N	I
L	E	T	S	G	O		E	V	E	N	T	S
E	N	O			M	A	R	I	A			
I	V	Y		G	A	G		M	C	G	E	E
			C	O	D	E			H	A	L	L
I	G	L	O	O		N	H	L		M	I	T
T	I	E	R	S		D	E	Y		M	A	O
A	N	O	D	E		A	X	E		A	N	N

Puzzle 129

N	O	G		E	E	G		C	E	L	L	O
B	A	A		A	L	I		A	R	O	A	R
A	T	L	A	S	E	S		P	R	O	N	E
			D	I	M			R	A	K	E	S
T	A	H	O	E			M	A	N			
O	F	A		R	O	M	E		D	O	L	L
L	A	T			N	O	S			R	O	E
D	R	E	D		M	O	S	S		C	U	T
			I	C	E			E	G	A	D	S
H	O	M	E	R			R	E	P			
E	L	A	T	E		R	A	T	A	T	A	T
I	D	L	E	D		N	I	H		H	M	O
R	E	T	R	O		A	L	E		O	P	T

Puzzle 130

S	I	L	T		T	K	O	S		T	O	P
A	W	A	Y		H	E	A	P		E	P	I
F	I	N	N		E	Y	R	E		M	I	T
E	N	D	E	A	R		S	C	O	P	E	S
				P	E	A		S	U	E		
S	H	H		P	I	P			C	R	A	B
K	E	E	P		N	A	H		H	A	L	O
I	F	S	O			C	O	P		S	I	B
		I	R	E		E	S	L				
A	S	T	E	R	N		T	O	S	S	E	S
C	P	A		R	A	G	E		T	A	X	I
H	A	N		O	P	U	S		A	L	E	G
E	M	T		L	E	T	S		T	E	C	H

Puzzle 131

D	A	D		L	I	A	M		B	A	W	L
U	S	E		A	S	H	Y		A	B	O	O
O	K	S		T	H	A	N		T	O	R	N
		I	N	C			A	R	O	U	S	E
A	B	R	A	H	A	M		I	N	T	E	R
L	O	E	B		S	E	R	B				
L	P	S			W	O	O			R	E	B
				N	E	W	S		F	E	M	A
A	L	T	A	R		S	E	A	B	A	S	S
W	A	R	S	A	W			L	I	L		
A	M	O	K		H	I	F	I		T	O	O
R	A	V	E		Y	M	C	A		O	F	F
D	R	E	D		S	A	C	S		R	A	T

Puzzle 132

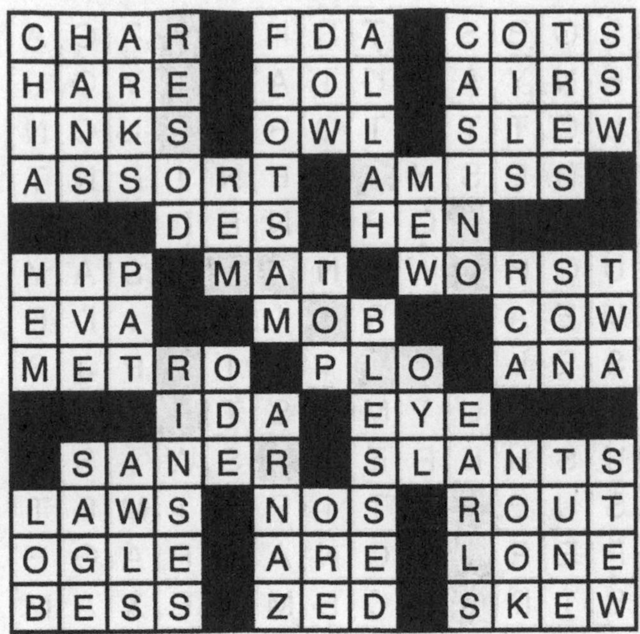

C	H	A	R		F	D	A		C	O	T	S
H	A	R	E		L	O	L		A	I	R	S
I	N	K	S		O	W	L		S	L	E	W
A	S	S	O	R	T		A	M	I	S	S	
			D	E	S		H	E	N			
H	I	P		M	A	T		W	O	R	S	T
E	V	A			M	O	B			C	O	W
M	E	T	R	O		P	L	O		A	N	A
			I	D	A		E	Y	E			
	S	A	N	E	R		S	L	A	N	T	S
L	A	W	S		N	O	S		R	O	U	T
O	G	L	E		A	R	E		L	O	N	E
B	E	S	S		Z	E	D		S	K	E	W

Puzzle 133

O	T	S		F	H	A		E	A	R	N	S
P	O	T		L	O	S		A	D	O	B	E
E	T	A		I	N	A	T	R	A	N	C	E
R	E	L	A	T	E		E	S	P			
A	M	E	N		Y	A	P		T	I	M	E
		M	G	M		L	E	M		N	O	G
I	M	A		I	S	L	E	S		T	W	O
F	I	T		G	O	O		G	R	R		
I	D	E	A		L	T	D		Y	A	R	D
			P	I	E		O	P	E	N	E	R
A	L	O	N	G	S	I	D	E		S	T	A
R	O	D	E	O		S	G	T		I	I	I
R	A	D	A	R		H	E	S		T	E	N

Puzzle 134

H	O	S	E		A	D	S			F	A	A
E	N	C	L		N	I	H		S	A	N	S
R	E	A	D		A	C	E		P	I	N	S
B	I	T	E	T	H	E	B	U	L	L	E	T
			R	U	E		A	M	A			
E	L	A	S	T	I	C		S	T	P	A	T
V	A	N			M	O	P			E	P	I
A	G	N	E	W		M	A	T	I	N	E	E
			T	A	C		Y	I	N			
M	U	S	H	R	O	O	M	C	L	O	U	D
A	R	T	Y		A	L	E		E	A	S	E
S	A	I	L		S	I	N		T	H	E	N
S	L	R			T	N	T		S	U	D	S

Puzzle 135

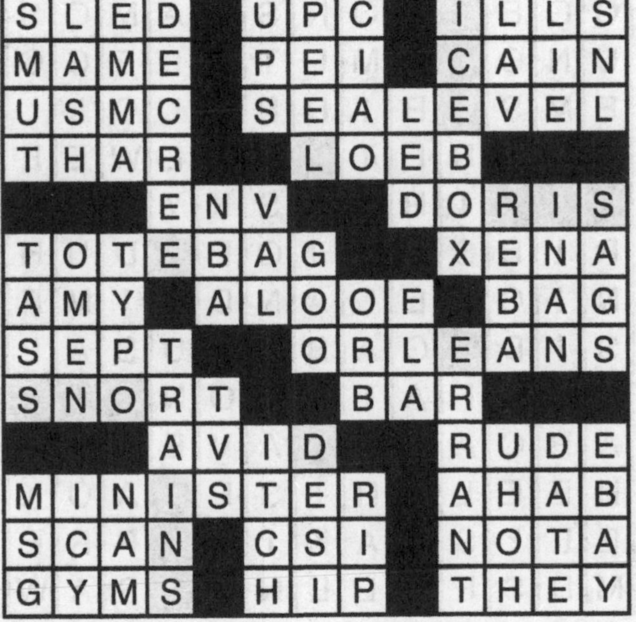

S	L	E	D		U	P	C		I	L	L	S
M	A	M	E		P	E	I		C	A	I	N
U	S	M	C		S	E	A	L	E	V	E	L
T	H	A	R			L	O	E	B			
			E	N	V			D	O	R	I	S
T	O	T	E	B	A	G			X	E	N	A
A	M	Y		A	L	O	O	F		B	A	G
S	E	P	T			O	R	L	E	A	N	S
S	N	O	R	T			B	A	R			
			A	V	I	D			R	U	D	E
M	I	N	I	S	T	E	R		A	H	A	B
S	C	A	N		C	S	I		N	O	T	A
G	Y	M	S		H	I	P		T	H	E	Y

Puzzle 136

Puzzle 137

S	O	B	S		T	S	K	S		P	G	A
E	N	Y	A		U	T	A	H		Y	O	U
L	O	T	T		T	O	R	I		L	O	N
F	R	E	S	H		L	E	N	I	E	N	T
				O	P	E	N	E	D			
U	G	H		W	O	N			O	S	A	Y
M	E	A	G	E	R		I	N	S	I	D	E
S	E	L	L			I	F	I		P	J	S
			U	T	M	O	S	T				
U	S	H	E	R	E	D		S	W	I	S	S
S	U	E		A	T	I	P		I	M	E	T
P	E	R		M	O	N	A		P	A	G	E
S	T	D		P	O	E	M		E	X	A	M

Puzzle 138

Puzzle 139

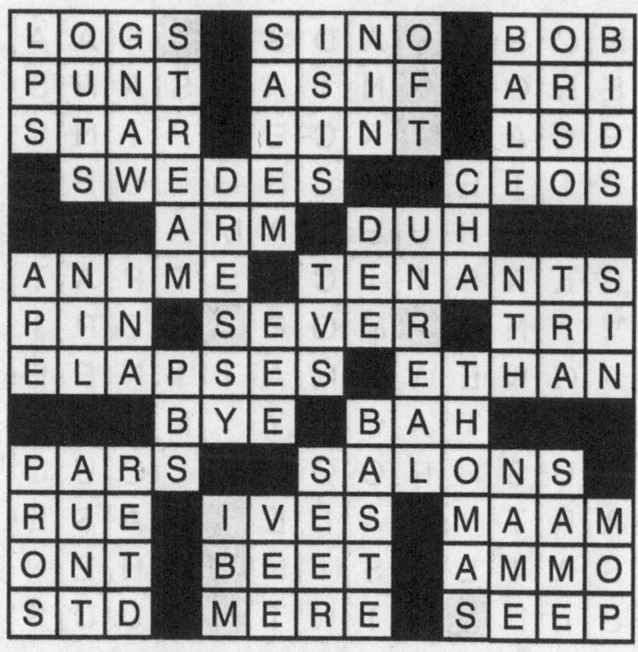

Puzzle 140

I	R	S			A	R	T			B	A	D
D	O	I	T		S	I	S		Y	A	L	E
S	E	P	A	R	A	T	E		O	N	A	N
			K	A	N	E		G	U	E	S	S
A	I	M	E	D		O	P	E	R			
L	S	A	T			F	A	R	E	A	S	T
F	I	S	H		O	P	S		S	O	L	E
A	N	T	E	N	N	A			O	N	U	S
			C	A	S	S		O	V	E	R	T
S	A	T	A	N		S	O	D	A			
A	M	O	K		H	A	N	D	I	C	A	P
D	O	L	E		A	G	E		N	A	P	A
E	S	L			W	E	S			R	O	N

Puzzle 141

U	R	L		S	O	L	I	D		C	R	Y
P	I	A		T	R	A	D	E		L	E	E
I	C	Y		A	B	B	O	T		U	N	S
N	O	S	I	R				E	B	B		
			Q	E	D		C	R	E	S	T	S
A	H	A	S		E	E	E		G	O	O	P
N	A	N			L	M	N			D	Y	E
K	N	I	T		H	U	T		M	A	S	C
A	S	S	I	S	I		S	A	O			
		E	S	C				T	W	I	S	T
A	F	T		A	L	A	M	O		N	O	W
N	U	T		R	O	B	I	N		C	S	I
G	R	E		F	O	S	S	E		H	A	T

Puzzle 142

S	C	U	D		E	R	M	A		L	O	A
D	A	Z	E		P	E	E	N		A	I	L
I	R	I	S		I	D	L	Y		K	L	M
			A	B	C	D		O	B	E	Y	S
D	A	L	L	A	S		A	N	Y			
S	L	O	T	H		F	R	E	E	S	T	
L	E	G			Y	A	M			L	A	M
	S	E	A	L	E	D		T	R	I	T	E
			L	I	P		E	R	O	D	E	D
S	M	A	L	L		O	T	I	S			
I	E	R		A	R	C	H		A	D	A	M
T	A	I		C	I	T	E		R	O	T	O
E	N	D		S	P	A	R		Y	A	M	S

Puzzle 143

A	L	P	S		E	P	A		S	L	A	T
T	A	R	A		L	E	D		P	E	E	R
E	Y	E	T	O	O	T	H		F	A	R	E
E	S	P		R	I	S	E	S		P	O	E
			H	E	S		R	O	S	Y		
T	A	M	A	L	E		E	S	T	E	E	M
A	R	A	T						E	A	S	T
R	E	C	E	S	S		A	L	E	R	T	S
		A	S	H	Y		M	I	D			
B	A	R		A	S	T	O	N		B	E	N
A	V	O	N		T	O	R	T	I	L	L	A
H	O	N	E		E	R	A		Q	U	I	T
S	W	I	T		M	E	L		S	E	A	L

Puzzle 144

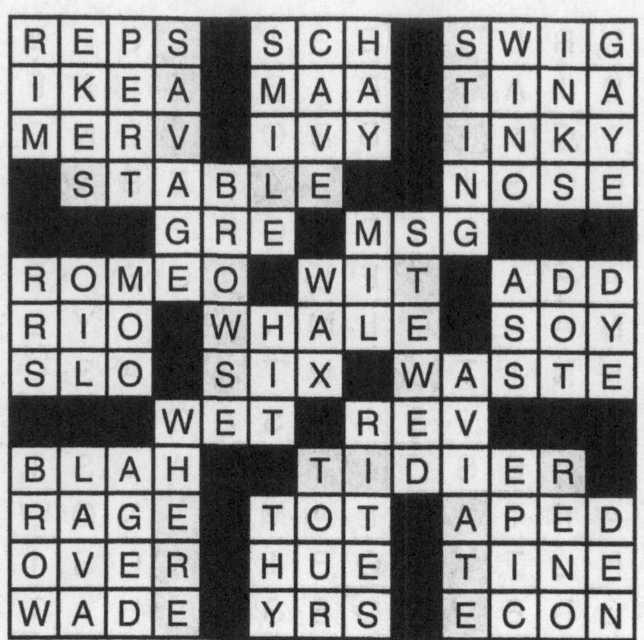

Puzzle 145

I	N	C			E	C	O			M	I	R
P	O	O	H		L	A	P		C	A	N	E
O	R	N	A	M	E	N	T		H	T	T	P
			N	O	V	A		Y	A	H	O	O
A	D	A	G	E		D	R	E	I			
T	R	O	I			I	N	A	R	U	S	H
M	A	N	N		F	A	A		P	R	E	Y
S	T	E	T	S	O	N			E	G	A	D
			H	E	R	B		F	R	E	R	E
S	C	R	E	W		A	W	L	S			
L	A	I	R		S	C	H	O	O	N	E	R
O	N	C	E		D	O	E		N	E	S	S
G	T	E			I	N	N			B	L	T

Puzzle 146

Puzzle 147

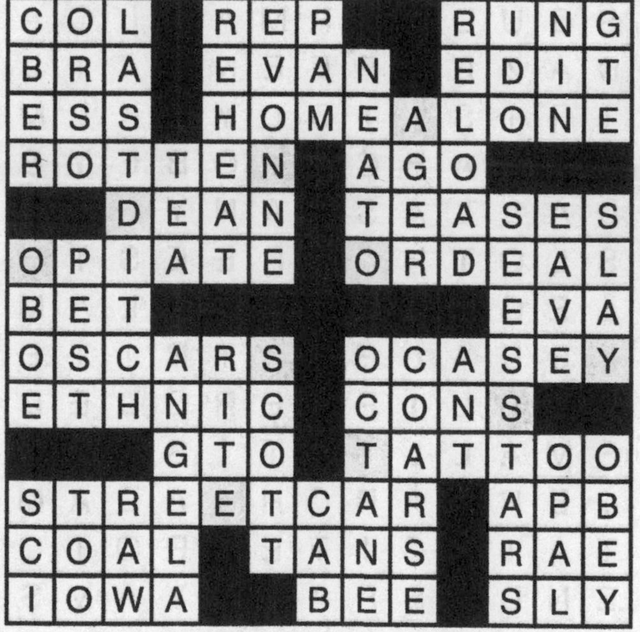

Puzzle 148

M	A	P	S		S	L	R			J	A	N
E	A	T	A		H	O	E		L	A	N	A
T	H	A	T		A	B	C		A	N	D	I
A	S	S	I	S	T		A	P	P	E	A	L
			R	S	T		P	C	S			
S	T	P	E	T	E	R		T	E	R	M	S
T	O	T			R	E	A			A	A	A
L	E	A	S	T		O	R	L	A	N	D	O
			A	H	A		R	E	D			
S	C	A	L	E	S		E	X	I	S	T	S
A	I	R	E		O	J	S		D	E	A	L
N	A	T	S		N	A	T		A	L	L	I
S	O	S			E	M	S		S	L	E	D

Puzzle 149

E	M	U	S		M	I	S		P	F	F	T
L	I	Z	A		A	W	L		A	L	L	Y
F	A	I	L		P	A	Y		B	E	E	P
			M	E	L	S			S	A	D	E
A	L	C	O	V	E		B	E	T			
B	O	O	N	E		D	A	Y		D	U	G
B	U	R		N	O	O	N	E		U	S	O
Y	T	D		E	T	C		L	I	N	E	N
			D	D	S		R	E	C	E	D	E
G	L	E	E			Z	I	T	I			
R	A	V	E		G	E	L		E	B	B	S
I	C	E	D		P	R	E		S	T	A	Y
M	E	S	S		S	O	D		T	U	R	N

Puzzle 150